Advance Praise for Content St

This book does the most important thing that people have been ignoring for *strategy from the perspective of your boss,* and there's a good chance that he or differently than you do. Understanding these differences is how you're going to get things done. To wit. Chapter 12, *The ROI of Content Strategy,* is worth 1000x times the cover price all by itself.

Deane Barker,
Business Development Director,
Blend Interactive

Content Strategy is an emerging field. As a consequence, there are complexities involved that cannot be sidestepped if you really want to understand what is involved. They are complexities that occupy the attention of practitioners working around the world to help organizations get a better return on their content investments. In their book, Rahel Anne Bailie and Noz Urbina, as leading practitioners in the content strategy field, do not shy away from these fundamental complexities and they provide decision makers with the tools to work through them.

Joe Gollner,
Gnostyx Research

This is the book that I wish I'd had every day for the last three years in my workplace.

Chris Opitz Hester,
Content Strategist

This work is what's missing amongst all the content strategy material that's out there. It completely answers the question "why content strategy" and expertly positions its business value for every single decision maker. If you have a vested interest in improving content, brand and product performance, this book is a must.

Kevin P. Nichols,
Director and Global Practice Lead, Content Strategy,
SapientNitro

At first blush you might think this is a book that, as a business manager, you feel like you should read – but that you don't really want to read. Let me tell you that with this book – it is the exact opposite. What Rahel and Noz have done is to create an incredibly readable, powerful and engaging argument for why businesses should take great care in managing the strategic asset of content. Anyone looking to understand the WHY of content strategy – and how it can have extraordinary impact on the business should read this book. It's quite simply an artful expression of how content, and our capacity to manage it well, is becoming one of the biggest differentiators a business has.

Robert Rose,
Big Blue Moose

This book is like a giant cheat sheet for me. As a content strategy recruiter, when preparing to present to clients, the book has everything I need to talk to clients in the non-technical, non-content-focused way that decision makers need. It helps them understand how valuable a good content strategy is to the whole organization's ROI. Content is not a cost center anymore!

CJ Walker,
Firehead

Content Strategy

Connecting the dots between business, brand, and benefits

Rahel Anne Bailie

Noz Urbina

XML PRESS

Content Strategy

Connecting the dots between business, brand, and benefits

Credits

Copy edit:	CJ Walker
Index:	Joy Tataryn
Illustrations:	Niamh Redmond
Cover image:	Francesco De Comite
Cover concept:	Rahel Anne Bailie
Dilbert cartoon:	Copyright © 2011 Scott Adams. Used by permission of UNIVERSAL UCLICK. All rights reserved.
XKCD cartoon:	Copyright © 2010 xkcd.com CC-BY-NC 2.5 (http://xkcd.com/773)

Disclaimer

Trademarks

XML Press
Laguna Hills, California
http://xmlpress.net

First Edition
ISBN: 978-1-937434-16-8
Library of Congress Control Number: 2012955383

Table of Contents

Foreword

For the last few years, my User Interface Engineering team has had the opportunity to study how decision makers make their decisions, up close and personal. We've watched as designers and managers made choices that influence the design of the websites, knowledge bases, training materials, and other things they worked on.

What became apparent almost immediately was that there are three approaches to decision making that almost everyone uses. Our research also turned up that the approach a decision maker chooses has a direct effect on the quality of the design. Choose the right approach, and you'll end up with something awesome. Choose the wrong approach, and your design will frustrate most of your users.

The first approach we encountered was when the decision makers made choices based on what they themselves would want from the design. It's what we call "Self Design," and it asks the questions: "How would I want to use this design?" or "What information would I want to see?" The decision makers use those questions to guide every choice they make about what the design contains and how it's presented.

Self Design works great for projects that are small and are used by people just like the decision makers. If the decision makers are using the design every day, then they'll see the holes in the content and design and make sure those holes get repaired. However, it doesn't work well when the design is large or is used by many different types of people.

The second approach we saw in our research was when the decisions about the design were made as an outcome of other decisions. Maybe the decision makers were making decisions about the underlying technology or the business decisions. In this approach, which we call "Unintentional Design," the resulting design evolves because other things are changing.

For example, imagine an ecommerce website where a change in the process by which new product descriptions are added to the site suddenly makes it harder to shop. What used to be very detailed information about each product is now missing the information the shoppers need to be sure they are getting the right product. This wasn't an intentional design outcome, just the result of new way the source material is compiled.

The third approach was the least common, but most effective. It's called "Research-infused Design" and it happens when the decision makers explicitly focus on the experience their users will have. They don't rely on their own needs, as in Self Design, but look directly at how people use the design and what those people need from it.

We found that the smart decision makers were the ones who took this last approach seriously. They would ensure that time and resources were available to make it happen. While it's slower and more expensive than the other two approaches in the short term, the long-term benefit from those investments provides exactly what users need when they need it. If you're designing something for the long term, this is best approach.

In this book, Rahel and Noz describe how to make this third approach work. Their wisdom and experience describe exactly what we saw in our research. Follow their advice and you're off to creating great designs for your users.

Jared M. Spool
Founding Principal of User Interface Engineering

Preface

If you've been asked to get funding for a *content strategy* initiative and need to build a compelling case, if you've been approached by your staff to implement a content strategy and want to know the business benefits, or if you've been asked to sponsor a content strategy project and don't know what one is, read on.

Who This Book Is For

This book is meant for those who are being asked to do more with their content and who feel they have taken all the steps they can on their own. It's for those who know they could do more with their content, but are struggling to figure out how to do so.

It's for those who know intuitively that content could contribute to their business, but can't quite make the content goals mesh with their business goals. It's for those managers who, because of outdated publishing practices, are prevented from making the power of content work for them. It's for those who want to save money on publication and redirect their investments to places that where they will make a difference.

This book includes case studies from our own clients and from the practices of those who generously contributed to the book. Some practitioners may read them and extrapolate how to use them to their own benefit for their clients or in their places of work. These are the people you want working on your project.

What This Book Is Not

This is not a how-to book. It's not a user guide for practitioners who want to understand the steps of how to devise a content strategy. Those books are out there already, and more will appear over time as the profession matures. This is also not a playbook that can be used as a template. Content strategies are highly situational, and what works for one organization may not work for another.

This book is not a web content strategy book. There are plenty out there already. Although we'll often use websites and web references as easily-understood examples, this book goes beyond the web. The web is technically not a type of content; the web is just an output channel where information gets published. And "web" is not a single output treatment, either. Whether you put content somewhere on the web – on a product site, online catalog, or knowledge base – in print, or into a PDF, you are publishing. And what you are really doing is publishing resources for multiple user types who have a wide range of information needs.

What's in This Book

This book provides practical advice on how to sell, create, implement, and maintain a content strategy. Here is what you'll learn from this book:

- What content strategy is
- Why you should develop a content strategy
- How content strategy fits into the bigger picture
- What value your organization can derive from content
- How to manage the complexities of content
- Ways to calculate the ROI of well-leveraged content
- What you need to know about the technical side of content, and why
- How to get a content strategy developed and implemented

Too Busy to Read the Whole Book?

If so, these chapters will give you a quick start:

- Need an overview of content strategy and its effect on the bottom line? You'll want to read Chapter 2, *The Content Strategy Imperative.*
- Want the condensed version of why you should care? The concepts are in Chapter 9, *Content in a Knowledge Economy.*
- Want to know more about the technical side of content? Read Part IV, "Content Under the Hood."
- Need some hard numbers to convince you? Look at the ROI the case study in Chapter 8, *Which Content Benefits from a Content Strategy.*

- Already convinced and want to get down to implementation? Jump to Chapter 23, *Implementing a Content Strategy.*
- Need to hire the right content strategist? Start with Chapter 25, *Finding the Content Strategy Skills You Need.*

Companion Website

The companion website to this book, TheContentStrategyBook.com, contains supplemental material that you are free to use in presentations or as part of a business case, as long as you preserve any attributions.

About the Authors

What happens when two kindred spirits find one another, by chance, across time zones and continents? For the two of us, it was an excited recognition of each other's ideas, and a desire to share knowledge, not only with each other, but with others. The idea behind this book is to look at content strategy from a wider perspective than just web-delivered content. We assert that an increasing number of organizations manage content in more diverse ways than simply the web, and web delivery suffers when it is not considered together with other channels. We hope to shape theories and bring ideas to organizations struggling to manage their content.

Two Authors, One-and-a-Half Perspectives

While it might seem that co-authoring a book cuts the work in half, that's not quite the case. We've collaborated and argued, encouraged each other and delayed each other, written and rewritten. We are two seasoned practitioners from, in some ways, similar, yet in other ways vastly different, professional backgrounds. Across two continents and cultures, we have come together to share our knowledge and experience. The challenges of creating a text and context that frame an issue for readers are compounded by merging two perspectives – though because some perspectives are shared, it's more like merging one-and-a-half perspectives.

In some ways, we are book-end professionals. We may come at the same problem from opposite ends, but in the end, we embrace the same body of knowledge. Sometimes, we've let our individual personalities and perspectives peek through. Yet whether working with massive content sets or re-imagining content delivery models, our underlying principles are the same.

Within the content strategy community, we are the two consultants least likely to fit into neat categories. We're not exactly "web" and not exactly "technical" and not exactly "enterprise" and not exactly "digital," though we are a combination of all of those, and then some. Whatever label we decide to take on, we trust that you, the reader, will be the winner and will find our perspectives valuable.

Rahel Anne Bailie

Rahel Anne Bailie is a recognized thought leader and is counted among the top content strategists in the industry. With over twenty-five years of professional content experience, she combines substantial business, communication, and usability skills with a strong understanding of content and how to manage it. She is known for her work with content "under the hood," particularly in connection with designing content during implementations of content management systems. Since 2002, her consultancy, Intentional Design,[2] has been helping companies leverage their content as valuable corporate assets. She is also a co-producer with Scott Abel of the Content Strategy Workshops[3] series.

Noz Urbina

Noz Urbina is an established content strategy thought leader, consultant, and trainer specializing in cutting edge, multi-channel, business-driven content projects. Since 2000, he has provided services to Fortune 500 organizations and small-to-medium enterprises and is a well-known workshop leader and keynote speaker at industry events. Since 2006, Noz has been Events Chair and Content Director for Congility.com and has earned a solid global reputation in the structured content community. Noz works as Senior Consultant and Content Strategy Practice Lead for Mekon Ltd.[5]

---

2 http://intentionaldesign.ca/
3 http://contentstrategyworkshops.com/
5 http://mekon.com

Acknowledgements

This book would not have been possible without the support and encouragement of our friends, colleagues, and industry peers.

Jointly, we would like to acknowledge the patience and stoicism of Richard Hamilton, who watched both of us and the book go through several metamorphoses, and our advance readers, particularly Scott Abel, Laurie Best, Chris Opitz Hester, SHN, and Kevin Nichols. We'd also like to thank Richard Ingram, who contributed his graphic talents to the book, Francesco De Comite, who created the cover image, and Niamh Redmond who turned our amateur attempts at graphics into pieces befitting the book. Additionally, our thanks to CJ Walker for turning her attention to editing, Joy Tataryn for the index, and Mark Poston for his help with the website. Thanks to Jared Spool for the Foreword. A special thanks goes to everyone who contributed case studies and anecdotes.

Rahel: Many thanks to Hedy Wong, for letting me off the hook as an absentee partner, friend, and housemate for the better part of two years; Lynna Goldhar Smith for listening to me vent about how I couldn't do this and assuring me that I could; to the rest of my family for putting up with fewer visits and less support while I locked myself in my home office to write. Thanks also go to my Jewish mother, Sharon Nelson, for her guidance and feedback. I'd also like to acknowledge Laurie Best, my Director on the City of Vancouver project, who read, gave feedback, and put up with my general distress about my writing – oh, and I borrowed one of your borrowed quotes.

Noz: Thank you first to my partner Elodie Eudier for her patience, support, understanding, strength, and level-headedness in the winding journey that is one's first book. To my mother who motivated and supported me towards writing a book since I was in diapers – she named me with a pen name already in mind – and who taught me to take editorial feedback in stride. To my father who taught me to always keep my creativity and spirit unfettered by tradition. Thank you to my first writing teacher, Flemming Kress, and my family and friends for continuing to contact and support me despite my having nearly abandoned civilized communication and social participation. Finally, thanks to my many clients over the years who always engaged and stretched me with their various challenges.

Introduction to Content Strategy

Here, we describe the fundamental principles of content and consider ways to think about content strategy within a greater business framework. Unless you are already involved with content at a strategic level, read this section. It provides the foundation for many of the concepts introduced throughout the book.

CHAPTER 1

Introduction

> If we were to sum up the mandate of a content strategy in a single phrase, it would be this: understand the gap between your user experience and your customers' needs, and fix it.
>
> —Rahel Bailie and Noz Urbina

As we publish this book, content strategy remains a moving target. Though the first book about content strategy was published a decade ago – Ann Rockley's seminal work, *Managing Enterprise Content: A Unified Content Strategy*[19] – the practice continues to develop and change as our understanding grows. This growth is not simply about new tools and technologies – like it or not, technology is a significant aspect of a content strategy – it encompasses the very nature of content.

In addition, the types of content we have to deal with have expanded. When we first learned to deal with content, instructors taught from a place of common understanding where two types of content existed: persuasive and instructional. Today, the categories have expanded to include not just persuasive and instructional, but also entertainment, social media, and user-generated content These are not necessarily new types of content, but they are more prevalent, more important to business, and on the radar to be dealt with as part of the content landscape.

This book shows how to revalue your content in the context of your organization's business model.

Publishing content is much more than writing copy within a communications strategy. That's because, contrary to the days of print-only publishing, content is not part of a linear supply chain where you create, publish, and archive. Digital content is produced and managed within a *content lifecycle,* often one that spans multiple iterations.

Publishing that starts with an electronic source – whether the final publication is in print or online – has unique needs, and the technical and editorial demands on content have expanded exponentially.[1] Planning, creating, combining, managing, publishing, archiving, localizing, iterating – the overall process is technically challenging.

Publishing requires a level of planning that addresses technical and business requirements along with editorial, social, and process requirements.

Publishing now requires a level of planning that addresses, in a holistic way, technical and business requirements along with editorial, social, and process requirements. This is called "content strategy," a comprehensive process that builds a framework to create, manage, deliver, share, and archive or renew content in reliable ways. It's a way of managing content throughout the entire lifecycle.

In other words, content strategy is to writing what house construction is to decorating. Decorating may be what denotes quality to the human eye, but it is construction quality that keeps the house standing strong. Similarly, writing (or copy) is what readers see, but it's the construction of that copy – the content strategy – that makes it useful to your customers.

Content strategy is an emerging discipline that is already making its mark by improving return on investment and increasing internal efficiencies in the ways that organizations provide information, support transactions, and foster customer engagement.

What Do We Mean by Content?

If it sounds like we're talking about enterprise content, we're not. To understand the difference, a quick word is in order about what enterprise content is. Enterprise content includes "all content within the entire scope of an enterprise whether that information is in the form of a paper document, an electronic file, a database print stream, or even an email message," including conversions from paper or microfilm.[2]

That definition extends to things such as wrapping email in XML for forensic e-discovery, human resources records, ERP system data, and related workaday content. Though you'd be hard-pressed to find organizations that agree on the scope of an enterprise content strategy, or two executives who agree on what enterprise content

---

[1] The expansion is exponential because the rate of change accelerates as more and more deliverables get multiplied by more and more target formats.

[2] Derived from "Enterprise Content Management" [http://en.wikipedia.org/wiki/-Enterprise_content_management#Definition] via Wikipedia.

actually includes, we can agree that the generally-used term refers to content beyond what is covered in this book.

This book is about *business-critical content* – information that has to do with your organization's products or services and that your organization depends on to operate. The important aspects are:

- The content is central to your business. We're talking about brand-building content: product content, marketing content, technical content, and pass-through content such as user-generated and social media content.
- The content either supports purchasing decisions, pre-sales, or it supports the relationship between you and your customers, post-sales.

In either of these cases, the content we're concerned with is, essentially, what content architect Joe Gollner calls "relationship content" – that is, content that serves to form persistent business relationships.

Content is a critical part of any product or service. A product or service is incomplete without useful information about those products or services. It doesn't matter whether you're supporting medical devices or courses for a post-secondary educational institution, travel services or government initiatives, embedding content into software or putting information into documentation and onto microchips; consumers want enough information to make informed decisions.

Content Is More than Marketing Material

The traditional view is that content development departments – technical documentation, customer support, and training – are cost centers and the goal is to cut and reduce. Many organizations have cut so much that they're absolutely anorexic, leading to product information that is inaccurate, outdated, inconsistent, or simply missing.

Yet in reality, technical materials, such as specifications, are often more important to sales decisions than traditional marketing materials. Customers will often bypass traditional marketing material and go right for the technical specifications. But technical specifications are generally considered "post-sales" material, and this is where companies skimp.

Technical materials, such as specifications, are often more important to sales decisions than traditional marketing materials.

Analysts and other high-profile voices frequently cite "lack of user support material" as a reason not to buy a product or use a service. This book helps you understand the disconnect between current and best practices and shows how to revalue your content in the context of your organization's business model.

Part of the disconnect between content valued by the organization and content valued by the content consumers – your website visitors, customers, potential customers, analysts, and investors – is that content is not being treated as a corporate asset. This is a fundamental shift in the way we think about product content. The content that people use to find out about your product or service – perhaps to decide if it is right for them, or if it will fix whatever problem they're experiencing – is a valuable asset. Content deserves to be treated with the care of other corporate assets; financial assets get reported monthly, and even bolts and screws get inventoried annually on a factory floor, yet content rarely gets managed with the same respect.

Often, the first impression that people have of an organization is its website, and that first impression is often lackluster, because the content that matters is lackluster, an unfortunate byproduct of poor publishing practices.

Christopher Cashdollar, Creative Director at Happy Cog, was quoted in a 2009 issue of .net magazine as saying "nothing can deter confidence quicker than a broken experience." We would add that broken experiences not only deter confidence but can damage brands – and damage them faster than ever, because social media and user-generated complaint sites and other mechanisms can affect perception at the speed of light. A positive user experience is a huge competitive advantage; without quality content at the center of your user's experience, that experience is simply broken.

But aside from what content consumers want, we need to be concerned with what organizations want, and ironically, it's the same thing. Organizations want to have brand-strengthening, useful content they can use to its fullest advantage, and they want to produce that content in the most cost-efficient way. This book discusses ways to make that happen. When you invest in content, you're producing some powerful content assets.

Be clear, though: it's not enough to write clever, accurate copy. There is far more to a content strategy than that. At the front end, there's the planning and, well, strategy. At the back end, there's technology, as well. These three things together – smart strategy, good content, and appropriate technology – increase the value your content delivers to your business. Sometimes, it's not about creating more content. Often, it is simply organizing and delivering content so that consumers can find everything they need to know about a product. In that case, with the same content and level of effort, you can produce great value for the organization and for consumer.

A content strategy is not something you do once and forget. The reality is that the bar is being raised for what content consumers expect – people go out and experience other sites and materials, and they bring their history with them. So in effect, inertia around content strategy actually means slippage. How you create your content, and how you architect its delivery becomes critical to being able to raise your own bar for continual improvement.

This book is also a place to find ways to look for potential return on investment (ROI) on your content, whether it is an Internal Rate of Return (IRR), or actual revenue-generation. If you're serious about managing your content, a good content strategy will ensure success. Technology can help, but it certainly won't fix any inherent problems with your content. The primary success factor is the content; the technology only supports it. It's actually not that hard to use your content to your advantage, once you realize the potential of your content and the potential of the technology to deliver it in the way you need it delivered.

Your Content Defines Your Brand

The consideration of brand is not limited to commercial, for-profit enterprises, or external communications. Brand is important internally and in public sector and non-profit organizations.

The discussion of brand fills many books and has many definitions, but in short, brand can be understood as the cumulative result of all user interactions with your organization. How users feel about your brand determines how willing they are to engage with your organization. Brand affects how easy it will be to get them to take a certain action, comply with a new policy, or even simply consume and be aware of a piece of content that you need them to consume. Every group that wants users to change their behaviors in any way must sell its message to those users such that they will take action. The strength of your brand influences how easy that task is.

Multimodal Content Strategy

Most of what has been written about content strategy has been focused on the Web. While the Web is a primary vehicle for delivering your content to customers, it is not the only vehicle, and your content strategy needs to be more comprehensive.

For example, a product description can end up in a user guide, on a website, in a catalog, in a brochure, or on a trade show banner – same content, different outputs. We also consider different modes of interaction, often called "modalities," which are important to particular types of content at different points in the content lifecycle and on different devices and platforms, such as mobile and smartphones, tablets, e-readers, large-surface interfaces, and those that support voice and gesture input and output.

We've called this approach a *multimodal* content strategy; it recognizes that the same content gets transformed for many modes of interaction and into multiple final products, across multiple channels. In this book, we describe how to build a multimodal content strategy.

CHAPTER 2

The Content Strategy Imperative

> When my mother was diagnosed with cancer in 2009, I, being the eldest of my siblings, went into hyper-responsibility research mode. I scoured the Web for any information I could find about uterine cancer so I could be informed and offer support, if not help, around her treatment. I would do a Google search, then head for information about symptoms, treatments, and survival rates.
>
> There is a lot of information out there, and a lot of conflicting information, so I went to a lot of websites. Sometimes, I found the information I was looking for and other times I didn't. When I found what I was looking for, I was relieved. But when I couldn't find the information, I didn't stop to marvel about the taxonomy or navigation, the color palette, the hover-overs, or the 3D effect on the buttons. What I noticed was that I had just wasted time on a site that was missing the information I hoped to find.
>
> It's not that I didn't appreciate the navigation and colors and affordance, and all the other good things that make up a smooth user experience. All I wanted at that point were answers to my questions.
>
> —Rahel Bailie

This story is an all-too-common example of the good-scent, bad-content user experience.[1] Many theories have arisen about why this has become a recurring theme in the web world. The most plausible one is a variation on Alan Cooper's *The Inmates Are Running the Asylum*[5]. The developers of software, and later web applications, drove the projects and had the power to determine the user experience. The focus was on technological possibilities, and the interface was an engineer's view into their world. They wanted to code, not plan.

---

[1] See "The Scent of a Site: A System for Analyzing and Predicting Information Scent, Usage, and Usability of a Web Site" [http://www-users.cs.umn.edu/~echi/papers/chi2000/scent.pdf] for a good explanation of web scent.

Cooper asserted that investing in the user experience was not only worthwhile, it was critical, and we saw the shift to emphasizing user-centered design. That morphed into user experience, experience design, service design, or any one of many other variations on the user experience (UX) theme. The commonality is that before any code is written, you need to understand the intended audiences, from how they will use the product to the cognitive processes that help them process information about the product to the human factors involved in using that information.

In the world of user-centered design, practitioners established processes that constituted best practices. This ensured that there was sufficient space within the process for the stages of user analysis, information architecture, interaction design, visual design, and usability testing.[2] While this was an important step toward the maturity of the field, there was still a conspicuous gap in who got a place at the table. Content was considered outside of the scope of the user experience. In a conversation with the Practice Lead at a prominent design agency, the idea of a content strategist was dismissed with a breezy, "Oh, we usually leave content for the client to deal with."

The Web doesn't *have* content, the Web *is* content. – Dorian Taylor

The problem with the model as it stands now is that content is still considered "the stuff that goes into the design." Content is populated into the design; it is migrated from its previous location to the new design. This development model treats content as an adjunct to the primary process, instead of placing content at the center of the process. Dorian Taylor, a system designer, captured the essence of this conundrum when he asserted, "The Web doesn't *have* content, the Web *is* content."[3]

Giving content a peripheral role creates spin-off problems that are not easily rectified through a tweak to the design or even through a change large enough to require a formal request for more budget and time. Positioning content at the center of a project – from the beginning to the end – means fundamentally changing the way we think about content.

---

[2] An explanation of each of these stages is outlined in a W3C post, "Notes on User Centered Design Process (UCD)" [http://www.w3.org/WAI/redesign/ucd#steps].

[3] From http://doriantaylor.com/the-web-doesnt-have-content-the-web-is-content on Dorian Taylor's website.

- **Form follows function:** This principle states that the form of an object must be based on its intended purpose. If the purpose of the site is to inform, sell, share, or entertain, then the consumption of content is the function. When the primary function for a site (or application or software) is to provide information to content consumers, then the design should be created to support the content. If enough representative content is not created before the design begins, then form is not following function. Instead, the function is being crammed into the form.
- **Content is the treasure, UX is the treasure hunt:** The elements of design – from the architecture and navigation to the look and feel to the code functionality and everything in between – are all components that come together to help content consumers reach the information they need as efficiently as possible. But in the end, if the content doesn't meet user expectations, the experience has failed. To return to our earlier metaphor, the UX treasure hunt was entertaining, but the experience will be remembered by the lack of treasure at the end.
- **Writers can't be experts at everything related to content:** Content development has become too complex to be left solely in the hands of writers, especially those writers who focus only on editorial issues and ignore the foundations that make it possible to implement a content strategy. Writers can't be expected to be experts at information architecture, though they know how to create folder structures on shared drives. Similarly, we shouldn't expect writers to be experts at content strategy, even though they know how to use a word processor. Writers cannot be expected to know enough about content standards and content modeling, reuse models, content for metadata, microformats, writing for *syndication*, writing for search engines, and componentization for content management systems to make informed decisions about how to pull all of the pieces together.
- **Content has become a major pain point:** Project managers have begun saying that content is the major pain point in their projects. For the most part, the design process has been figured out. There are processes and best practices, and the various professionals know how to work well together. Where the processes break down is at the content stage. This breakdown can be attributed to a number of key failures:
  - **The existing content is unusable:** The existing content is unusable in the new site, software, application, or wherever the content is destined to be pub-

lished. The old content may describe outdated functionality, or may not be chunked in ways that are suitable for integration with the new site structure or other delivery mechanism.

- **The migration failed:** The migration of the content didn't go as planned because of the garbage in, garbage out principle – the existing content on the old site was unsuitable, unstructured, or unmappable to the new site.
- **The content was trapped:** The content was trapped in attachments, such as PDF files, which couldn't be migrated without labor-intensive manual intervention.
- **The new design is inadequate:** The new software, application, or site design doesn't accommodate the content. There is no way to provide the necessary information or instructions within a design that was just, no doubt, approved in a lengthy and painful sign-off process.
- **Content is missing:** There is simply no content for certain sections – often the new, key sections – because there was no understanding of how long it takes to create suitable content, or there was a lack of understanding about why accurate, readable content is important.
- **There is no budget:** Content is a major budget item. When organizations hire project teams, the proposals often omit content in order to lower the cost. Then, the organization is told they are responsible for content development, and they realize they lack time, budget, and/or expertise to start creating content.
- **There is no governance:** Poor content often reflects poor business processes. The processes may simply be outdated, in the sense that print or PDF documents are created with the afterthought of "put this on the website." More likely, the processes reflect departmental silos where creating and publishing content serves internal needs, but does not respond to user needs.

Enter Content Strategy

The creation and delivery of content is often examined during periods of change, perhaps during a website refresh project, implementation of a content management system, or a knowledge base upgrade. The circumstances may be different, but the commonalities are similar. On the technical side, developers own the code. When a design element is involved, the UX professionals own the design process. Yet when it comes to the technical and design side of content, there is often a vacuum, and as the saying goes, nature abhors a vacuum. As a result, content strategy has begun to fill the vacuum in what is generally an unclaimed and misunderstood space.

A content strategy is a repeatable system that governs the management of content throughout the entire content lifecycle. This is a brief statement, and looking at it more closely gives us some insights into the nature of content strategy.

When it comes to the technical and design side of content, there is often a vacuum, and as the saying goes, nature abhors a vacuum.

- **It's strategic:** It governs what happens to content during the implementation phases. This is where the planning and analysis happens. It's not only where the "how" is addressed but also the "why." It's about processes within an organization and how they align with corporate goals.
- **It's repeatable:** A content strategy is not a one-off activity. It's a way to handle content within a corporate context where a commitment has been made to achieve a level of process maturity that can manage and sustain the content lifecycle. A maturity model for content strategy is being developed, and is included in Chapter 21, *Leveraging Content Strategically*.
- **It's about process:** The processes within a content lifecycle are software- and platform-agnostic, though any organization with a large corpus likely uses some sort of system to assist with process management. The processes are established as part of the planning phase and implemented throughout the content lifecycle.
- **It's governing:** Content strategy is the guardian of content. It helps you make the important decisions about how content is created, collected, managed, published, and curated.
- **It's a system:** It's not a technology, though it can be technology-assisted. It describes an organic system that covers content from cradle to grave, and all the iterations along the way.

Content Strategy and the Bottom Line

Having a content strategy acknowledges that content is an asset that needs as much management as other corporate assets – physical, financial, and information. It also acknowledges that managing content is different from managing other assets. Content is more complex and nuanced. Therefore, it needs its own strategy.

Measuring ROI can be done by looking at how content helps meet operational goals.

The bottom line for any effort undertaken by an organization is Return on Investment (ROI), and content strategy is no exception. The expectation is that developing and adopting a content strategy will create a benefit, either through increased revenue or operational savings. This is the fundamental rationale for managing any asset. The Institute of Asset Management (IAM) defines asset management as "the art and science of making the right decisions and optimizing these processes" to determine "the operational performance and profitability of industries that operate assets as part of their core business."[4] From this point of view, having a content strategy puts into place a framework that allows organizations to measure investment and results.

These measurements are highly situational and are generally tied to an organization's marketing or operational goals. A content strategy allows an organization to look at effort throughout the content lifecycle. If content is tied to entering a new market, with a resulting increase in sales, ROI becomes readily apparent once the numbers are crunched.

The ROI for an investment in a content strategy can be shown through increased brand equity, increased sales, reduced product returns, shortened content development cycles, reduced translation costs, reduced service and training expenses, or fewer call to service centers. Whether you increase ROI through increasing revenue, reducing costs, or both, a content strategy is a critical part of achieving the greatest possible benefit from your content.

---

[4] "What is Asset Management?" [http://theiam.org/what-asset-management]

CHAPTER 3

Understanding the Disconnect between Content and User Experience

> The elegance of a user experience is negated if the content at the end of their search is outdated, missing, or outright wrong. It's like going on a treasure hunt. Even a five year old will tell you that if there's no treasure inside the chest at the end of the hunt, the whole treasure hunt sucks. Simple (and brutal) as that.
>
> —Rahel Bailie

Before we go any further, we need to address a proverbial elephant in the room: the notion that there needs to be a tug-of-war between what an organization wants to provide and what a user wants. This sometimes *is* a very real tug-of-war, but it need not be.

In market segments where delivering a good user experience to customers has significant, immediate impact on the bottom line, there is no disconnect. Providing a good user experience means more revenue.[1] Organizations have started to understand that there is a lot at stake when it comes to user experience; more and more organizations are adopting processes designed to improve the user experience.[2]

The big disconnect has moved downstream. Designing a customer experience has often stopped short of providing the content needed to complete the experience. The content the organization wants to provide and the content the user wants to have should be like two sides of a coin. It's often not.

---

[1] A striking illustration of that was made in an interview by Dr. Eric Schaffer of Human Factors International with the Director of Usability at Staples, who demonstrated that a small improvement to the user experience had a half-million dollar ROI impact in the first year. The transcript of "Keeping Users Stuck to Your Site" [http://www.humanfactors.com/downloads/keepinguserstranscription.asp], is available on the Human Factors site.

[2] User Interface Engineering has an excellent example of an *experience map* [http://www.uie.com/articles/-experience_map/] that shows how to connect the user experience across various touch points.

To illustrate, let's look at restaurant websites. We can all relate to the user experience of restaurant sites as an example of a common business-to-consumer enterprise. They are also excellent examples of an industry sorely in need of content strategy. Currently, they serve as a kind of "What Not to Wear" for the rest of us, though it wouldn't take much of a make-over treatment to transform the tarted-up into the tried-and-true.

A de facto standard has developed that dictates restaurants should have a splash page. The home page is inevitably built in Flash and offers slick photographs of the restaurant interior or fake people in fake fun poses meant to suggest they are patrons cavorting in the restaurant. To gain access to actual content requires a click, after which the landing pages generally look like the home pages of other sites, with a menu bar containing links to information such as menus, group rates, restaurant locations, newsletter signups, and so on.[3]

Customers Want Cute *and* Smart

Consumers don't visit a site to poke around, they come to do something such as find information or complete a task.

No doubt, the eye candy is appealing to those who appreciate a visual aesthetic, but what seems to be missing in the equation is a focus on the customer's need for information – that is, a strategy for determining which content is served up, to whom, and when.

Consumers don't visit a site to poke around and see what's there. They come to do something – either find information or complete a task. So why does the typical consumer go to a restaurant website? An informal poll conducted on Facebook and Twitter ranked the top tasks as:

- Finding contact information, specifically the location and/or phone number
- Viewing the menu
- Making a reservation
- Getting directions

[3] This website model is so pervasive in the restaurant industry that the popular comic website, The Oatmeal, created a comic specifically about restaurant websites [http://theoatmeal.com/comics/restaurant_website].

Compare that with a quick look at the content on a typical restaurant website. Extrapolating from the list of common tasks on offer gives us an idea of what restaurateurs think people want to do. Here's a synopsis from the site of a restaurant chain that has some 50 restaurants. They have devoted a fair bit of space to these tasks:

- Find a gift card or check the balance on a gift card
- View the "drink of the day"
- Read about the chef's exploits in a cooking competition (read the blog)
- Read about the newest restaurant to open (a 12-hour drive away)
- View the specialty menu for an upcoming holiday
- In smaller print, and at least a click (or two or three) away, the consumer can:
  - Find a restaurant address
  - View the regular menu
  - Learn about the restaurant chain
  - Watch a television commercial
  - Follow the restaurant on Twitter
  - Become a fan on Facebook
  - Sign up for a newsletter
  - Fill out a feedback form
  - Vote in a food poll
  - Learn about jobs at the restaurants
  - Contact the head office

This is an example of a common but ill-advised strategy that says that if you make people work hard to find information, you will keep them engaged. When potential customers are stopped, semi-legally, on the side of a road trying to find the address of the restaurant on their smartphone because they're lost and running late, they don't care about what the restaurateur wants them to consider. They just want the information, and fast. In fact, if the address and phone number were in the search link, or at least in the search result, they would be happy campers (see Figure 3.1).

The Chef's Table **Restaurant** In Chatham, Ontario | **Phone** 519-436-0559

The Chefs Table **restaurant** at 397 McNaughton Ave. W. Chatham, Ontario. **Phone** 519-436-0559. Great service and fabulous food in intimate atmosphere.
chathamchefstable.com/ - Cached

Downtown Restaurants - Vancouver **Restaurant** - Restaurants Directory

Andales Mexican **Restaurant** 1175 Davie Street Vancouver BC, Canada **Phone**: 604-682-8820 ... Chili Club Thai **Restaurant** 1018 Beach Avenue **Phone**: 604-681-6000 ...
www.downtownrestaurants.com/ - Cached - Similar
www.cbc.ca/canada/british.../bc-phony-restaurant-inspections-scam.html

Figure 3.1. Telephone numbers in restaurant search results

Who Wins, Who Loses?

This approach goes for the cool factor, but does it work for the consumer? This standard was likely developed, and allowed to perpetuate, through a combination of non-technical restaurant owners who appreciate the esthetic, and the egos of web designers who found one industry that allowed them to continue with the Flash intro, without even a "skip intro" option.

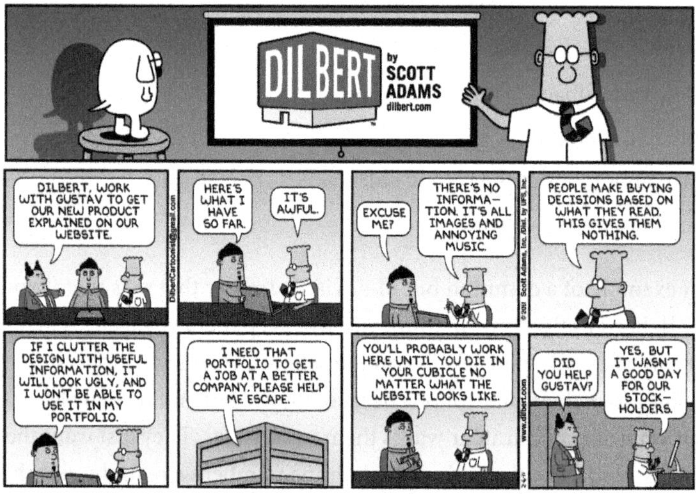

Figure 3.2. Dilbert comic strip that reflects corporate reality[4]

---

4 DILBERT ©2011 Scott Adams. Used by permission of UNIVERSAL UCLICK. All rights reserved.

So how could we turn an efficient user experience on restaurant websites from the exception into the norm? If we look at restaurant sites from a strategic point-of-view, the process unfolds differently. It would start with content and back its way out to design in a way that ensures both the organization and the consumer are winners.

Content Rules

What your customers want is to get some information – in other words, consume content. It doesn't matter whether the content is text, audio, graphics, or video, and it doesn't matter whether the content is persuasive, instructional, or entertainment. The people who come to your site are content consumers, and they have searched out or navigated to your site, slogged through your knowledge base, or picked through your instructional material to find specific content to consume.

When content consumers find what they're looking for on your site, they consider the endeavor a success. In other words, they went on a treasure hunt and found the content "treasure." When the hunt leads to no treasure, the time and mental energy spent is considered a waste, no matter how good the rest of the user experience is.

While each audience may have a different reason for consuming content, there are broad categories of content consumers that you should be aware of.

- **Potential customers:** These consumers are looking at your content with a critical eye. Whether they are doing product research, feature comparison, or looking at terms and conditions, your content contributes to building a trust relationship.[5]
- **Existing customers:** These people aren't looking to be sold. They already use your product or service. They may be looking for technical information, product updates, troubleshooting tips, or customer support.
- **Stakeholders:** These could be, for example, shareholders of public corporations. They are a small but influential audience that will look for a small amount of specific information.

---

5 Karen Donoghue's book, *Built for Use*[6], explains how users judge each step of a transaction as a point toward, or away from, trusting the organization behind a website.

- **Internal staff:** Another specialty audience, they may use the public-facing content, but in different ways. For example, customer service representatives may use content to answer technical questions.

Understanding who your consumers are, what types of content they need, and how they consume that content is critical to success.

Understanding who your consumers are, what types of content they need, and how they consume that content is critical to being successful at producing good content. Yet how many writers create content without ever talking with even one user? This is usually not because writers are lazy or callous. Many writers who have never talked with a user will say things like "we're not allowed" – their management thinks that talking to users is a waste of time or believes that sales representatives are "good enough" proxies for users.

But sales people aren't consumers. Sales people don't necessarily understand how consumers think; they know how they want consumers to act. If you don't observe how users look through your site for product information, how do you know what content to provide?

This is where we can turn to the field of user experience. To create a good user experience, you first need to understand the audience by developing *personas* and scenarios. Personas help you understand the behavioral characteristics of typical content consumers. From that information, it's possible to anticipate what the most common tasks will be and what information will be in highest demand.

In the section titled "Content in the Context of User Experience" (p. 228) we discuss the idea of developing personas and scenarios in more depth, but to jump ahead a bit, an exercise from a content strategy workshop illustrates how this can be applied to content. Participants are asked to create a persona around the typical buyer of a specific consumer product. Despite differences in the details – and those details vary wildly – each group that has ever completed this exercise has identified common key behaviors exhibited by the typical product buyer. In turn, these behaviors influenced how that typical customer would buy and set up the product, and how the customer relates to the company throughout the life of the product. This has a direct effect on what content is produced, how it is delivered for optimum consumption, and how post-sales content is delivered so that all of this content can be consumed at the right time by the right person in the right medium.

Why Content Strategy and Why Now

This section illustrates how content strategy might benefit your organization. If you like case studies as a helpful way of discussing an issue, this section is for you. The case studies illustrate how content can be leveraged as a business asset to benefit, or hinder, an organization as it strives to meet its business goals. We'll use examples from life sciences, travel, and enterprise financial software to demonstrate:

- How even in the face of great complexity – complex systems, user interactions, publishing problems, regulatory constraints, and a dizzying number of products sets – we can still develop effective content strategies that support brand and strategic goals.
- The vital nature, role, and ROI impact of content governance in an organization.

CHAPTER 4

Strategy Beyond Surface Beauty

> One of my most frustrating clients was a luxury consumer electronics company that was so deeply siloed that different departments had no idea what was going on elsewhere in the organization. Customers were drawn in by strong search results, a lovely website, and the ability to easily buy online. However, offline and post-sale, the content experience quickly went down in quality, leaving people disconnected from the brand and sometimes even returning products because they couldn't figure out how to use them. A couple of years later, I discovered that they were struggling against their competitors despite their technically stronger product.
>
> —Noz Urbina

Your content, and particularly your website, is the public face of your organization. It represents you before, after, in between, and in some cases instead of, direct user interactions. Aside from the aesthetic aspects, our faces expose how we balance our lives and how we take care of ourselves: whether we exhibit clarity or confusion, are rested or fatigued, are well-nourished or malnourished, are fit or not. Like it or not, websites also expose your internal corporate health. How well a website hangs together and its overall impact as a vehicle to support marketing and provide customer support are intrinsically linked to the care given by the organization that feeds it.

Your website is the public face of your organization.

More Than Cosmetics

Our faces have expression and mood, which influence how people perceive us. Similarly, websites have distinct looks, express messages, and convey tone and mood. This we know; this is one of the first things that creative directors focus on during the design phase. However, without a healthy supply of nutritious content, a website decays quickly and betrays bad habits. One response to this decay is to have the marketing group apply makeup and glamour; but masking a problem does nothing to actually improve health. Underlying performance problems cannot be rectified by a single department within an organization. Nor can a single department properly represent an organization. It takes a clear strategy supported by strong processes, the right technology, and good content to promote the type of collaboration that makes a website deliver the experience demanded by its users, and stack up against its competitors.

Below the Surface: Untapped ROI

The parts of an organization richest in customer-facing content – marketing communications and technical communications – have for years regarded each other as different beasts with different motivations. Marketing moves units, technical communication then takes over and helps people use them.

Today, marketing departments take the position that brand moves units, and experience creates brand. However, marketing departments are still avoiding – sometimes desperately so – the reality that they must deliver end-user experiences that compel users to return to the organization and become repeat customers or even evangelists. This means partnering more closely with the departments that have the knowledge and content that affects the overall brand. Changing your face means not only changing what feeds you, but changing deeply embedded habits and behaviors as well. It means focusing on health as well as beauty. It means making an effort and changing how you live, think, and care for yourself.

Changing your look may mean changing deeply embedded habits and behaviors: how you live and think.

The separation between departmental silos is often mirrored in the formats each department uses. During content audits, we have found organizations that expressed their marketing messages with well-honed copy on beautiful, search-engine-friendly web pages. Yet on these same pages the core substantial content – the content users really want – was only offered in low-quality, print-based PDF-download deliverables. The print deliverables weren't low quality because they were unaesthetic (sometimes they were quite pretty); the problem was that the PDFs were neglected and malnourished. The content budget was disproportionately spent on drawing users to the site and delighting them visually, but the in-depth product information that would help make the sale was an afterthought. Invariably, we found that web and PDF deliverables were the responsibility of different departments with different budgets, processes, and tools. In the end, the users and the brand suffered because of this silo divide. Any beauty was only skin deep.

The lesson to take away from all this is that content consumers don't just want an application, a website, or a print deliverable; they want them all, so they can get what they need as they move between contexts and devices. Similarly, they don't just want a good pre-sales experience or initial engagement, they want a good relationship throughout the lifecycle. When customers have issues, good service will not make up for a bad product and vice versa.

Modern consumers are faced with unprecedented choice – each year globalization and the internet provide us with ever more suppliers for products and services. We are reaching a tipping point where we as an industry face a paradigm shift that affects all aspects of our work. Our old departmental and technological divisions need to come down so we can collaborate to deliver the content services that our colleagues, management, and users want. That will be a lot of work, but the result could be truly beautiful and good for a healthy ROI.

Case Study: Nurturing the Health of Corporate Content

Content strategy is far more than a cosmetic exercise. To stretch the metaphor, content strategy goes beneath the skin and looks at how to improve corporate health.

The Organization

This case study looks at a top life sciences company that has a large line of chemical and hardware products that are sold around the world for use in labs and hospital emergency rooms. When a patient comes in, possibly unconscious, various tests must be done before physicians can begin administering treatment. This company's machines are used to conduct the tests, and their chemical products are used in the machines during each test.

Because the users are medical staff, not technicians, and because the industry is regulated, reliability and ease of use for all the company's products and supporting content are critical.

The Problem

The organization has complex, inter-related product lines with extensive reuse. Each chemical they sell for use in medical analysis has an associated kit of "helper" chemicals. One kit is called the "Control Kit" and the other is called the "Calibration Kit." These kits are used to set up the machine before a live run with the main chemical, which is called the "Reagent." Inside the machine, the reagent reacts with a sample from the patient and provides information about the patient's condition that the doctors can use to give the appropriate care.

Each helper kit works with one reagent and reuses and repurposes some, but not all, of that reagent's information in its insert leaflet. All the kits – main and helper – have labels on the boxes that repeat the information in the kit inserts, but these labels are formatted according to separate specifications for each geographic market.

To summarize, the content for each product consists of:

- Reagent, Control, and Calibration Kit inserts (x 1 each)
- Kit labels (x 15)
- Translations into 19 languages (x 19 each)

Total content deliverables for a single chemical product: (3+15) x 19 = 342

The Challenge

The immediate challenge is specific: how can they reduce the size of the inserts from 8 to 4 pages? Customer feedback was that the inserts were too long, and the competition managed to have shorter inserts. The company had heard through the grapevine that the competition used a content management system to handle all sorts of content operations automatically, and they thought they might use the same technique to manage their content.

The problem with the inserts was not only the excessive length, but also their form: print. Customers wanted to read the inserts online as HTML with related-item navigation, but the organization could barely keep pace with delivering content in sync with product releases for the print deliverables.

Beyond the immediate challenge, the organization had two broad concerns:

- **Editing the content:** They needed to deliver content in two output formats, but were using tools (Word and InDesign) that were not conducive to producing content suitable for reuse across deliverables.[1] And the team was already overloaded keeping up with the demand to:
  - Reproduce kit inserts for the different regions making slight differences in each insert to conform to local regulations.
  - Tailor each kit insert, including updates, to meet specific marketing objectives.
  - Synchronize the shared content between the various places that the content needed to be printed: inside the box, on the box, on the main product, and on the companion products.
  - Manage change requests. Every time a change was requested, it sent a ripple of updates through other deliverables, which had to be updated manually.
- **Retaining the content:** Interviewing internal audiences uncovered a contradictory pull to the desire for shorter inserts. The support staff – internal content consumers who answer external customer queries – wanted to keep all the insert content because some of the information was not available elsewhere.

One staff member said, "When a customer can't find information in the kit insert or the website, I have to make a dozen phone calls to track the information down." This staffer's concern extended to the troubleshooting guide, which is the same as a kit insert, but with added information that support staff used to answer customer questions. The staffer said, "I have no idea who creates the troubleshooting guides. I just get the same kit insert PDF the public gets, plus a totally separate PDF of the troubleshooting guide. I'd love all the information to be available through the intranet instead of via two PDFs."

Here we see the challenges in having an environment with multiple content inputs, multiple content outputs, and content creation and publishing silos. The product content is used by different users in different ways, and often the content teams and

[1] See the section titled "Mastering the Next New Thing is Not Enough" (p. 155) for more about format lock-in.

their respective managers are not even aware of other uses. For example, the main project contact did not know the products had a troubleshooting guide.

Content is often used in ways the organization is not aware of.

Eventually, it was discovered that the content for the kit inserts and troubleshooting guides was copied from research and development department documents into two different Word templates: one for the troubleshooting guides and one for kit inserts. The documents were then formatted and translated separately (so the repeated content was translated twice) and sent on to create box labels. In addition, lab technicians had requested a new type of document, "technical summaries," which would contain only the technical facts and key content that they thought customers and support staff would need. Figure 4.1 shows the end deliverables and their components.

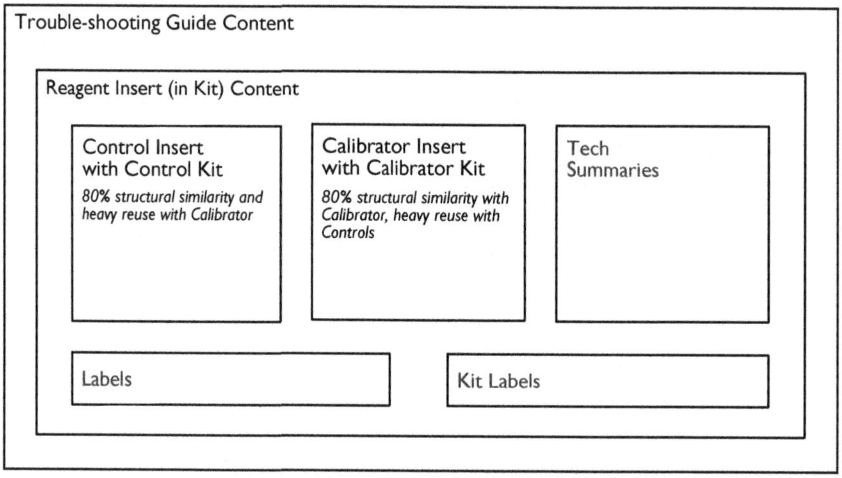

Figure 4.1. The content reuse relationships of various end deliverables

For each main chemical they had the following deliverables:

- Main Reagent chemical kit insert, control and calibration inserts, troubleshooting guide, technical summary (x 1 each PDF, with demands for x1 each HTML)
- Kit labels (x 15 PDF)
- Translations into 19 languages (x 19 each)

Total content deliverables for each chemical product: ((5+15)x19)+5 = 385

To put things into the larger perspective, the organization sold between 50 and 100 different reagents at any one time.

The stream of content from source to customer and back was rocky and winding. The various content teams used the same source to create deliverables, but they didn't communicate laterally across silos, nor did the product development team communicate with teams responsible for other parts of the content lifecycle.

The content needed to live multiple lives to make sure the product would look competitive during pre-sales and deliver the desired customer experience. Plus the content needed to support the post-sales relationship to drive repeat sales. Although there was extensive duplication, every single deliverable was independently reviewed, by multiple reviewers, to meet regulatory requirements.

The Goal

In this case study, there was no single goal. Instead there were several intertwined goals, some from different departments. These goals bear some discussion to help understand the tensions between the various content requirements.

One set of goals came from content consumers, who did side-by-side comparisons with the competition's products. They were concerned about how content affects usability, repeat business, pre-sales marketability, and brand impression. For them, content forms part of the product experience, and they want all of their suppliers to measure up. The content consumers suggested they consider a content management system and indicated that the competition might be using one. This speaks to the close and forgiving relationship that this organization has with its user community.

The support teams had a completely different set of goals. Their key performance indicators concern queries resolved, and good content helps them improve those indicators. They had no stake in content creation, so effectively they were customers.

The company was spending a lot of money to produce content that wasn't quite right for anyone. Because so much effort was put into simply getting the content up to standard, the website only showcased a library of downloadable PDFs, which none of their audiences wanted. Without a holistic content strategy, they might never discover that there was no navigable, friendly way to consume all this valuable content. And if this problem was never identified, it could never be communicated to the administrators of the website.

Without a content strategy, you might never discover that there is no navigable way for users to find your valuable content.

Was the problem that they lacked a content management system? A system might have helped, but without first developing a content strategy, it's difficult to identify and qualify the opportunity, and therefore, it's that much harder to justify and create a budget. How do you do a proper requirements analysis to select a vendor if you never learn about a whole host of content requirements because your content departments don't talk to each other? If they didn't work out what they wanted the system to do and align content strategy with corporate strategy, they were exposed to a host of risks, including:

- **Buying the wrong system:** Too many projects begin with the statement, "We have (name a software application here: Moodle, Drupal, Joomla, SharePoint, etc.)" instead of choosing technology that matches a good set of requirements.
- **Poorly integrating the system:** Some organizations choose a system that theoretically could work, but then don't implement it in a way that addresses their business needs.
- **Missing opportunities:** Any time content doesn't present customers with an engagement opportunity, money is left on the table. Presenting content online that would otherwise be in PDFs or printed materials provides an opportunity to craft messages and announcements into the experience.
- **Doing all of the above:** It's frightening how many organizations do all of the above, without ever noticing.

The Strategy

Our recommendation was to address the immediate competitive challenges regarding the external deliverables, but at the same time to go deeper into the business and look holistically at the broader issues and processes across silos.

It has been a recurring theme in our project experience that it is difficult to get web practitioners to recognize that web strategy and content strategy are more than just marketing, copy editing, and good design, and that there is more to metrics than comparing page impressions to conversions.

It is difficult to get web practitioners to recognize that web strategy and content strategy are more than just marketing, copy editing, and good design.

We suggested that this organization build processes and systems to support modular reuse across deliverables and audiences and to track effectiveness for both internal and external content consumers. The plan was to check the product facts once, review them once, then reuse them in different target contexts and automatically push them to as many formats as required, including:

- HTML for the intranet troubleshooting guides
- Adobe InDesign for print deliverables like guides, labels, and inserts

This content would not be managed on the intranet alone. The management would begin at the source – on the cross-channel repository that fed the intranet and other channels with verified, ready-to-format content.

The labels for physical printing sometimes needed visual layout changes, so we suggested a mostly automated publishing system that:

- Takes the latest content from the shared repository (of XML modules)[2]
- Lays out the content as a "nearly there" version of the print layout
- Allows publishing specialists to jump into the process to tweak the layout as needed before going to production

It was not full automation, but in this case, the client did not want full automation. With this process, the business could benefit from the following:

- Partial automation for all print and full automation for HTML and some simpler print deliverables
- Up-to-date, accurate, and signed-off information
- The ability to apply last-minute tweaks

[2] Modular XML content is discussed in Chapter 18, *Right Content, Right Context.*

Because life science companies like this are highly regulated, the ability to eliminate expensive review cycles, while still keeping an audit trail in the management system that is valid across multiple deliverables, increases efficiency.

All in all, to start achieving customer experience and delivery improvements, the best approach requires modularity and standardization across departments. It isn't essential for everyone to use the same tools, but the content has to be correctly written and marked up so it can be fit together as assemblies of format-agnostic components ready for web-based and print-based output.

The Risks

Although breaking down silos for enterprise benefit was the best way to go in this case, it is almost always difficult. The strategy was to keep cross-departmental systems integration to a minimum and focus on sharing editorial standards. Not everyone has to be an XML author. If everyone can follow guidelines, and if an editor can check the content before it hits the system, then it can be compliant and ready for machine-processing.

A cross-departmental project is more complex than a project that has one executive champion and budget umbrella to fall under. The benefits have to be sold carefully and repeatedly to get buy-in from the various stakeholders.

The Results

As hands-on content strategists, both authors of this book like to be around for the implementation of our recommendations. Unfortunately, it is not possible in every project to be engaged up to the roll-out of a change-heavy strategy. In this case – with multiple international offices, budgets, and decision-making stakeholders involved – we were only engaged in the delivery of some content strategy auditing, process re-engineering, and information architecture. In a knowledge transfer model, the team was empowered to take the initiative.

This case study provides a real-world example that shows how disassociating content from format and taking a more holistic approach addressed this business's strategic goals. This case study illustrates the potential benefits of moving to a reusable component content architecture in organizations that require a diverse set of content deliverables.

With a good reuse strategy, content can be targeted to both internal and external users.

With a good reuse strategy, content can be targeted not just to the Web, but also to internal and other external users throughout the customer lifecycle.

Good content strategy ensures that your content deliverables don't undermine your brand. Tempting users to engage, then frustrating or disappointing them, is a sure way to make them deaf to future communications.

CHAPTER 5

Content as Part of a Complex System

> I worked for a client who was shifting their business model so that they were selling technology to the general public through major national department store chains, when previously they had only sold the technology to enterprise customers. Because they could support the problems that their enterprise customers had with field engineers, the company was doing okay financially and didn't really see a critical need to invest in documentation.
>
> However, when they started selling to the general public, they started getting huge numbers of phone calls at the help desk and lots of returns at the retail stores because of the poor documentation. They went into a death-spiral, losing an average of $12 every time a help desk call came in. The company's profit margins were so low that it only took a couple of calls to put them in the red. So the more retail systems they sold, the more money they lost. They ended up losing the whole division which manufactured that technology for the general public, small-office/home-office, enterprise, and all their markets. In this case, poor documentation took down what had been a very successful product.
>
> —Dr. Tharon Howard

During a lively discussion on whether good content was important, or even necessary, Dr. Tharon Howard contributed the preceding anecdote, which connects content quality directly to bottom-line results. Content cannot be handled with the certainty of action-reaction or with the knowledge that processes put into motion will yield intended consequences. However, as described in his story, the effect of content can accelerate the success or, in this case, the demise of an organization that does not understand the potential impact of content.

Poor documentation took down what had been a very successful product.

What We Mean by Content

In conversations about content strategy, the question continually arises about what constitutes content. For practitioners, the boundaries of what constitutes content may seem quite clear. For others, those boundaries are ambiguous. The word "content" is conceptual and doesn't resonate for people who work outside our field of practice.

The word "content" is conceptual and doesn't resonate for people who work outside our field of practice.

To practitioners who live and breathe content the entire working day, the idea that we can say "content" and not be understood seems unthinkable. Yet we have to admit that the term is industry jargon. A content professional – a lawyer and gifted editor who works for a legal education organization – asked that very question: what is content? Her organization publishes information for the legal profession, and her role is to work with legal authors to ensure that the work comes together and is edited to the high standards set by the organization. In one view of the world, she would be considered a content developer. She works with subject matter experts, in this case lawyers, to rework their writing and to shape articles and books for publication. Yet in her world, this is not content.

However, a traditional definition of content – say, of a book – is all of the words on and between the covers, including all of the illustrations, photos, tables, and so forth. Content also includes the stuff generated by the printing process – the page numbers, the headers and footers, and any icons in the margins. Content includes the organizational and navigational materials such as index and glossary. The physical book is the container, and the content means everything within the container.

Similar conversations happen with people inside the web publishing industry as well. They want a definition of content that will give the concept boundaries. When practitioners ask "what do you mean by content," they are often trying to identify what content they are responsible for. Text may be content, but what about the lines on a page? What about buttons on a website? The text on the buttons is content to a content strategist because of factors like spelling, appropriate tone, and translation, but what about the button itself? Is that content? And what about different aspects of the button: its size, color, shape, shading, and what we call "affordance" (the shading that makes a button look clickable)? And what about the behind-the-scenes metadata and XML elements? Are they content, too? Which of these constitute content to a content strategist? In an article on the industry-popular Boxes and Arrows site, content strategist Rachel Lovinger puts it succinctly, "Everything is content," and she goes on to name some examples of content: text, graphics, lines, colors, structure, and so on.[1]

Lovinger is right, everything is content. Any writer who has seen a line in a graphic that points to the wrong caption or points to an empty spot on the page (the "oops, we moved the graphic and forgot to move the text to go with it" moment) knows that lines are important. However, to a content strategist, some content is more important than other content. The lines that are meant to enhance a graphic might be important to the designer from an aesthetic perspective, but if those lines don't help readers understand the content better, then those lines aren't really important. In fact, they may be a distraction.

Lovinger is right, everything is content. But to a content strategist, some content is more important than other content.

Content and Complexity

When software developers want to learn a new coding language, they read a book that outlines the rules for code, they apply the rules, and the code works. There is a temptation to think that content strategy works the same way. Read up on it, follow the rules, and it works. Yet translating code from one language to another is far more predictable than translating content from one language to another. (Just ask anyone who has suffered through instructions written by non-native speakers or translated by machine.)

This is because of a seemingly small but important difference. Software is *complicated.* Content strategy is *complex.* Explaining the distinction is worthwhile. A complicated system, like a car, may have many parts, but it is predictable if you understand the parts. A complex system has elements, like human interactions, that make it harder to predict. The inherent nature of complexity is uncertainty.

---

1 "Content Strategy: The Philosophy of Data" [http://boxesandarrows.com/-content-strategy-the-philosophy-of-data/].

We work in complex organizations, which operate in a complex world.

In fact, we work in complex organizations, which operate in a complex world. Content needs to be adaptable to various market conditions, which in turn must adapt according to the systems in which they live. How we understand content within the framework of a *complex adaptive system* can mean the success, or failure, of the content, a project, or even a business.[2]

To explain how we'll use the term complexity and apply complexity theory in this book, it's helpful to understand the differences between ways that organizations plan, create, and maintain content. The Cynefin framework, shown in Figure 5.1, is a helpful way of describing this.[3]

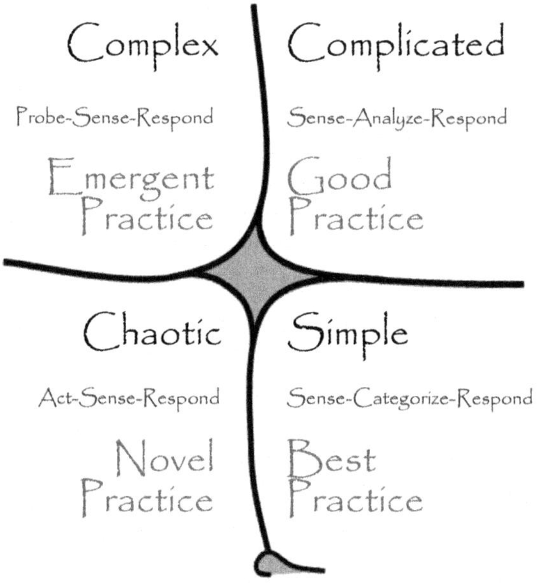

Figure 5.1. Cynefin Framework

[2] We can learn from Robert Axelrod and Michael D. Cohen in their discussion of complex adaptive systems in *Harnessing Complexity*[1].

[3] The Cynefin framework, from C.F. Kurts and D.J. Snowden in "The new dynamics of strategy"[11], is a practical application of complexity theory which forms the basis of a leader's framework for decision-making. It is particularly helpful as a framework in which to understand content strategy.

To interpret the framework, we begin in the center, then go to the lower left-hand corner, and then move counter-clockwise around the framework:

- **Disorder:** This domain is a state of ignorance, in which unawareness leads to failure. (In Figure 5.1, disorder is the dark space in the center, which belongs to no quadrant.) In a content world, this is the state where decision makers retreat to their comfort zones or choose not to make decisions and let the changing tides create an outcome – usually ending badly.
- **Chaotic:** The relationship between cause and effect does not yet exist. A typical situation would be a start-up company where no systems are in place, and content is created ad-hoc, as time and opportunity allows – hence, a *novel practice.* There is no strategy, let alone a content strategy.
- **Simple:** The relationship between cause and effect is straightforward and easily seen. Because of this direct link, *best practices* can be established. In a content world, this would apply to formulaic writing, where writers are expected to produce content by following established templates. If there is a content strategy, it is very simple as content is likely destined for a single deliverable.
- **Complicated:** The relationship between cause and effect in this domain depends on some level of analysis and requires a certain level of expertise during implementation. This could apply to the practice of multi-channel or cross-channel publishing, where each implementation is sufficiently situational that there can be no single *best practice,* only *good practice.*
- **Complex:** The relationship between cause and effect is not readily apparent; the nature of complexity forces this to continually be an *emergent practice,* which can be understood only in retrospect, not in advance. In the content world this is content strategy, which operates within a framework of guidelines that are subject to a high level of analysis before setting out a course of implementation with continuous course-correction as events unfold.

Functioning within a complex system is all about strategy.

The idea of complexity makes a great deal of sense when we think about content strategy. Functioning within a complex system is all about strategy – and content strategy is no exception. In technical terms, the strategy defines how an *agent* – a person, organization, or thing within a system – responds to its surroundings and pursues a goal or solution. In practical terms, it means that strategy governs a wide spectrum of circumstances, with the goal of effecting a positive outcome.

Complexity theory is generally used to describe sweeping changes that complex systems such as the Grameen banking system[4] made for micro-lending in developing countries. For our purposes, we can use their theory in the context of content strategy to look at how selection and adaptation in an organization's content ecosystem make a difference in the success of that organization. Let's use an airline check-in process to illustrate.

Content as an Agent in Complicated Systems

In this example, the agents are an airline customer and either an airline employee or an automated check-in kiosk.

Airline check-in software is *complicated*. There are tens of thousands of lines of code that govern every possible action you can take. The software that governs transactions at an automated check-in kiosk attempts to cover every possibility: what happens when you enter your information (correctly or incorrectly), when you use an authorized or unauthorized ID, when the machine issues a boarding pass, and so on. Nothing is left to chance, and there's no room for leeway. Therefore, when you approach the kiosk with a situation that is not covered, you come to an impasse.

Human systems, on the other hand, are *complex*. Anyone who has ever worked with the public will tell you that there is no end to the potential "send and receive" combinations of communication. When the complicated system fails – in other words, when the rules for every anticipated eventuality don't cover a particular situation – the complex system takes over. Humans use a limited set of principles that apply to the majority of circumstances to reason out the solution to a problem. In this case, the customer service strategy likely includes: identify and anticipate needs, look for ways to help the customer, follow the applicable guidelines fairly, provide courteous service, encourage feedback, and apologize when something goes wrong.

---

4 http://en.wikipedia.org/wiki/Grameen_Bank

When a customer service interaction succeeds, the positive social outcome is not only a successful transaction, but also a deeper trust relationship between your customer and your brand.[5] However, the organizational agent (software or human) isn't the only agent in the transaction who has a strategy. Customers come to the counter with their own strategies. Their strategies may include guidelines such as: when the software doesn't work as expected, seek human intervention; be firm when requesting service; avoid conflict; keep explanations short; and when in doubt, ask to talk to the manager.

Now, put these two strategies together, and you can see there is a wide range of possible outcomes to any transaction. The interaction between the two agents affects how they will interact with other agents in the future. For example, if bypassing the check-in kiosk and engaging with an airline employee works well once because of the positive social outcome, then the customer is more likely to bypass the kiosk in future transactions. If using the kiosk results in a satisfactory outcome, perhaps because of a shorter completion time, then the interaction encourages the customer to return to that option for future transactions. The outcome may also affect the airline's strategy and systems as it learns from repeated transactions.

In the airline example it may not be obvious, but transactions revolve around processing content. The success of a transaction depends on the system providing content – responses from the kiosk software or the airline employee – that leads to a positive outcome for the customer. Customers only care about whether the content moves them ahead in their tasks or stops them from being successful. The airline employees may be as pleasant as possible, but it is the content – articulated decisions based on guidelines – that customers will remember as solving their problem, or not. In other words, the success or failure of the visible content determines how successful the system is and may lead to changes based on how easily and effectively customers can use the content to complete a task.

It may not be obvious, but transactions revolve around the processing of content.

On a smaller scale, the same principles bear out. Consider businesses such as hotels, where consumer confidence brings bookings and a good customer experience encourages repeat business. The importance of engaging customers to give their approval –

5 *Built for Use: Driving Profitability Through the User Experience*[6].

a tweet on Twitter, a "like" on Facebook, a good tip with a Foursquare check-in, a positive review on Yelp or Trip Advisor – fuels the marketing strategy.

If an enterprise concerns itself with managing only its own content, it misses an opportunity to manage customer expectations and satisfaction. The one-way transmission of information only allows for a one-way action-reaction from the customer.

When an enterprise concerns itself with managing its content and user-generated content, the enterprise has created a dialogue, and the action-reaction moves the conversation forward. Each interaction changes both the customer and the organization. Unhappy customers feel heard, happy customers get an unexpected perk. The organization understands customer frustration points better, and may be able to make simple changes to improve customer service.

Taking a wider view of content means managing incoming content *and* shaping that content.

In addition, taking a wider view of content means not just managing the content that comes in, but also helping to shape that content. Studying customer behavior to determine how users contribute content may uncover patterns. For a hotel, positive feedback is likely to be given while the customer is in the hotel, while negative feedback is given after the fact. Positive comments tend to occur in the moment. When customers are happy with customer service, they will spontaneously register their pleasure. When the experience leaves customers frustrated, they are more likely to hang onto that frustration until they can express it.

A creative strategist would look for ways to encourage more positive feedback. As frequent travelers ourselves, we know that smartphone users turn off their data plans while traveling to avoid exorbitant roaming fees. Without an infrastructure – in this case, free wifi in the restaurant, the bar, the spa, the front desk, and anywhere else hotel guests may have the opportunity to have a good experience – the hotel may inadvertently discourage customers from giving spontaneous feedback. The savvy content manager would figure out a way to test how to improve the infrastructure in order to tip the balance for incoming content.

Content as an Agent in Complex Systems

For several years, a number of conferences focused on internet strategy or digital strategy without acknowledging that what was being discussed was content strategy. For example, the Internet Strategy Forum – aimed at managers responsible for driving internet strategy and implementation – included keynotes by a senior social media analyst at Forrester and Vice Presidents from Hewlett-Packard, Intel, Intuit, and Xerox. The Gilbane conferences – whose delegates cover IT and business line managers and staff with departmental representation from IT, Operations, Marketing, Manufacturing, R&D, Customer Support, and Product Support – have industry panels where content management and publishing strategy has been debated. Yet until recently, the term "content strategy" had not been part of the conference vocabulary. There seemed to be a reluctance to identify strategy as being about content.

It was interesting to listen to keynote speakers discuss the strategy for delivering content without actually articulating that content is a central part of the strategy. They attributed the success of their strategies to many aspects of delivering content, but never explicitly acknowledged that the quality of the content was important. Yet, taking content out of the equation would have made their presentations fall flat as, without content, their strategies would have failed. However, this is changing rapidly. A number of conferences have started including presentations, or entire tracks, on content strategy, and there are now conferences solely devoted to content strategy.[6]

There is a reluctance to associate strategy with content.

As Axelrod and Cohen note in their book, *Harnessing Complexity: Organizational Implications of a Scientific Frontier*[1], "many moving parts" means complicated, not complex. Complexity is more. It indicates that a "system consists of parts which interact in ways that heavily influence the probabilities of later events." Content is not simply a moving part within a content delivery system. Content isn't even just a type of artifact – an item used by an agent – within the system. Content is a primary player, perhaps an agent unto itself. After all, content is a means of communication and can effect change in a way that other system components cannot.

---

[6] 2012 saw two landmarks: the call for papers for the Society for Technical Communication's annual conference received more proposals for content strategy than for some of the more traditional topics such as management, and a two-day content strategy workshop [http://www.contentstrategyworkshops.com] event was held in Portland, Oregon.

A shift in content can cause a shift in the organization, which, in turn, can cause a shift in the relationship between an organization and its customers.

Content is what provides information that the brain can process to make decisions. A shift in content can cause a shift in the organization which, in turn, can cause a shift in the relationship between an organization and its customers. Once you recognize that content governs the relationship between an organization and its customers, the folly of talking about publishing or communication strategies without talking about content strategy becomes quite clear. What can this shift look like? Using a contemporary example, let's look at social media. Content is a prime agent in how adoption of social media affects customer relationships, as shown in Table 5.1.

Table 5.1 – Content as an agent in customer behavior on social media.

Before social media, customers would:	After social media, customers would:
Consult website for product information	Consult website for product information
Talk to an in-store sales person	Verify reputation on support sites or forums
Consult with a friend to verify choice	Verify choice with multiple friends through Facebook or Twitter
Make a decision	Make a decision

We discuss this in terms of social media but a more a more accurate name would be media for delivering social content. The shift to social content – from the micro-content of Twitter and Facebook to customer community sites such as Get Satisfaction[7] to social recommendation software such as GetGlue[8] – profoundly changes the way organizations engage with their communities, and in turn, can profoundly change the way the community reciprocates.

[7] https://getsatisfaction.com
[8] http://getglue.com

As organizations gain more experience with social content, they are starting to realize how it fits within, and changes, their current content ecosystem. C.C. Chapman, co-author of *Content Rules*[4], said in a presentation to Vancouver's Third Tuesday group of social media professionals, "share, don't shill." His statement was indicative of the fundamental shift in the way that organizations talk with customers about themselves and their products. They are moving away from the polished marketing voice to a more genuine conversation.

As organizations gain experience with social content, they see how it fits within, and changes, their content ecosystem.

Social media opens up a brand, exposing its identity to consumers. Bryan & Jeffrey Eisenberg note that consumer "BS meters operate in high alert mode – consumers can spot a false claim, a hyped pitch, or an over-reaching associative clue in a nano-second."[9] Instead, consumers are calling for a conversation. Part of that conversation is sharing information with as much transparency as possible. Consumers *will* define the brand, and influence the overall conversation about the brand. The question becomes whether the brand will be defined with your input – or without it.

Selection and Adaptation

According to Axelrod and Cohen, a major aspect of change in complex systems occurs through change in the agents and their strategies. When discussing content strategy, we could say that populations have interaction patterns, which influence behavior and reactions. This happens through the following mechanisms.

- **Selection:** In the context of content, selection refers to learned behavior. For example, website visitors have learned that clicking on the logo in the top left corner takes them to the home page.
- **Adaptation:** Adaptation is improvement leading to greater success. For example, as search engines have improved, site visitors have adapted their strategy for finding content from browsing to searching.

Together, selection and adaptation change the behavior of website visitors, which in turn causes website designers to change their websites. Selection (learned behavior) helps us find information, and adaptation helps us improve our interactions to find

[9] *Waiting for Your Cat to Bark*[7].

what we need faster. The selection and adaptation process changes the way we structure content. For example, we might find that because they use search more frequently, website visitors miss content that we think they should read. To compensate for that change, we have to create new content models. And new content models will, in turn, change the way visitors read what's on the page. And so the cycle continues.

When a system is complex, there are interactions among elements that influence the system and its outcomes. In our social media scenario, potential and existing customers ask questions questions about products, and they expect virtually real-time answers. Answering those questions means changing the nature of the content provided, often making it shorter and easier to find. However, if a customer's problem cannot be answered in 140 characters, that customer still need help. For many organizations, these changing and expanding needs will require beefing up user assistance content.

At the same time, social media becomes a conduit for user assistance. Need information about a particular feature? Here's a link to the content from the User Guide. Haven't figured out the advanced features? Here's a link to a short training video. Troubleshooting gone awry? Here's the right article from the support site. A population changes, and the agent needs to change strategies to stay effective.

Content strategies change over time because systems change.

In other words, our strategy for communicating with customers changes over time because systems change over time. Systems demand better content within a better user experience, and better content makes better business sense.

At some point the drive to improve ROI has implications for the production and management of content, leading to improvements in the quality of content, which then contributes to the bottom line. Done well, the process can improve with each iteration. Done poorly, as recounted by Dr. Tharon Howard at the beginning of this chapter, the process can unravel with unanticipated results.

The idea of content existing within a complex adaptive system not only means that content has an effect on its environment, it also means that the environment influences the content. A good strategist – marketing strategist, digital strategist, or content strategist – recognizes this synergy and is prepared to factor it into the making of a good user experience.

CHAPTER 6

Managing the Complexity of Content

> I once worked with a CIO on a project to source and implement a new product information management system for her company's online retail operations. She presented her case to the rest of the executive committee, and they committed to funding the project. However, she told them that committing the funds was not the issue, it was their commitment to making the project a success. When they asked what she expected from them, she explained that without their commitment to a *governance* model, the risk of failure was too great. When, inevitably, some teams resisted the change, would management stand up and insist that those departments get on board? Once the executive committee and the CIO worked out the governance issues, she took the project forward. She's one of the few CIOs I've met who really gets the impact of a governance model and the havoc that can be wreaked in the absence of one.
>
> —Rahel Bailie

Governance, compliance, and risk are the business trifecta in regulated industries.

Managing content, processes, and people can be a complex endeavor, and managing them in large systems exponentially increases the complexity. Governance is a critical tool for managing complexity. At a corporate level, governance determines who has the authority to make decisions, and for your content strategy, it defines who is allowed to create, approve, and publish content. Governance also defines how those decisions are made on a daily basis.

Governance is primarily a human management issue, but elements of governance can be programmed into software systems to, for example, require a particular sequence of steps to ensure the quality of content.[1] Technologists think governance is irrelevant, content strategists find it frustrating, and management avoids it. Yet, make no mistake, without governance, the most technically brilliant project can be derailed.

[1] For a detailed description of the nature and mechanisms of governance, see Lisa Welchman's article: "Web Governance: A Definition" [http://welchmanpierpoint.com/blog/web-governance-definition].

In this chapter, we look at how to manage content within complex systems, with an emphasis on the role of governance.

Governance, Compliance, and Risk

To discuss governance is to discuss compliance and risk. Content strategist Chris Opitz Hester calls governance, compliance, and risk the business trifecta, particularly in industries where compliance with regulations is at least in part achieved by publishing information.

Governance and compliance go hand-in-hand and, ultimately, provide a mechanism for managing the risks inherent in publishing content. Governance also determines how compliance is achieved. For example, are all departments required to publish content to particular standards, or can they opt out and work within their silos?

Managing Content through Content Channels

There are three universal content goals: inform, transact, engage.

Each organization, and each business unit, has specific business goals for its content that can be grouped into three universal goals:

Inform: This is the most basic goal, yet getting users to the content they need, as quickly as possible, is difficult. Users may come to your site through search or through navigation, but either way, the path to your content has to reflect their mental model – in other words, you have to think the way they think.

Unfortunately, too many organizations still organize their content by internal department or business unit, a practice known as "showing your corporate underwear." This is a governance issue because deciding to publish within departmental silos may make it easier for staff to manage content, but it puts the needs of your site visitors second. Re-arranging your content to match the mental model of your site users and to provide information in a way that is useful to them doesn't come about easily, but it is often the first step toward discussing governance.

Transact: Transactions are processes in which there is interaction between the user and software. The user enters some information, then the software processes that information and displays the result. Typical transactions include searching for a product or paying for a purchase. Transactions may account for relatively few content pages on a website, but that content generally supports a high number of transactions.

The goal is to explain the context and instructions of the transaction clearly enough that anyone who needs to complete a transaction can do so online. The more people who can complete their transactions online, the fewer resources will need to be diverted to assisting those stymied by unusable instructions or applications.

The success of transactions depends on two factors: the quality of the application software and the quality of the instructions. The second factor, called *transactional content,* comprises the instructions and terminology embedded within the application. Transactional content should be coordinated with the content on the rest of the site. Using consistent terminology makes it easier to understand and complete transactions. Also, content such as feedback messages extend the corporate brand and may be the content that customers see the most.

However, this content is often held hostage by the software developers and sometimes trapped within the code. A common stumbling block to project success is the power of development groups to simply refuse to cooperate. Sometimes they don't recognize the importance of content and other times they may see content as a low priority. Or they may resist transferring control of content to content developers. Having a governance model that is clear about roles, responsibilities, and expectations is the only way to ensure that all parties work towards the same outcomes.

Content such as feedback messages, is an extension of the corporate brand, and may be the content that customers see the most.

Engage: Engagement can mean different things, depending on whether the organization is part of private industry or the public sector. Yet despite some superficial differences, the outcomes are virtually identical. Engagement is meant to change behavior. In the marketing industry, this is known as "conversion." In the private sector, conversion means increasing the percentage of viewers who complete a desired action such as making a purchase or registering to get information. In the public sector, conversion means increasing the trust and loyalty of existing and potential constituents. When organizations fail to share content in ways that make it easy for their users to become engaged, something will fill the vacuum – often social media and often in communities that don't have the organization's interests at heart.

Engaging users is a strategic, not a tactical, activity

Building the opportunity for user engagement into a website cannot be done at a tactical level; it is a strategy-level activity that needs to integrate content from across the site and present it to the content consumer at the right time and place. Without a governance model in place, creating a strategy for the required number of social media channels and accounts becomes almost impossible.

Managing Risk through Content Processes

If it sounds presumptuous to say that good content management processes are an effective risk management tool, think again. Content is often the manifestation of business processes, and content is the primary evidence of communication, so content becomes the focal point during risk management crises. Consider these examples:

Content often becomes the focal point during a crisis.

- In 2005, Transport Canada revoked an airline's operating certificate when it discovered that certain content was missing from the airline's operating manuals. The airline went bankrupt soon afterwards.[2]
- In 2006, a US District court ruled that Target Corporation discriminated against the blind because the content on their website was inaccessible to the blind. Target settled the class action lawsuit for $6 million.[3]
- In 2011, Enbridge paid over $1 million in fines for failing to provide sufficiently accurate information (i.e., content) regarding the location of underground natural gas pipelines as required under the Technical Standards and Safety Act.[4]
- In 2011, a Massachusetts Supreme Judicial Court voided foreclosures because they were based on improper or incomplete paperwork.[5]

---

2 "A Steep Price for Bad Documentation" [http://intentionaldesign.ca/2006/09/24/-a-steep-price-for-bad-documentation].

3 "Target Settles Accessibility Lawsuit for $6 Million" [http://www.sitepoint.com/-target-settles-accessibility-lawsuit-for-6-million/].

4 See "Bloor Street Explosion Update" [http://www.kodiakdrilling.ca/articles/page/2/].

5 A New York Times article "Massachusetts Ruling on Foreclosures Is a Warning to Banks" [http://-www.nytimes.com/2011/01/08/business/08mortgage.html] provides a more detailed account of this case.

These are not isolated cases. Instances of fines levied, lawsuits settled, product launches delayed, sales in certain markets denied, and even companies put out of business happen on an all-too-regular basis. We may not hear about the pharmaceutical company that loses $1 million a day for delayed FDA approvals or the lawsuits won because of sloppy safety instructions accompanying industrial products, but we know that in all of these cases, good management of content would have made a difference.

Managing Key Stakeholders through Governance

Over the years, our experience and our conversations with peers tell us that implementing an appropriate governance model is the single most common stumbling block when it comes to achieving project success. Governance is about getting everyone on the same page, from creation processes to approval processes, from brand and relevance to site mandate. The common concerns about governance can be distilled to a few main areas.

Sponsors: Executives – management or sponsoring stakeholders – want to support the adoption of governance in theory, but they find it difficult to overcome organizational obstacles. Sometimes, sponsors who are prepared to roll up their shirt sleeves to tackle technical issues will wither at the thought of the amount of personality-handling – the so-called "soft side" of a project – required to get agreement on governance models.

Management: Unit or project teams tend to collaborate well at the operational level, and they can reach agreement between themselves and subject matter experts, but tensions among upper levels of management over control of features, quality, and resources are not as easily resolved. Organizations often have "elephants in the room" and other issues, like unarticulated de facto standards, that must be surfaced and dealt with. This requires an informed authority at a higher level, such as a director or general manager, to make governance decisions with which the organization must comply. Without good governance, the content team is left vulnerable in its ability to move forward efficiently. Without the authority to implement content and related standards – and sometimes without governance guidelines to enforce those standards – the team cannot prevent business units or content owners from digging in their heels about their particular content areas, or refusing to engage in any exercise to cull or bring added value to the content.

Executives who have little technical knowledge can unwittingly make decisions that have serious technical implications.

Executives who have little technical knowledge can unwittingly make decisions that result in serious technical implications that have a huge impact on the design, user experience, and larger content strategy. The problem is compounded because the content team generally has insufficient time to respond to directional changes; often they have little or no access to the executive level in order to explain the consequences of straying from tested best practices.

Fear of Change: Inevitably, there will be change-resistant staff who fail to understand how publishing has changed over the years and who insist on staying within their comfort zone. They can derail a project by holding up publication with unduly long approval processes. In some organizations, time-sensitive content may take weeks to get publishing approval. This is far too long for content such as responses to social media posts, product defect announcements, or other content that consumers expect to be published immediately.

Increasing Success through Governance

If governance is the single most common issue that can derail a project, then it makes sense to tackle fear of governance early. Content strategists and other communications professionals are always looking to identify the governance issues encountered in the course of their work and the factors that can be leveraged for success in future projects. Here are some guidelines from our experience:

Recognize the Web as a tool and asset. Unlike print publishing, which is by and large under control, most websites continue to be treated as secondary to their brick-and-mortar and print presences. Use of the Internet and mobile devices to access information and resources has grown by leaps and bounds. Developing a common vision for how business will be done online, and then creating the infrastructure to do so, is the foundation for all the factors that follow.

Adopt Web Operations Management guidelines: A fundamental aspect of moving web operations up the content strategy maturity model (see the section titled "Assessing Your Organizational Readiness" (p. 212)), is to acknowledge *Web Operations Management (WOM)* as an extension of governance. Web Operations Management is a concept introduced by Lisa Welchman to describe the governance decisions needed to allow an organization's website and related assets to function.[6] Web Operations Management provides a common framework by which an organization can measure its success and then continuously improve to keep pace with demand, which is a necessary component of content maintenance after the initial site launch.

Invest strategically in a technology infrastructure: Use the expertise of your vendors, but own the process. Resist the temptation to outsource the entire project because it feels complicated. Your organization needs to manage those complications in the long term, so use vendors to help the organization understand and conquer those complications, whether they be governance, technology, or user research.

Invest in specialized content skills: Organizations have tried the decentralized authoring model – where subject matter experts, department assistants, and other staff are asked to contribute to the website without being trained in writing for the Web – and it has not worked. The allure of a decentralized authoring model is reduced head count and budget, but this has proven again and again to be a false economy. Your organization probably lacks the skills required to manage content from the editorial, technical, and strategic sides of content, and the need for advanced content skills will not disappear after the project is "complete." Investing in content strategy will ensure that the content does not deteriorate after the initial product or site launch, and it reduces the need later on for a costly rectification project.

Have form follow function: Consider the design as a treasure hunt and the content as the treasure. No matter how much consumers may enjoy the hunt, they expect to find treasure at the end of the hunt. This is a departure from the idea that "user experience" consists of navigation, interaction, and visual design, where content is the just

---

[6] "The Web Operations Management Primer" [http://www.welchmanpierpoint.com/article/-web-operations-management-primer].

the stuff poured into the design. The design and architecture should support the content, not dictate the content.

Set priorities and boundaries: Trying to "boil the ocean" may jeopardize project success. Triage the content to be reworked, or spread the depth of content over multiple publishing phases. It is best to start with less and carefully add more quality content during subsequent phases.

Align content with business objectives: Users must be able to do business with your organization online as smoothly as on paper or in person. You can make that happen by ensuring that content rolls up to the tasks that people want to accomplish online in the context of the organization's business goals. This alignment cuts out the ambiguities that lead to content clutter.

Ideally, content strategy exists within a larger governance structure as part of a corporate digital strategy. This gives it the authority of a corporate-wide mandate and makes it easier to build a strong content strategy. While having a strong content strategy is a good starting point, success rides on all aspects of the system being equally strong, which can only happen with a strong, coherent governance structure that can handle complex systems.

CHAPTER 7

Content, Complexity, and Governance

> Lisa Welchman, an industry leader on web governance, talks about how the organic growth of the corporate website has led to governance conundrums. Once upon a time, some technically-minded person bought a domain name, put up some web pages, and voilà, that was the web presence. There may still be an element of anarchy, where various business units try to assert authority and may even succeed in implementing or blocking activities in some areas. But authority is likely still randomly placed, and the web presence is not thought of as an area needing strategic governance.
>
> It reminds me a little of the saying by Albert Einstein: "You cannot solve a problem from the same consciousness that created it. You must learn to see the world anew." Getting governance under control requires you to consider your content and your strategy for its delivery through a new business lens.
>
> —Rahel Bailie

A content strategy can only succeed within a governance framework that supports content within the larger organization. Governance can be enforced through two basic channels: policy or technology. However, a governance framework can be developed and maintained in several forms: governance by committee (hand-picked council), governance by autocracy (I'm the boss), governance by democracy (majority rules), governance by standards (benchmarking against industry standards), or governance by technology (encoding of rules into your software tools).

Organizations that value and tend to infrastructure quickly recognize that content strategy is essential.

As best practices for developing and maintaining content progress, the focus has moved from practices that are technology-driven to ones that are operations-driven. Along with technology and process, content is one of the infrastructure pillars needed to support a good user experience. When organizations value and tend to their infrastructure, they quickly recognize that content strategy is an essential component.

Case Study: Management as Content Roadblock

Understanding that content is a "moving part" within a complex adaptive system is one thing. Understanding the far-reaching effects by decision makers within that system is another. Decisions about content can affect far more than simply content; a single decision can cause a domino effect with serious consequences. The following case study demonstrates how failures in governance can derail a project.

The Organization

The organization is a multinational that develops financial software. This particular branch produces enterprise accounting software. The organization is in a highly competitive industry with relatively few players, and it was losing sales to the competition because the way it delivers its product is outdated.

Enterprise accounting software is a large investment for customers, who recognize that their purchase means they are entering a multi-year, often multi-decade, relationship with the software vendor. It makes sense, then, that potential customers will closely scrutinize the vendor's product before they buy it. It also makes sense that if an existing customer has been unhappy with the product – particularly in a head-to-head comparison with the competition – that customer will scrutinize the product development roadmap before renewing a contract.

This organization recognized that its product needed a remake, not simply to a more contemporary look-and-feel, but also in the way the product was offered.

The Problem

The plan was to transition from installed software with a desktop interface to a web-delivered *software-as-a-service* interface.[1] The company wanted to offer an online or cloud-based accounting option, but it couldn't do that in one big leap.

An interim step was to offer a desktop product, with a new code base, in a browser-based interface. In other words, it would still work like installed software, but the

---

[1] If this phrase sounds like industry jargon, it is. Installed software would be like buying Microsoft Office and installing it on your laptop, whereas Web-delivered software-as-a-service would be like Google Docs.

look-and-feel would get users accustomed to the eventual online product. The new interface was created by a user experience team that redesigned it with best practices in mind. The task-based interface used *portlets*, small plug-and-play application windows for specific functions that users could configure for their particular workflow.

The content needed to support the legacy product fell into several categories:

- **Technical documentation:** Manuals, which would be moved to an online help system containing more than 12,000 topics
- **Training material:** Training guides based on material from the technical documentation
- **Knowledge-base articles:** Customer support material written by the customer service representatives

There was no reuse strategy between the content streams. The customer service representatives did not realize they could use the existing content rather than create their own. The training staff admitted that, because they charged for training, they rewrote the technical documentation to give the illusion of value. And in one odd instance, instructions for report creation that would have been appropriate for end users were replaced with copy from marketing communications.

In addition, product content was translated into four languages, but only about twenty percent of that content was translated. The writing team recognized that this was inadequate. Not only had much of the translated content fallen behind the English version, but because the content had become bloated and inconsistent, translating all the product content was economically unfeasible. However, the organization realized that with the new interface, customers would expect content to be in the language of the version they had purchased, including the content for training and post-sales support. Therefore, they had to address the cost and efficiency of their translation processes.

The Challenges

The major challenges involved the user interface, the code, the content, and the seemingly intractable relationships among them.

The User Interface

The *wireframes* – a sort of web page blueprint – that the user design team had drawn for the product interface showed extensive changes. The old interface looked like a typical desktop financial application with data input fields that you navigate with a mouse or the tab key. User assistance was accessed by pressing F1, which would invoke a new window with the Help file. Users would either use the Search function or browse through the Table of Contents to find an answer to their problem. The new interface used *embedded assistance* that required complete and clear, yet concise and consistent, content. Consistency became critical because content coming from different places would appear side-by-side in the new interface.

The Code

The software was a mature product going through a change of code base and development methodology. This was the perfect opportunity to change the way the interface content was stored – both text strings and external resource files.

The new method needed to facilitate the multiple ways content would be used in the new environment. This required the content to be: integrated with the new interface, pulled into a single body of work for translators, re-incorporated into the interface and knowledge base for consumption, and consistent to minimize translation costs. The organization was adopting certain syndication standards, which could also be used to syndicate content within the software; this would make it easier to synchronize menu labels with help content.

The Content

The content quality was of the old-school help variety and often self-referential. For example, if the software didn't recognize what was typed into the Date field, the user could press F1, open the help file, search for "Date field" and, with some luck, get the associated help topic. However, the helpfulness of "Enter a date into the Date field" is questionable; the user would have been better served to know why the date was not recognized and what to do to fix the problem.

In an ideal situation, the bulk of the product content could have been reused across the three content streams, as demonstrated in Table 7.1:

Table 7.1 – Content reuse example

Online help topic	Training material	Knowledge base article
Short introduction	Learning objective	Product version, etc
Procedure Step 1 Step 2 Step 3 Step 4	Procedure Step 1 Step 2 Step 3 Step 4	Procedure Step 1 Step 2 Step 3 Step 4
Example	Exercise	CSR notes

Instead, the content was rewritten by each group, leading to inconsistent content across the product line. A user might be told to click [X] in the help file, press the [X] icon in the training material, and click the [X] button in the knowledge base article. This was confusing to users and expensive to translate; each content set was considered unique content and had to be separately translated.

Then came the complication of the new interface. With the new interface, the content set expanded to include ten to twelve places in the interface where content was built in, in the form of embedded assistance. (See Figure 7.1 (p. 60).)

When the user experience (UX) team was asked how the content would populate the interface, they said they would write instructions for each area. Aside from the obvious sharp increase in translation costs, the lack of consistency in a fourth content stream would negate some of the great design work done by the UX team. When the team discovered how many help topics had to be integrated into the interface, they quickly agreed to listen to alternatives.

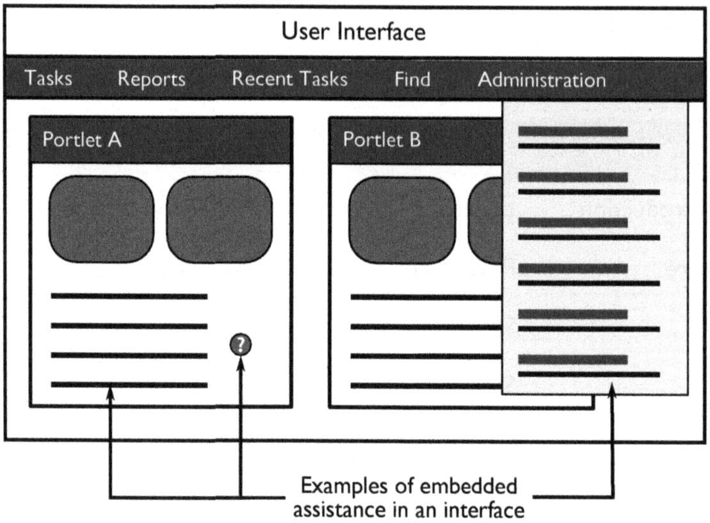

Figure 7.1. New user interface with embedded assistance

High-quality content is a key market advantage that influences user confid-ence.

The Goal

The overall goal was to update the product look-and-feel and ensure that the interface would enable customers to use the new product without a dip in productivity. The content teams wanted to provide high-quality user assistance content that seamlessly answered user's questions. The marketing team explained that user confidence is contagious, both within and between organizations, and is a strong consideration in purchasing decisions.

The internal goal was to provide content in the most cost- and time-efficient manner. After reworking the content – eliminating duplication and unneeded variants – they would significantly decrease ongoing production and maintenance costs. The impact on translation costs was also dramatic, reducing the cost of translating all of the content into four languages to less than the cost of translating it into a single language.

The Strategy

What quickly became apparent was that the new product could not be launched if the content didn't support the interface. The success of the interaction between interface and content depended on a functional content lifecycle. We discuss the content lifecycle in Part V, "Developing a Content Strategy."

This organization could potentially leverage the existing content across all user-assistance content channels, including the embedded assistance in the user interface, as illustrated in Figure 7.2. However, this would mean developing a strong content strategy with tight reuse.

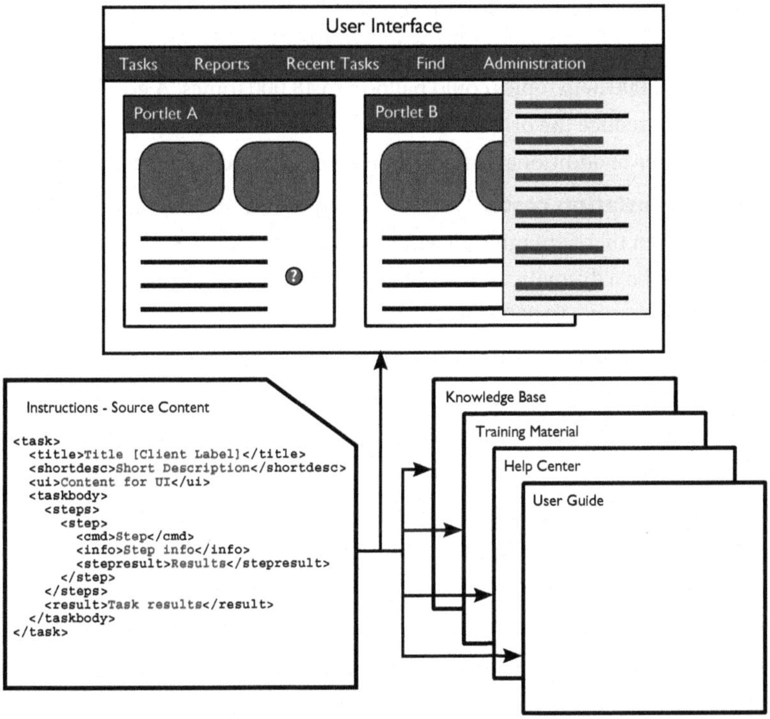

Figure 7.2. Content reuse from a single source

The strategy had the following components:

- **Break down content into topics:** Their content primarily described "how to" tasks that support the bookkeeping staff. Topic-based content would allow the core task-based content to be created in one place. Most would be created by technical writers, but some would come from training and perhaps some from customer service reps. The term "object-oriented content" was adopted to explain this concept to the developers.
- **Bring consistency to the content:** Consistent terminology would address three issues. First, it would make the product easier to use by standardizing terms. Second, it would increase the reliability of search. Third, it would increase consistency, which would lower translation costs.
- **Reuse content as much as possible:** With four groups creating parallel topics, the initial 12,000 help topics could balloon to 48,000 topics. A good reuse strategy would likely reduce the original number by 30% to 50%, assuming that only a small number of additional unique topics would be added by each group.
- **Reduce translation costs:** Translation requires a substantial investment, particularly when there are multiple languages involved. Given the per-word cost, there would be a dramatic reduction in translation costs from reducing the number of topics to 10,000 from 40,000 or more.
- **Break down silos:** To realize the time and cost benefits of content reuse, each team needs to contribute content in a much more integrated way. The total amount of content that the teams could produce barely covered the basics; creating duplicate content was certainly not a good way to spend scarce resources.
- **Streamline content production:** The technical writing team had been reduced to twenty percent of its former size, and the training and customer service teams were recreating the same content with different wording. Content creation and publication needed to be consolidated to eliminate duplication and overlap.
- **Eliminate the need for separate transactional content:** Content destined for the interface should be created and maintained in the context of the related task to reduce the risk of disconnected content and inconsistent terminology and to reduce the administrative overhead required to coordinate topics across content channels.

Table 7.2 – ROI estimate

Content creation	
Current cost per topic:	$220
Projected cost per topic:	$120
Current number of topics:	12,000
Projected number of topics:	7,500
Content requiring updates with each release	
Current percentage:	30%
Projected percentage:	15%
Content integrated from other business units	
Current cost:	$20,000 – 3 months
Projected cost:	$500 – 1 day
Translation	
Current product size:[a]	over 5 million words
Projected product size:	3 million words
ROI after capital expenditures	
Current content production cost:	$3 million over two years, dropping to $250,000/year for maintenance
Projected content production cost:	$600,000 over two years, dropping to $250,000/year for maintenance

[a] Only 18% (average) was translated into 3 languages, and much of that was out of sync with the product functions due to budgetary priorities. Reducing the words per topic by over 35% and the number of topics by close to 40%, then translating into 3 languages still averaged out to 60% of the original word count.

The Risks

The strategy had all the inherent risks associated with adopting a new and unfamiliar methodology: the projected ROI might be less than expected, the new methodology might cause some friction during implementation, and the production efficiencies might be less than anticipated.

The other option – continue the current production strategy – also had implications. The new user interface could not be launched, as it would be missing critical components. The ongoing quality of the product would be compromised, and the market benefits of adopting the new interface would be negated. The volume of content would remain higher than they could handle with the available resources. The product could not be fully translated, which would severely affect the new interface and limit their ability to extend into other-language markets. There would also be no reusable content for other groups, such as training and customer support. The project team determined that the potential benefits far outweighed the risks.

The Results

An analysis was created and presented to the stakeholder groups. The ROI and IRR were carefully calculated for all possible scenarios, both adoption and non-adoption (see Table 7.2 (p. 63) for details). The risks were calculated, and the content creators were briefed as a first step toward changing their production methods.

However, the strategy hit two snags, both related to governance.

The first roadblock came in the form of a director-level engineer who would fly in, every other week, for an afternoon of managing the team. His reliance on the software development group, combined with his physical separation from the project, exacerbated his tendency to be risk-averse. He asked whether any other teams in the organization were using such a methodology, and he was skeptical that such a methodology could be sound if it wasn't already being used elsewhere in the organization. His rationale for non-adoption centered around fear of failure; he didn't want his project to be the test case.

The second roadblock was the senior manager of the development team. He initially indicated that he was on board with the changes, saw the implications for product improvement with integrated content, and understood the product degradation that would occur if the content could not be delivered as planned. However, by the time the presentation was made to his director, he had recanted, citing a difficulty with code changes.

The user design and user assistance managers were left in an unenviable position. Without agile content to dynamically populate the new design, they could not adopt the design that was supposed to catapult them past the competition. Later that year, the company launched with a compromised interface. The plans to improve content delivery were abandoned; the plans for content optimization did not fit within the small portion of the project that did launch.[2]

Realities of ROI

This is a case where adaptations to a complex system went off the rails because governance lay in the hands of two agents with tunnel vision: the director-level engineer and the senior manager of development. Had a cross-departmental governance committee been formed that could balance project decisions between the needs of the marketing, user assistance, and technical teams, the organization might have reaped the benefits of a much different outcome.

When the product launched – months after the content strategy had been derailed – only a few of the much-anticipated interface enhancements were implemented. This was partly because circumstances conspired to prevent content from being ready and partly because the interface was unable to show the content according to the design. Aside from the hard cost savings that were not achieved, there were significant soft costs, such as lost opportunities associated with sales and license renewals. By all measures, the anticipated ROI from content production efficiency was not attained.

---

[2] Because the consulting engagement was only for the strategy phase, the information about the outcome comes from publicly available marketing material.

The Value and ROI of Content

This section is for you if you need to demonstrate the value of a content strategy to decision makers higher in your organization. We can't cover every possible calculation of content value, but we try to cover a variety of situations that can be transferred and adapted to come up with the numbers you need.

We provide concrete examples and some cautionary tales that look at how:

- Content affects the user's experience of your organization or brand
- Good content helps satisfy user expectations and foster ongoing, mutually beneficial relationships
- Meeting user expectations helps attract and retain customers, be they enterprise buyers or private consumers
- A poor content strategy can significantly undermine investments around your organization

CHAPTER 8

Which Content Benefits from a Content Strategy

> Many years ago, I worked on contract in the finance department of a large corporation. The corporation had a paper division (this was in the days before the Web, when printing on paper was the only option for sharing information). The executive whom I assisted was in charge of maximizing profits by moving money around the world, taking it from one fund and putting it into another, moving from one currency to another, looking for new ways to eke out more return on their investments. The amounts seemed ridiculously fantastic to me, a naive 20-something-year-old at the time, and translated into today's currency, those numbers still do.
>
> What I learned from my short stint working there was the importance of keeping a close eye on corporate assets. Millions of dollars were huge amounts of money back then, and the consequence of investing the funds a half-day ahead was the equivalent of the value of at least a luxury mansion or two. It wasn't enough to put the money into a bank vault. They didn't speculate that when the vault was opened a year or two later, the money would have sorted itself into stacks by currency type and replicated itself into little stacks of interest. ROI on the currency was managed as closely as ROI on the goods the corporation manufactured.
>
> —Rahel Bailie

There are some important differences in the way content strategy can be defined, both in terms of what constitutes content, and then what constitutes an appropriate strategy for that content. To discuss what types of content would benefit from a content strategy, it is important to have a full appreciation of those differences. Richard Sheffield, author of *The Web Content Strategist's Bible*[20], distinguishes between a technical and a practical definition of content as follows: "Web content can be anything that appears on a website, including words, pictures, video, sounds, downloadable files (PDF), buttons, icons, and logos" and he clarifies that he is "... usually talking about the editorial content – the paragraphs, sentences, and words on a web page." That is a useful definition, but it stops short of the type of content strategy being discussed here.

In this book, we introduce the concept of *business-critical content.* Our definition of content involves a wider view, including content that goes beyond the Web, beyond the page, beyond the source and the outputs, to the infrastructure that supports the publishing of content to meet organizational business objectives.

Business-critical content is whatever your organization uses in the context of forming and maintaining persistent relationships with consumers of your product or service.

The definition of the body of content that will give an organization the biggest ROI is highly situational and certain to vary between organizations. Depending on the organization, that range of content can vary wildly. The content that is business-critical may be product content synchronized across many publications: from product packaging to instructions for use, from marketing content to training content, from user-assistance content to social content. It could also be behind-the-scenes content such as *metadata* or *transactional content* – for example, user prompts integrated into a web application – that is the starting point for embedded assistance. Business-critical content is whatever your organization uses in the context of forming and maintaining persistent relationships with consumers of your product or service.[1] The following important distinctions help define business-critical content.

- **It's central to your business:** The content contributes directly to, or is a necessary part of, whatever product lines or services the organization puts into the market. In other words, it's content that the organization needs to plan, produce, sell, and maintain the product or service. We won't cover enterprise-level content such as internal reports or retention of human resources records. That's not to say that enterprise-wide content isn't important, but that is fodder for an entirely different book.
- **It's part of the customer lifecycle:** The content supports purchasing decisions, pre-sales, or it supports the relationship between the organization and its customers, post-sales.

---

[1] From email correspondence with Joe Gollner, whose blog, *The Content Philosopher* [http://www.gollner.ca], contains many content strategy resources.

- **It's part of the product lifecycle:** The content supports marketplace consumers, or it supports the engineers who develop, integrate, or otherwise handle the products or services.
- **It supports a competitive advantage:** The content provides an advantage in the marketplace by being better than the competition's content.

Estimating the Value of Content

When we think of assets, we often think of manufacturing, where assets mean bins of components on the factory floor waiting to be assembled into finished products for sale. Or we might think of a wholesale context, where assets mean finished products sitting in a warehouse waiting to be put into a retail store. These assets are managed with some sort of system that scans barcodes and reports on how much stock is on hand, where it is located, and which downstream location it gets moved to.

Case Study: Making the Case for Efficiency

Help documentation is a requirement for any company that sells an enterprise product or service. But for most companies, online help is the end of the road in terms of innovation. Aside from updating their help authoring tools, most companies have not gone beyond creating online help topics for user support materials.

For one company, though, this was only a rest stop on the way to something better. Many organizations talk about continuous improvement, the operative word being "talk." The organization in this case study not only talks about continuous improvement, it practices it. The drive to widen the gap between quality delivered and production costs is ingrained in this company's corporate culture. So once the production of online help became comfortable, they began looking for ways to produce their user support content better and faster, while reducing the resources needed to do so.

Most companies have not gone beyond creating online help topics for user support materials.

The Organization

Jack Henry & Associates provides computer systems and ATM/debit card/ACH transaction processing services for financial services organizations. Their clients, a range of banking industry institutions, use the documentation to install, operate, and maintain the software, as well as to ensure that they comply with regulations. The banking industry is subject to various types of regulations. The industry thrives on precision, from their mathematical calculations to the supporting information that explains the models in the software. This extends to the work ethic at Jack Henry, where gains and losses in productivity and resources are measured and calculated carefully. The cost of user support material is not exempt. Jack Henry and Associates recognizes the potential of good content, done well.

This Fortune 500 company has over twenty writers, one project manager, and three managers in the documentation department. There are eight subject matter experts currently using the *content management system* (CMS) to review documents and another eight lined up for training.

The Problem

User assistance in the form of help is still the de facto standard for user support materials, but for Jack Henry & Associates, this was only a step towards a better solution. The documentation group at Jack Henry & Associates had none of the business upheaval that often drives a major overhaul of technical content. They had a content publishing system that allowed them to produce the usual range of product documentation. In the spirit of continuous improvement, they sought to widen the gap between quality delivered and production costs. Once the production of online help became comfortable, they began looking for ways to produce their user support content better and faster, while reducing the resources to do so.

In the 1990s, Jack Henry & Associates used word processing software to create book-like help, which was printed as paper manuals. In 1999, they moved to PDF output. Then, in 2001, they changed their technique for delivering product documentation. Using a popular HAT (Help Authoring Tool), they produced topic-based content. This single-sourcing exercise allowed them to create topic-sized WebHelp and .CHM files – typical online help – as well as reuse this content to continue producing traditional product manuals in PDF format.

The Challenge

Jack Henry & Associates realized that, while the move to topic-based content was sound, using a HAT was only the first step to increased productivity. The documentation team still did a fair amount of manual processing. Each set of documentation was in a separate project file in the HAT. Each writer contributed to multiple products and could be responsible for as many as 64 separate project files. And each project had unique challenges. For example, different types of manuals or variations to accommodate multiple GUI screens. The writers depended on old-fashioned manual coordination to enforce documentation standards. The writers could reuse content within a project, but not between projects. The benefits associated with sharing content were outweighed by the risk that content would be inadvertently overwritten or otherwise compromised.

Another challenge was capacity planning. Creating capacity in this context meant anticipating future needs for technical content and creating an environment that could handle the growth in the workload. In a technical communication department, that can generally happen in one of two ways: keep the same work methods and technologies and add more staff, or maintain staffing levels and improve production methods and/or tools. In other words, they wanted to increase the quality and quantity of documentation without incurring additional costs. However, one product had some thirty components and two graphical views for a total of 62 sets of help files. With new products on the horizon, they realized they needed to investigate other ways to manage their technical content.

The Goal

Jack Henry & Associates wanted to publish superior documentation that could be used as the first line of support with minimal cost. The idea was to do more with less and in a way that reduced waste in its various forms: repetitive and rote tasks, working in silos, inability to reuse content, and manual processing that could be handled by technology tools. The additional capacity would support more product lines with reusable content.

They wanted to publish superior documentation that could be used as the first line of support with minimal cost.

It made sense to protect the organization's intellectual capital – the writing team – and focus on making technology and methods work harder for them.

It made sense to protect their intellectual capital – the writing team – and focus on making technology and methods work harder for them.

The project team realized that to succeed they would need new methodologies and new tools, and they knew that management wouldn't be swayed by weak arguments. Management buy-in depended on a solid business case, strong ROI, and an implementation plan guaranteed to succeed.

The Strategy

The move to componentized, structured content was a two-stage process. In the first stage, They looked at standards and methods, and in the second stage, they looked at tools and technologies.

They began by looking at structured content, first HTML and then XML. They knew they didn't want a "book" or linear type of architecture. They could see the advantage of a topic-based architecture, and they wanted to be able to mix-and-match topics across publications, products, and product lines. When Jack Henry & Associates discovered DITA (Darwin Information Typing Architecture), they realized this structure fit well with their plans. It would facilitate information sharing in the ways that they envisioned, and it would allow them to meet their business goals.

The next step was to migrate the content to DITA. The deconstructed HAT files turned into approximately 40,000 topics, which they put into a flat file system. They realized that it wasn't an ideal solution, but it was a noteworthy move, and it allowed them to begin building a reuse model. The anticipated reuse was in the range of 20% to 25%; the actual reuse was closer to 60%.

This significant benefit was realized through a change in writing styles and methods, targeted graphics, and using the DITA standard. They were sharing content across product lines and reusing content effectively in multiple ways: components, topicrefs, conrefs, and conditional processing.[2]

---

[2] topicref and conref are DITA facilities that support content reuse. They allow authors to include content by reference (conref) and build maps of topics (topicref).

The Requirements

Unfortunately, given the complex reuse model, tracking content took considerable time and effort. They had started by using an Excel spreadsheet to track files and reuse, but the process had become unwieldy. Even a task as simple as moving a file to another folder took considerable time and effort to ensure that all of the references – and with the reuse model, those could be substantial – were recorded and updated.

As the number of files grew, the amount of time spent on tracking grew exponentially. They realized they had, in effect, been using staff as a manual CMS. However, unlike a software CMS, their staff could not increase capacity past a certain point. To handle the projected workloads, Jack Henry would need a series of clones – or a CMS. Now, they had enough ammunition to make the case for moving to a CMS.

They had been using staff as a manual CMS.

Here are the requirements they assembled:

- Produce single-language documentation
- Support structured content through DITA
- Work with an XML editor
- Reuse common words and phrases in any topic-level file
- Reuse topic-level content in any product document or online help system
- Search for content within the CMS
- Share content among multiple documents
- Track content everywhere it's used
- Prevent accidental data loss with workflow and recursive versioning
- Allow topic review by SMEs
- Support effortless output to multiple formats
- Separate content from format, to easily tailor the output formats to each purpose

The Search for Tools

Selecting a CMS is tricky at best, but for a neophyte to the world of content management, particularly component content management, the experience can be like a journey through a minefield.

The requirements they assembled included everything needed to create the multiple outputs they wanted. However, the price estimates for a fully-featured system ranged from $300K to $500K and would have taken a year to implement. The project team knew that they would not see any ROI for several years.

Management wanted to see a better business case, so the project team narrowed their focus to requirements that would have the greatest effect on ROI. In the process, they looked at a much more cost-effective content management system. After all, why pay for a system that has features such as translation capability when they're not needed? Through this process, they demonstrated where the ROI would be seen and how long it would take to break even.

The new CMS met the bulk of the requirements, and its high value and low adoption cost increased its appeal. The team encountered so few issues during the evaluation phase that they decided to recommend this as their tool of choice. The most significant gain came from switching XML editors to an easier-to-use tool that increased adoption and efficiency.

The project team returned to management with a strong business case, this time asking for less than $25K. The proposal had a winning combination of ROI and budget numbers: the system cost 10% of previous systems and implementation investment was negligible.

The Implementation

Once management agreed to proceed, the project team wanted to be sure the CMS they chose would perform as anticipated.

An implementation team was assembled – two writers and a project manager – whose task was to learn, test, customize, and implement the CMS to optimize it for Jack Henry's documentation. The implementation went very smoothly. The simplicity of the system meant an ease of customization. There were no exceedingly complex features to work around, and no excessive customizations were needed. During the content migration, all content was transferred smoothly, without any data loss. The writers were ready to work in an XML editor, supported by the CMS, within a few weeks of installation (see Table 8.1 for the high-level schedule).

Table 8.1 – 61 Days to full productivity

Pre-installation	
Test Environment	10 days
Day 0: Installation and Setup	
Installation	1 day
User training	10 day (2 days x 5 groups)
Testing before migrating pilot project	25 day
Day 36: Content developers begin using the CMS	
Ramp up to full productivity	15 days
Day 61: Full productivity levels achieved	

The Results

When project funding was approved, they expected the ROI break-even point to occur within six months. They beat that estimate, breaking even within three months. The cost-savings in staff-hours was also significant. An estimated 4,000 staff-hours were saved through decreased processing. The major inefficiency during the flat-file days involved searching through the files. That pain point disappeared because files were now tracked by the CMS. 300 hours of the saved staff-hours could be attributed to decreased processing through the adoption of a common publishing tool, 1,800 hours to link management, 90 hours to streamlined version control, and the other 1,380 to workflow improvements.

The project was funded assuming a six-month break-even point. They broke even in within three month.

About the time of the implementation, two writers decided to move on; this represented a loss of 4,000 staff-hours. However, because of the productivity improvements, their work was easily absorbed by the existing writers.

Table 8.2 – ROI calculation – Jack Henry & Associates

Operational area (ROI Calculated as savings)	Savings
Gains in publishing efficiency	300 hours
Improved content search through CMS	1,840 hours
Improved file and link management in the CMS	1,080 hours
Efficiencies associated with automated versioning	100 hours
Improved workflow by editing directly in CMS	1,380 hours
Calculated annual savings	**$117,500**
Publishing efficiencies, user confidence, and file integrity	
Decreased content processing	4.000 hours
Increased capacity deployed elsewhere	4,000 hours
Internal return through capacity building	$200,000 hours
Total first-year ROI	**$317,500**

These cost savings were significant, and there were additional, harder-to-quantify savings that went beyond pure numbers:

- With the CMS in place, the team could go beyond simple conditional processing (DITAval files) to include variable processing.
- The time-intensive Excel spreadsheet was retired, and its tracking function absorbed by the CMS.
- They no longer needed to worry about data being inadvertently compromised by the little slip-ups that always happen during rush times.
- Despite the decrease in staffing through attrition, the CMS added enough production capacity that they could tackle a long list of requests for writing services.

This organization had two reasons for adopting a CMS: to move the production process to the next step in the publication maturity model, and to address some specific pain points. The ROI – over $300,000 in the first year – was only possible through better-than-anticipated efficiencies and by applying the right technology to support the business objectives. Table 8.2 summarizes the project's ROI.

What is Typical ROI

It may seem startling that an organization can achieve this magnitude of savings, and in fairness, this case may be at the higher end of the ROI scale. However, it is not that unusual for an organization to realize massive first-year savings with what is essentially some process re-engineering and application of some appropriate tools.

Producing content without efficient processes and tools is like trying to produce automobiles without a production line. It's messy, inefficient, and expensive. The year the production line goes into effect, there will be a significant drop in costs.

Producing content without efficient processes and tools is like trying to produce automobiles without a production line.

Managing Content Assets

Content deserves to be managed with the same care as other corporate assets. Let's take a quick look at some other corporate assets and how they're managed:

- **Financial assets:** Virtually all organizations have extensive financial management systems.
- **Product designs and inventory:** Product components, from nuts and bolts on up, are designed using product lifecycle management software and inventoried through asset management modules or discrete software packages.
- **Customer relationships:** Companies invest in customer relationship management software to keep track of information about customers and their transactions.
- **Software source code:** Source code is a corporate asset in any development environment and is managed through a source code control system.

Content is a highly visible asset. It is the first thing people see when they come to your website, pick up a brochure, or unpack a product.

Unlike other corporate assets, content is highly visible. It is the first thing that visitors and customers see when they come to your website, pick up a brochure, or unpack a boxed product. Your content may form the customer's first impression of your organization, no matter where that content is first encountered. Yet content is one corporate asset that rarely gets managed with the same care and respect as other assets.

Remember the stereotype of the person who stuffs money under the mattress? This is the corporate equivalent: stuffing content randomly into envelopes and sticking those envelopes into a mattress, often a big mattress called the website. When the mattress gets too overstuffed and lumpy to allow a good night's sleep, many corporations and public sector organizations exacerbate the problem by just getting another mattress and stacking it on top of the first.

This problem became so pronounced in the UK public sector that it made national news. In 2010, The Guardian reported that the National Health Service spent millions on 2,873 websites that "are difficult to find, badly designed and irrelevant to patient needs..."[3]

In Chapter 9 we look at some not-so-secret ways to get more out of your content.

[3] "NHS spends millions on websites that fail patients, says government report" [http://www.guardian.co.uk/-society/2010/aug/04/nhs-websites-failing-patients]

CHAPTER 9

Content in a Knowledge Economy

> Interesting content lives in the Venn overlap of an organization's expertise and the audience's interests.
>
> —Margot Bloomstein on Twitter

In a knowledge economy, content becomes an important corporate asset. Potential customers see, and judge, your content assets before they ever see your physical assets. They visit your website to see what you have to offer. They search to compare product specifications or service offerings. They look through your documentation to see how a product works.

You cannot deliver a complete product or service without good information about it. Your content is not only your intellectual property, it is the ambassador of your brand.

Whether you create content from scratch, assemble it from content *components,* converge or aggregate content that was created somewhere upstream, or in a sophisticated content model, do aspects of all of these things, it doesn't really matter. Whatever the case, you are creating and managing powerful corporate assets. Content is a critical part of your product or service. You cannot deliver a complete product or service without good information about it. Content is not only your intellectual property; content is the ambassador of your brand.

The traditional view of content is that content-producing departments are cost centers and the goal is to cut and reduce. Content is viewed as "nice to have," but peripheral to the bottom line of the business. Many organizations have cut so much that their product information has become inaccurate and inconsistent, and content is sometimes simply missing. The marketing content may be robust, but the post-sales content has succumbed to budget cut-backs.

However, consider how a lot of people (maybe most) buy a gadget. They bypass the hand-crafted, market-tested marketing material and go right for the technical specifications; they want specific technical information to compare products.

Many organizations have cut so much that their documentation teams have become anorexic.

Ironically, the content that potential customers use to help make buying decisions is generally considered "post-sales" material – technical specifications, user guides, training material, and knowledge base articles – yet this is where companies skimp. They view this material as unimportant because, after all, who reads the manuals? Yet in reality, this material is just as important – or more important – to sales decisions as traditional marketing materials.

It's true that we don't sit down and read user documentation the way we read novels, but when a product doesn't work, we find ourselves poring through whatever information we can lay our hands on and praying that we find the answer as fast as possible. It costs plenty for a technician to spend time searching for information. Consumers can afford to be more fickle. There's always another website, another site containing peer reviews, another way to get some semblance of missing information (Twitter, anyone?). The trouble with this method is that you can't guarantee that the information a consumer finds will lead to your website. And if you haven't provided good information to existing users, they're likely to point that out to the active leads who have turned to social media for feedback from their peers.

Getting a product without the expected content is like buying a luxury car that has no windshield wipers. Imagine that as you're taking possession of your new car, it begins to rain outside. The car salesman tells you that they didn't get around to putting on windshield wipers because, well, the company didn't really think they were that important. You'd probably be outraged, right? You'd question the company's reputation and probably some of the other features – did they skimp on seat belts or brakes? In fact, you'd probably cancel the contract before leaving the lot and shop elsewhere, this time with a little more caution. Yet many companies provide incomplete, incorrect, untranslated, or outdated documentation. It might not matter for dollar-store items, but the more costly the purchase, the more it makes a difference.

In fact, it's important enough that analysts and other high-profile pundits frequently cite "lack of user support material" as a reason to avoid a product or service. A 2012 poll conducted by content strategy consultant Sharon Burton found that consumers overwhelmingly associate the quality of a product with the quality of its documentation, and they will question their brand loyalty when the documentation fails them.[1]

Manufacturers already assume a 25% return rate on products, and in some product sectors, the average rate of "no fault found" returns runs as high as 50%. The costs add up in other areas, as well, from costly integration work to failed acceptance tests to lengthy project delays.

User documentation is important enough that analysts and other high-profile pundits frequently cite "lack of user support material" as a reason to avoid a product or service.

Locating the Disconnect between Content and Value

So where is the disconnect? It starts with organizations that are in denial about being corporate publishers. Organizations publish content all the time. Their various audiences don't care where the content came from or how it got there. If the content can be found online, someone will use it for some purpose, whether that be pre-purchase decision-making, post-purchase troubleshooting, or ongoing maintenance.

It's also not particularly useful to categorize the material being published based on how it is published. We think of information as being on the Web, in print, or downloadable in PDF form. Each type of output may have specific publishing needs, but in the end, they are all just output channels.

What is more helpful is to discuss content in terms of *genre,* because comprehension is closely tied to editorial structure. Organizations publish product information such as product descriptions and technical specifications, marketing material such as white papers and case studies, and user assistance content such as user guides or support articles, training material such as how-to videos or online help, and a plethora of other forms of content, much of it published to a variety of media. What you are really doing is publishing resources for multiple user types with a wide range of content needs. That published content is valuable and gains value over time.

---

[1] "Why Your Customers Are Mad at You" [http://sharonburton.com/-recording-of-why-your-customers-are-mad-at-you/]. Contains the results of the survey and a recording af the accompanying webinar.

Value gained over time has a number of layers and nuances, from the SEO value of a link to ROI on referrals through social media to brand loyalty fostered by content findability. All of these are a way of saying that content – information about your product or service that people use to make a buying decision or fix a problem – is a valuable corporate asset.

The Nuances of Content

The basic definition of content is this: "Human-usable, contextualized data."

Let's make that concept a bit more real.

The number 12 is data. It may have a context in the sense that we know it is more than 11 and less than 13, but it doesn't have any meaning for a reader until there is a practical context, such as:

- a dozen eggs
- December
- players on a team
- children on a school bus
- price of a product in dollars

In each case, the context helps us process the data. Here is an example of a practical application of this definition of content. An item in a catalog will have content attached to it: a product description, a photo, and perhaps a video of the product in use. There will also be data attached to the content, such as a SKU or a price. If someone were to ask you whether $127 for a pair of shoes was a good or bad value, you'd be hard-pressed to give an answer unless you had some context. For some shoes, $127 might be considered exorbitant; for other shoes, that price might be considered a bargain. In other words, once the data can be understood in context – for example, the specific type and brand of shoe – that data has become content under our definition.

The Pain Points of Ad-Hoc Systems

Unsophisticated or ad-hoc systems are prone to error. Although they are systems in the sense that they involve some process, they are not management systems and were not built with organizational goals in mind.

The pains and costs that ad-hoc systems introduce include:

- **Inaccurate content damaging brand and efficiency:** The more times you copy content, the greater the chance that errors will be introduced. With the passage of time, what was once good content will go bad. It will go out-of-date or out-of-sync with brand, brand goals, or the reality of the current product line. Duplicated content can mean duplicating errors, which must be tracked down and corrected individually. The classic, extreme case is a legal statement that needs to be updated in hundreds of deliverables across various channels.
- **Interdepartmental "broken telephone":** In both the private and public sector, fragmentation of content across teams is an issue which plays itself out on the customer's doorstep. Content gets mangled or simply contradicts itself when delivered. Customers need to know the org chart just to know where to look, and they can never feel 100% confident that they've found the right answer.
- **Missed opportunities to nurture brand advocates:** In Chapter 13, we examine how the overall content experience affects a business's ability to deliver a solid end-to-end consumer experience. Without this overall positive experience, it is extremely difficult to make consumers into community advocates and enthusiasts who are essential to brand development in a social, online world.
- **Letting the competition in the door:** If you don't have a system that enables you to understand your audience's needs *and* align content strategically, you are giving your competitors the opportunity to convert and poach. What could have been loyal, engaged, repeat customers look around and evaluate their options.

  At the enterprise level, it means customers may put out RFPs instead of renewing their contracts. In the private sector, it means alternative content sources may arise that are out of your control. At the consumer level, it means customer's exercising their options to look elsewhere instead of continuing with you because of brand loyalty.

If your system doesn't enable you to align content with audience needs, you are giving your competitors the opportunity to convert and poach.

Ultimately, a content strategy delivers the peace of mind that comes with knowing that your content assets are present and accounted for and that you can use them to their fullest potential without the machinations and tribulations associated with ad-hoc or rudimentary systems.

CHAPTER 10

All Content is Marketing Content

> Have you ever watched a guy look for a gadget online? He goes for the specs, right for the specs. Never mind the lovely photos and the polished marketing content. He wants to know watts and amps and horsepower. Oh, and the cursing when he can't find it!
>
> —Rahel Bailie

A long-standing practice in marketing departments and product management is to create a multi-tier hierarchy of importance when it comes to product content. Organizations invest in marketing content and decline to invest in technical content. The decision is based on the assumption that marketing content helps bring in business, whereas technical content is simply an expense that requires constant cost-cutting.

A long-standing practice is to create a multi-tier hierarchy of importance when it comes to product content.

Case Study: Stratifying Content Limits Potential

The concept of content silos is not new and, as discussed earlier, we understand the limitations of content when that content is isolated into departmental silos. The same holds true when content is isolated into silos by genre – that is, content created for marketing is isolated from content created for training, which is isolated from content created by technical writers, which is isolated from content created by customer support. This arbitrary cultural stratification is as toxic as arbitrary content stratification and can easily backfire, as demonstrated in the following case study.

The Organization

The organization is a privately-owned company that designs and manufactures mobile power products such as battery chargers, power inverters, inverter-chargers, and backup power devices. The company was preparing for its Initial Public Offering (IPO) and decided that the website needed a facelift as part of the preparations. In addition to adding a tab for investors, they wanted to "tweak" the user experience so users could select and purchase products on the website.

The project was short and intense, and during the process, we discovered that the biggest barrier was not what we anticipated.

The Problem

As part of the revamp of the site, some guerrilla testing was done with owners of recreational vehicles and pleasure boats to determine how they would search for products on the site. Likely customers were asked which product they would consider for their boats or recreational vehicles. The results were definitive. The participants were mostly men – even when couples were asked, the wives would defer to their husbands – who began their search by entering a particular wattage into the search bar looking for the technical specifications. On the site, their searches were mostly unsuccessful. They would then revert to browsing the site. However, once they got to a product page, the technical specifications were often missing, and there was no easy way to compare products in the product line.

The Challenges

The challenges users faced when trying to make a purchase from the website stemmed from several factors that had nothing to do with the user experience:

- **Corporate culture:** The organization valued marketing material over technical material. As a result, they invested in marketing material while treating the technical documentation as a barely-necessary cost. Technical material was considered less important than content that they thought "got the sale." This stratification also meant that management did not have a robust system for managing and producing technical content.
- **Lack of investment:** The stratified corporate culture meant that resources were not evenly allocated. As a result, the technical documentation team was understaffed. The lack of a robust system for managing content hampered the technical documentation team's ability to produce user support content as quickly as the product schedule demanded. The team was often left scrambling to produce content on a compressed or delayed schedule. This meant that new products were always at risk of having no technical material available.
- **Inability to structure content for *dynamic delivery*:** The dearth of content management tools prevented the team from creating content that could be easily

integrated into the sales side of the website. Instead, they published specifications as PDF files, as they'd done for years. This made it easy for them to pass content to the marketing group and on to the webmaster to be posted to the website. Unfortunately, the trade-off for this convenience was the inability to leverage the content locked in the PDF files.[1]

- **Devaluing of technical content:** The marketing group gave the PDF files to the IT department whenever they got around to it. Because they didn't see the value in the content, they didn't see the value of getting it onto the website as soon as possible. Compounding the problem, the webmaster didn't see uploading the files as a priority, it was just another task for "whenever you have time."
- **Lack of user experience research:** Because no one had observed how users actually used the website to research and make their purchases, the site was not designed with features, such as a comparison chart, that might have been helpful.

The Goal

The marketing department, which had responsibility for the website, had two goals, one specific and one general:

- The specific goal was to create an area on the site where investors could find information of interest to them – in time for the IPO.
- The general, and secondary, goal was to improve the user experience, particularly around product selection and purchase.

The Strategy

It quickly became apparent that they needed to liberate the content from its PDF format and put it into a *content repository* from which a CMS could find and retrieve content and present it dynamically. This would make it possible for customers to compare products side-by-side, search for technical specifications, and choose the right product for their purposes.

---

[1] Not all PDF documents are searchable. Some files are not searchable at all, and many others lack basic navigational components for a usable search.

The Results

The product pages were standardized, so similar information was displayed in the same area for each product. The new architecture allowed for a page structure that included a section for the specifications, and they created a comparison chart. Most importantly, content was published without delay, and likely buyers – those who knew what the devices were and needed only to determine which one was the best for them – could search the technical product specifications. The pages were revamped to make it easier to find local retailers and service centers for each product; previously, this was a painful exercise in frustration.

Prioritizing Content

Knowing which content supports purchase decisions is knowing where to invest your content dollars.

Knowing which content supports purchasing decisions is critical, because that is where to invest your content dollars. In Chapter 22, *Feeding the Customer Lifecycle*, we discussed the impact of content on one person's attempt to research and purchase an LCD projector. The example may be several years old, but the research style is still valid today.[2]

Over the course of forty-four minutes, the purchaser carried out thirteen searches and went to fifteen sites to find the information she needed. She looked at product descriptions to understand important purchase parameters, product reviews to see what industry experts recommended, product pages and specifications, pricing pages, and several other pages for information related to replacement part costs to determine the total cost of ownership (TCO).

One of the lessons learned from this exercise is how much effort users will spend to find the information they want. Knowing what visitors want and providing that content makes it likelier that they will remain on your site.

---

[2] See "Websites Visited during a B2B User Session" [http://www.useit.com/alertbox/-sites_visted_transcript.html] for the complete transcript.

A 2012 survey conducted by Sharon Burton[3] concluded that consumers expect products to come with documentation that meets their needs. The more costly the product, the higher the expectations. By and large, consumers are not happy with product documentation, and when the instructions are confusing or incomplete, consumer confidence about the product is compromised.

If you think that providing a Hansel-and-Gretel-style trail of content to your shopping cart is the only investment you need to make, think again.

These two examples demonstrate that businesses must determine what types of content are valuable in order to prioritize the content they produce. This conclusion may seem obvious, but some prominent brands continue to make the mistake of investing selectively in some types of content and skimping on other content they assume is "second class." The best organizations understand the value of content and how it directly contributes to the bottom line. These organizations make the effort to distinguish between content as a "nice to have" cost center peripheral and valuable product collateral.[4]

[3] "Consumer feelings about product documentation." [http://www.sharonburton.com/-consumer-feelings-about-product-documentation-results-are-in/]

[4] From an email exchange with Kevin Nichols, Director of Content Strategy at Sapient.

CHAPTER 11

Content as Business Asset

> There are two ways of looking at content: the disposable tissue and the linen handkerchief. Tissues are for single-use situations – they're cheap and flimsy so you can justify the use-and-toss model. Fine linen handkerchiefs, on the other hand, are better quality and cost more, and they can be reused with dignity. It's the linen hankie content you want to invest in and care for.
>
> —Rahel Bailie

It's only now, over twenty years since the first web browser was created, that organizations are recognizing that they need a content strategy to manage their content assets. Managing content as a corporate asset is a critical baseline before those content assets can be used to build a competitive advantage.

Categorizing Content Assets

Before we look at the qualitative aspects of content, let's look at the quantitative aspects:

- **Single-use assets:** They're cheap and disposable. Tissues, toilet paper, and tongue depressors all fall into that category. Use-once content like meeting announcements and news releases are examples of single-use assets.
- **Multiple-use assets:** The value of an asset multiplies with its quality and compounds based on the number of times it can be reused. Multiple-use assets include technical content for products that share common attributes, and therefore, common content.

From a pure numbers point-of-view, it makes sense to reuse content wherever possible. Content is expensive, and creating unique content can be pricey. It's pricey to create, it's pricey to maintain, and it's pricey to translate. So it makes financial sense to reuse content, as long as it doesn't hurt the customer experience. For instance, product descriptions can be reused in multiple ways. They can be reused in their entirety, or they can be broken down into components, which can be reused in a variety of configurations across public websites, intranets, applications, and printed material. Table 11.1 shows an example of the multiple reuse opportunities for a product description – in this case, a book.

Table 11.1 – Reusing content components

	Search results	Details page	Catalog	Book Listing	Ad	Flyer	Special offer
Title	■	■	■	■	■	■	■
Author	■	■	■	■	■	■	■
Price	■	■	■	■	■	■	■
Short Description		■		■	■	■	■
Long Description		■				■	■
Product Details		■				■	■
Reviews		■					■
Cover Art	■	■		■	■	■	■

It is tempting to conclude that managing content is a matter of managing the technology. After all, many content management system projects are funded with a single year's savings in translation costs. Get a good content management system, configure the content, and you're on your way, right?

Post-sales material has tremendous reuse potential.

Not so fast. The ROI from implementing an efficient technology such as a content management system is only one part of the equation. We also need to look at content from the qualitative side of things.

Recognizing the Reuse Potential of Content Assets

There is lots of content that can be reused. On the marketing side, reuse is often limited to product descriptions and sales sheets. However, post-sales material also has tremendous reuse potential. We sometimes call this content the *triumvirate* because it gets reused across three departments: technical documentation, training, and customer support. In many organizations, the amount of technical content vastly outweighs the marketing copy.

In terms of volume and visibility, the marketing copy is like the icing on the cake – its job is to entice and persuade – and the technical content is the cake itself – its job is to satisfy the appetite for hard-core, how-to material. Without massive amounts of technical information, there would be no foundation to hold up the marketing copy. Therefore, it makes absolute sense for the technical information to be managed with the utmost attention to content reuse.

In terms of volume and visibility, the marketing copy is like the icing on the cake – its job is to entice and persuade – and the technical content is the cake itself

It's generally obvious when organizations are managing their content efficiently. The text is identical, even though the styling is different, and there is so much content that it wouldn't be economically feasible to have a stable of writers creating each page manually. The content is accurate and consistent across the site. Since they created content once, instead of three times, they likely reduced their content creation effort by somewhere between half and two-thirds. Pretty good value, as assets go.

The missing piece is the user experience. Across the Web, corporate silos are alive and well. For training, users are directed to a training area of the site. For documentation, users are sent to a technical documentation area. For user assistance, users are sent to the customer support area. And user-generated content is divorced from all of this, buried in the detritus of user forums, yet another silo. Figure 11.1 captures the nature of all these silos.

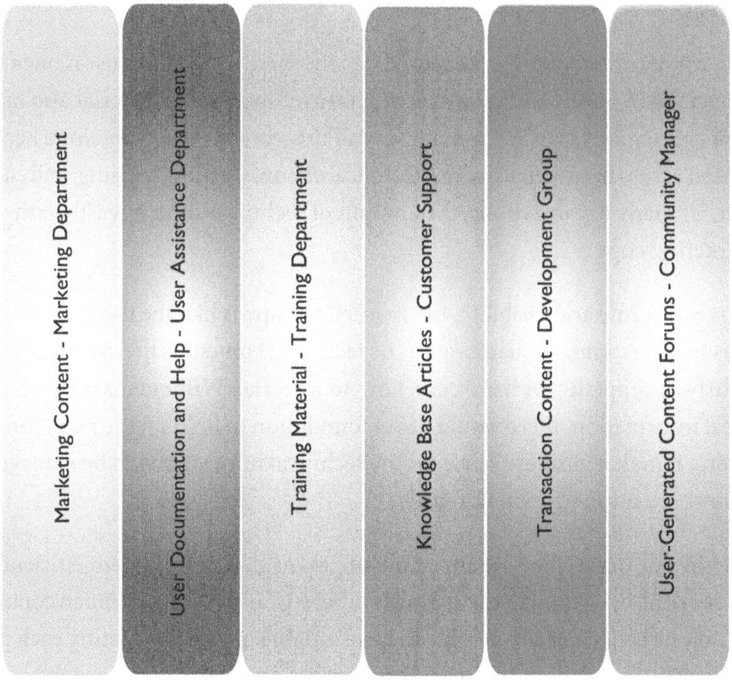

Figure 11.1. Content is often produced and published in silos

Publishing information in vertical silos is known as showing your corporate underwear.

Publishing and presenting information in vertical silos has been around as long as organizations have had hierarchies. This is sometimes referred to as "showing your corporate underwear." This arrangement is convenient for the organization – each department has dominion over a separate area of the website. However, this is not convenient for customers, who are left jumping around the site looking for the information they need.

Figure 11.2 is an example of this type of content presentation. Notice that superficially, the content is well-managed. There is consistency in terminology and presentation. The styling is different, which is appropriate to the presentation of the information in each genre. At first glance, there does not seem to be anything really wrong with the way the information is presented.

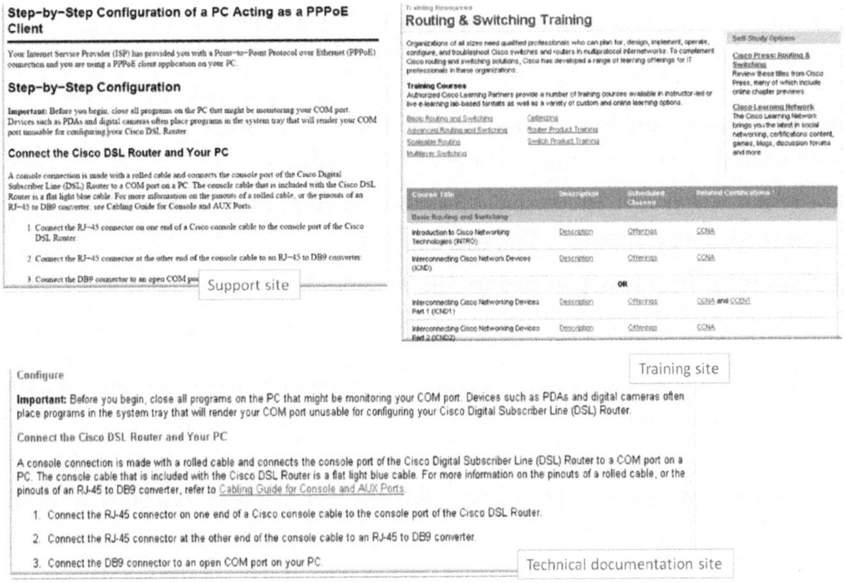

Figure 11.2. Content published in three channels

Yet a closer look shows the content silos. When users want instructions for using the product, they go to the technical documentation section of the site. When they need to troubleshoot the product, they go to the customer support section of the site. And when they need training, they go – provided that they realize that training material is available online – to the training section of the site.

We know that virtually any robust technology, notably content management systems, can present content in any place and order we want. Our challenge, then, becomes knowing what types of things customers want to do and making those things as easy to do as possible. This is where the qualitative side of content, its presentation, becomes a value factor.

Content that Connects: Helping Users Find Success

From a thirty-thousand-foot view, website visitors generally want to do one of these three things:

- **Get information:** Search for information, look up information about a product, service, or resource, or find resources to solve a problem.
- **Complete a transaction:** Log into an account, make a purchase, submit a trouble ticket, look for training, or find user support.
- **Engage with your organization:** Share their experiences or knowledge, connect with other users, give feedback and suggestions, and so on.

The tricky part is that users may want to perform tasks you didn't anticipate.

Aside from this, and this is the tricky part, they may want to perform tasks you didn't anticipate. For example, if you met two people who hacked into the code of a robotic vacuum cleaner to make it play holiday music at Christmas, you might think they represented a marginal user group, until you discover that there is a book available through Amazon on that very topic.

We've already discussed how the user experience is broken if a user goes on a treasure hunt for content and there's no content treasure at the end of the hunt. These two examples make it clear that you need to provide the right information to your visitors. However, from a content strategy perspective, the challenge is more like providing the right content from the right source to the right users at the right time in the right format on the right platform in the right language for the right product version.

The more competitive the industry, the more likely you are to see user-centered content presentation. Figure 11.3, which shows the HP page for an industrial printer-plotter, is a good example. Considering how many products HP has, it makes sense to give users a single page to bookmark, where they can find virtually every piece of information about the product they could ever want to know. Users can read about product features, examine the specifications, find and buy supplies and accessories, download drivers, get support, find compatible products, and even arrange financing.

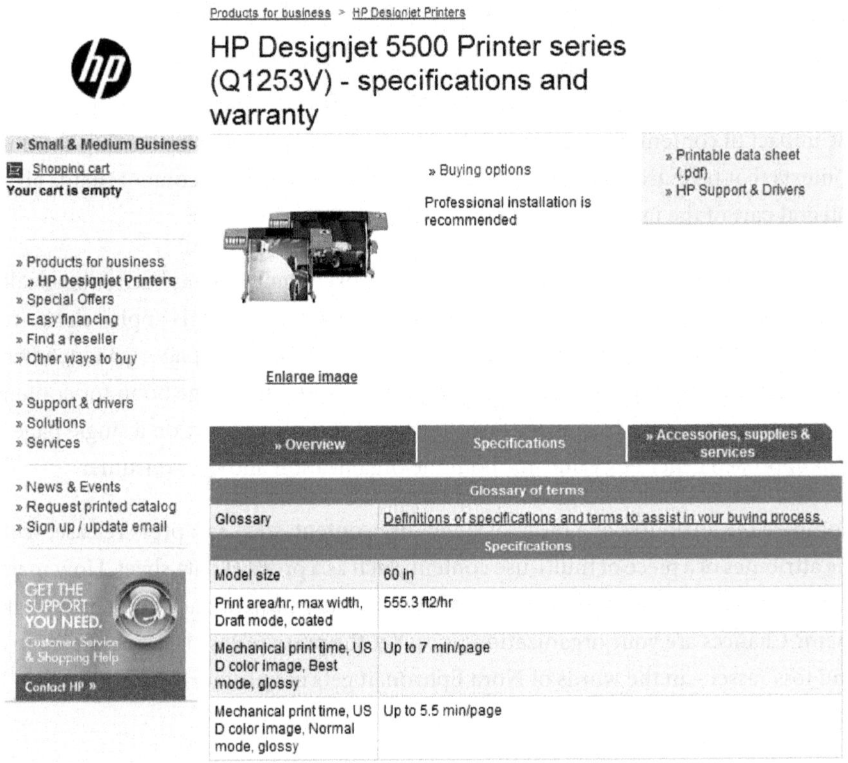

Figure 11.3. Content gathered into a product page for a better user experience

This is a great example of taking content out of organizational silos and presenting it in a way that is useful to users.

But what about the organization's objectives? Unless it is in the business of providing news, it is not focused exclusively on publishing. Yet corporations do want the same things consumers want, even if they express things differently. Organizations want:

- Brand-strengthening, useful content that explains enough about the product or service to entice the target market
- Findable, searchable, and filterable content
- Cost-effective processes to produce content

Turning Content into High-Value Assets

To strengthen their brand and to be more cost-effective, organizations need to turn their best content into high-value assets. We have already discussed ways to amplify the impact of content. By creating high-value content assets and presenting them in contexts that help users be successful, organizations can deliver content that is an integral part of the user experience they want consumers to have.

The HP site in Figure 11.3 is an excellent example of content that has been strategically structured to be more useful to the customer. In all likelihood, this approach has reduced service calls. It's not about creating more content. HP's web pages gather content into a single product portal. Same content, same effort, but a huge boon for content users because they can find everything they need about a product on a single page. This approach generates value, for both the organization and the consumer.

Compare the attributes of a piece of single-use content, such as a press release, with the attributes of a piece of multi-use content, such as a product data sheet. How many organizations consider press releases to be high-value content and invest heavily in them? Chances are your organization does. Yet the press release is a single-use, "use and toss" asset – in the words of Nora Ephron, it gets used tomorrow to wrap fish. It gets skimmed and tossed, if it's read at all.

How many organizations consider a product data sheet a high-value piece of content? Not very many, yet a product data sheet can be used in multiple places – for example, as a decision-making tool or as part of a training course – and it will be studied closely by its readers. So how do we realign content to reflect its true value?

We need to recognize that people use product content far more than they use marketing content.

First, we need to recognize that people use product content far more than they use marketing content. Marketing content is the icing on the cake. Product content is the cake itself. So it's not really about marketing content. Yet it's all about marketing, because if your content says one thing in one place and something different in another place, you've got a consistency problem. And a brand problem. And a credibility problem. And, depending on the industry you're in, you may have a liability problem.

You need to have accurate, up-to-date information anywhere your content is used – in your marketing materials, on your site, in your print documents, in your PDFs, on your product packaging, and in your service agreements. Your content should be able to do the following three things:

- **Integrate:** Integration means taking pieces of data, and including them in a larger content chunk to create context, such as adding a price to product or a time and date to a course offering.
- **Converge:** Convergence means combining chunks of content into a cohesive display. Think of catalogs, where multiple product descriptions come together and get displayed on the same page or screen. On a clothing site, the convergence could be a shirt, pants, and belt to create an "outfit." On a consumer electronics site, the content could be similar laptops to encourage users to compare products.
- **Syndicate:** Syndication allows your users to request that content be pushed out to them automatically, rather than forcing them to go to your sited continually. This can extend your reach tremendously, and it keeps your brand in front of your audience.

These three techniques are possible when you invest in the technical side of content. They allow you to leverage your content assets in new ways. To reiterate, it's not enough to write clever, accurate copy. Technology provides tools that can increase the value of your content; we discuss this in more detail in Chapter 17, *Planning for Power Publishing*.

The technology side always seems more daunting than the editorial side, but don't be in denial about the value of taking on the technical aspects of content. The bar is being raised for what content consumers expect – people go out and experience content presentation on other sites, in other printed material, and so on, and they bring their history with them. So, in effect, inertia around content strategy actually means slippage.

The technology side always seems harder than the editorial side, but take the technical aspects of content seriously.

Let's take a look at an example (see Figure 11.4). Visa lets customers download their transactions month-by-month. A small business can send its downloaded files to its accountant and save the trouble of transferring expenses into a spreadsheet. The download takes about fifteen minutes. For those fifteen minutes, Visa provides a great user experience.

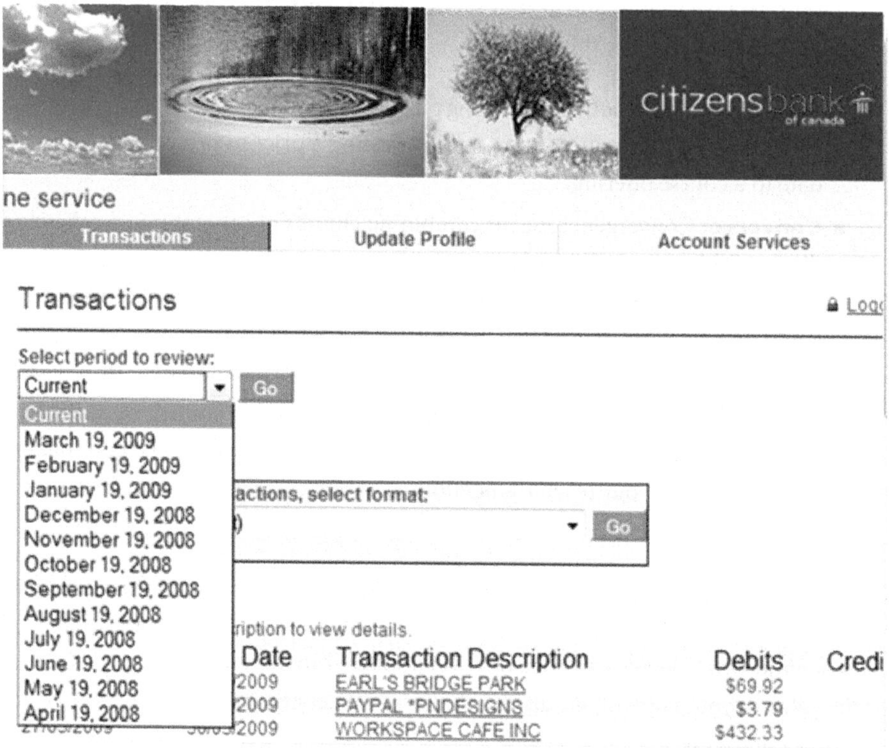

Figure 11.4. Credit card statements limited to month-by-month download

Now, compare that with the experience at a relatively small credit union site (see Figure 11.5). They let customers get to the equivalent information for their accounts, and they do it with many fewer steps. Customers can download up to two years' worth of statements at one time by simply choosing the start and end dates. The download time takes less than a minute.

Once you experience the credit union site, you see the Visa experience in a whole new light. Users bring their experiences from elsewhere, and they compare their experiences. So how do you ensure that you are providing a good user experience? How do you use your content strategically?

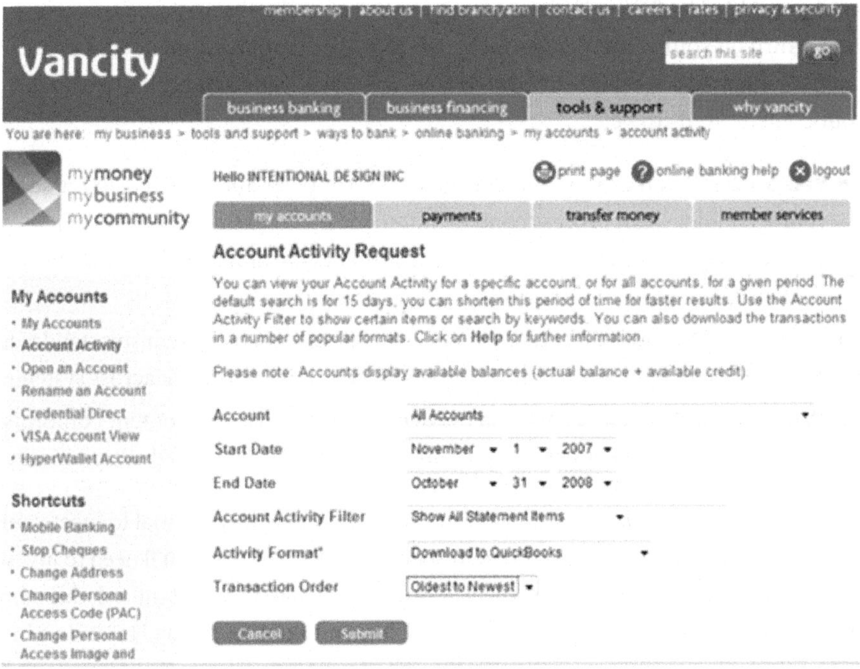

Figure 11.5. Credit card statements downloaded more efficiently

You need extremely nimble content to be able to deliver the best user experience.[1]

What you need to determine is, in this order:

- What user experience you want to deliver
- How to organize your content to be able to create that experience – in other words, a content strategy
- What technology will help you deliver that experience – in other words, the best content management system for that purpose

---

[1] Rachel Lovinger of Razorfish coined the phrase *nimble content* [http://nimble.razorfish.com/publication/-?m=11968&l=1] to describe content that supports publishing in the digital age.

In Chapter 12, *The ROI of Content Strategy*, we discuss the five basic ways you can get a return on your content investment, but to realize that investment, your content must be prepared so that it can be integrated, converged, and syndicated. To do that, your content needs to be:

- **Semantic:** This means adding metadata that supports automated delivery so your technology can process content automatically as customer needs change. Metadata also make content findable for content consumers and sortable for content developers.
- **Standards-based:** This means structuring your content using industry standards like XML. You don't want content locked in; you want it to work across systems.
- **Well-formed and properly structured:** This means your content conforms to a *schema* that creates predictable content that can be processed automatically.

If your content has those qualities, you can start exploiting its potential to meet your organizational goals. If your content doesn't have those qualities, you'll need to invest in reshaping your content to become well-formed, semantic, and standards-based. And it will likely be a substantial investment. To paraphrase Kristina Halvorson in her book, *Content Strategy for the Web*[8], "good content costs money. Get over it."

CHAPTER 12

The ROI of Content Strategy

> In a discussion that arose from a serendipitous meeting during the accidental double-booking of a meeting room, I chatted with a communications professional whose job included developing and implementing a content strategy off the side of his desk. He tried to do this while doing his main job, which was managing community forums for a product line for one of the largest enterprise software companies in the world.
>
> His challenge was to convince his manager that a content strategy was worth it. The management attitude boiled down to this: they couldn't care less about content unless it made more money or cost them sales. Saving money on production and maintenance of content was not a priority, and content that was seen as peripheral to the traditional marketing and sales cycle was definitely not a priority.
>
> —Rahel Bailie

For all of the complexity of business, there are some commonalities across business models, and in those commonalities lies the answer to gaining ROI in a content strategy. The bottom line is profitability, and there are five basic ways to improve profitability: increase revenue, increase efficiency, extend scope, manage risk, and build brand loyalty. These five options fall into two broad categories: make money and save money.

Management couldn't care less about content unless it makes money or costs sales.

The options are not mutually exclusive; in fact, you should consider all five options as you build your content strategy to maximize ROI. The five options are shown in Figure 12.1 (p. 106).

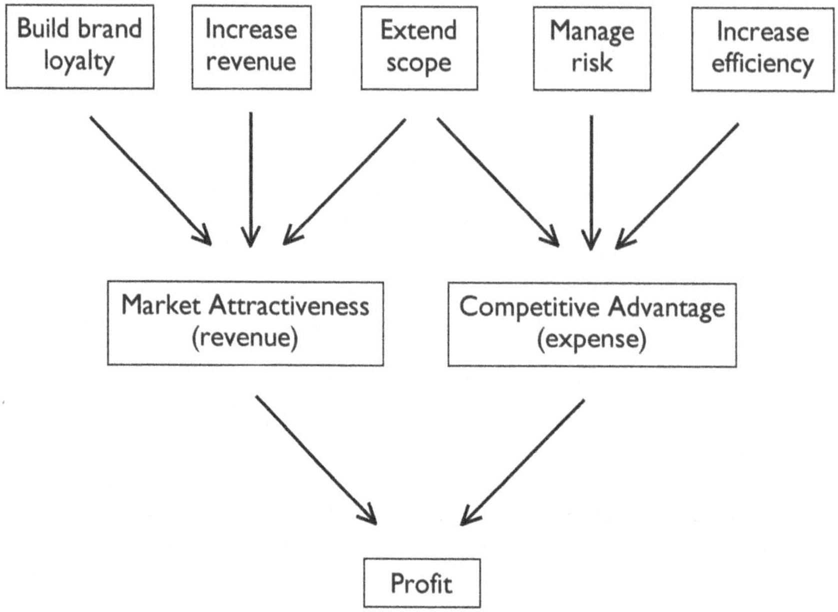

Figure 12.1. The business case for content strategy

On the expense side, you can:

- **Extend scope:** Shift from unnecessary, rote work and focus on mission-critical tasks such as producing better content or content in more languages.
- **Manage risk:** Accurate content isn't just good for your customers, it also helps prevent loss. A lawsuit or regulatory penalty can put a dent in your budget.
- **Increase Efficiency:** Increasing production efficiency, reducing support calls, reducing translation costs, or reducing time to market can all be measured in hard dollars. If your organization cannot efficiently manage content in-house, then outsource the job to an organization that can.

On the revenue side, you can use content to:

- **Build brand loyalty:** More than ever, a better user experience is an important market differentiator. Keep the confidence of your customers and garner the trust of potential customers through better delivery of better content.
- **Increase revenue:** Opportunity cost is harder to measure, but if you look, you will discover ways to use your content to increase sales. Examples include: providing better specifications, more accurate product descriptions, or better comparison tables. All of these respond to consumer demand in new ways that you might not have been able to afford to do before. You may also be able to derive revenue directly from your content. For example, media outlets and training organizations can offer paid content that drives sales.

It's actually not that hard to improve ROI, once you realize the potential of your content and the potential of the delivery technology. If you're serious about leveraging the value of your content, then using a content management system is an obvious, major step toward efficiently managing your content. But it's a good content strategy that will ensure success. The technology will help, but it will not fix any inherent problems with your content. The primary success factor is the content; the technology only supports the content.

Calculating Content ROI

What gets management attention is a lost sale that can be attributed to inadequate content.

It is not surprising that management at the corporation mentioned in the anecdote at the beginning of this chapter didn't think of content as part of a complex adaptive system (see Chapter 5, *Content as Part of a Complex System*). Therefore, their investment in marketing and sales content was not unexpected. What was a surprise, however, was the lack of motivation to save money on content. Never mind that lowering the cost of content production, when done well, generally shows spin-off benefits such as faster time-to-market, increased consistency and accuracy, and greater consumer confidence. However, unlike the team mentioned in the case study in Chapter 8, this company, did not focus on improving the bottom line.

Enter James Mathewson, former Editor-in-Chief of ibm.com, now head of search strategies. During a chat over lunch at a conference, James put this type of thinking into perspective. Not only that, but he created additional context that demonstrated the flaw in that way of thinking.

Considering the size of IBM, the potential for savings in production is in the millions, yet saving a couple of million here and there on new production methods is sometimes a lost cause, as it would cost substantially more to implement the new tools and systems to realize those savings. What gets management attention is when a lost sale can be attributed to inadequate content. "That always gets their attention," Mathewson deadpanned over his coffee.

Unless it's easy to continue down the path toward the first sales interaction, consumers can slip away undetected.

Linking Poor Content to Lost Sales

Mathewson explained how his team was looking at how people interpret information and how their interpretation affects their thinking and behavior, particularly around the journey of software adoption.[2] In this context, Mathewson demonstrates the role that content – pre-sales (marketing), post-sales (customer support), and user-generated – plays in purchase decisions.

The larger a purchase, the longer the sales cycle leading up to the purchase. For enterprise software, the cycle can easily be over a year long. The due diligence required for such a purchase demands multiple touch points, and content gets examined several times before a potential customer interacts with a sales representative. A potential customer can abandon due diligence at any point during the journey. Unless it's easy to continue down the path toward the first sales interaction, potential customers can slip away undetected.

IBM set out to nurture those preliminary, self-directed transactions and then measure the effect of those efforts. The idea was to demonstrate the effectiveness of the process and remove any barriers that could stop potential customers from continuing along the sales path. To evaluate the strategy, IBM conducted usability studies using mar-

[2] The methodology behind Mathewson's explanation is *Attribution Theory*, which looks at how people construct the meaning of events based on their motives and their knowledge of the environment. The article, "Attribution Theory" [http://webspace.ship.edu/ambart/Psy_220/attributionol.htm], from Shippensburg University, elaborates on the topic.

keting content. They then tracked what customers did online to determine what information they needed to have before purchasing a product.

They discovered that potential customers quickly progress from the best-foot-forward marketing material to post-sales documentation and user-generated content such as forums. Customers are looking for post-sales behavior. They want to see what problems exist, how the company approaches those problems, how they solve them, how responsive they are, and so on.

One of the first hurdles is the language used in content. It's often filled with organization-specific jargon. This may work for existing clients, but it creates a barrier for prospects, who will likely search for content. Users increasingly search for content; they only browse when search fails. Content needs to be both searchable and navigable by product categories, using common, familiar search terms that prospects are likely to use.

Users increasingly search for content; they only browse when search fails.

Another hurdle is addressing the concerns of those who don't see themselves as part of the prime target market for a particular product. Customers recognize that software is never designed for every buyer; it's not economically feasible. In a world that runs on the Pareto principle,[3] what happens to those who think their business need falls within the outlying twenty percent? A company can either ignore that market or show prospects how the product can be customized to work for them.

This could be called a risk management strategy. Prospects know that the software won't be a perfect fit, but they are more likely to continue their pursuit if they are confident that the company will work with them to create a solution that works.

---

[3] The Pareto principle, commonly known as the 80-20 rule, says that 80% of results come from 20% of the effort, or 80% of sales come from 20% of customers.

As part of their research, prospects consult content usually considered post-sales material.

People are impatient, Mathewson discovered. Prospects don't spend a lot of time looking for information; they expect to find it quickly. But post-sales documentation is often not easily found through search. And search is critical in an organization that has vast amounts of content. Mathewson points out that IBM's documentation is complete because they comply with ISO standards. However, with some 18 million pieces of unique documentation, content must be findable through search. IBM research showed that prospects get to information most often through search, with navigation as a fall-back. Therefore, quickly and reliably serving content that mitigates the concerns of a potential buyer encourages the buyer to continue searching.

Mathewson warns that complete documentation does not necessarily equate to good documentation. When management does think of documentation ROI, they think about cost savings – "Let's produce content because we have an ISO requirement" – and then they focus on producing content more cheaply, even though studies on the pre-sales side of content quality show that this strategy backfires. They tend to focus on measures like the following, which may reduce cost, but also reduce value:

IBM research showed that prospects get to information most often through search, with navigation as a fall-back.

- Letting content lapse into inaccuracy
- Using machine translation instead of human translators
- Removing editors from the production cycle
- Letting subject matter experts publish documentation

Pursuing such measures may reduce the cost of producing content, but corporations can miss sales opportunities because shoddy content quality compromises the company's reputation. Substandard content doesn't show the company in a good light – a light absolutely needed when potential customers need to justify a purchase.

Critics and cowards may want to minimize the issue because it's always easier to ignore the elephant in the room. But the evidence shows that it's smart to learn how the entire suite of product content affects the bottom line. Mathewson's studies have shown that about 60% of prospects used post-sales material as part of their sales cycle.

Content is not only a critical aspect of selling a service or product, it also helps ensure that new customers keep the service or product. It's no longer IT departments that are left in charge of buying products. Now, it's business users who decide, and they're more discerning. It's not uncommon for them to request a 30-day "try-before-you-buy," or to put the vendor through a proof-of-concept which may last 60 or 90 days. That's when substandard documentation can become evident, creating a predictable series of problems with installation, integration, training, and use. It's common to see customers move from vendor to vendor until they find a "win," and often the deciding factor is sufficient documentation, where the customer decides what is "sufficient."

In Chapter 13, we look at how a leading world brand opened the door for the competition because they didn't have the right content at the right time.

CHAPTER 13

Content Strategy in Business to Consumer

> Knowledge is power. And consumers today have access to knowledge that gives them a much greater level of power in the vendor-consumer dynamic than they had in the days when access to information and information itself were almost solely under the control of vendors. Customers are forcing vendors to cater to a new and expanded set of demands. Rather than trying to win back control from customers, communication professionals working at product companies need to deal with their customers' new needs and partner with their colleagues to meet those needs.
>
> —Noz Urbina

Content can make or break a business-to-consumer experience. Here, we look at how this happens by examining a detailed personal account, based on an interviewee's experience. As strategists, we look at transactions through two simultaneous perspectives. One perspective is the customer experience; we are consumers having the same experiences, good and bad, as other consumers trying to negotiate a typical marketplace transaction. The other perspective is that of the critical analyst, pondering noteworthy service anomalies, good and bad, and figuring out what they mean in the greater scheme of things.

The following experience demonstrates how a content strategy that does not sufficiently consider and cater to the different phases of the customer lifecycle will negatively affect the brand. Although anecdotal and specific to one interviewee – a European male, mid-30s, referred to from this point on as "the buyer" – the analysis of the experience through the dual perspective of a strategist exposes some of the ways that the right content in the right format delivered at the right time can make a critical difference in how consumers relate to a brand.

The Pull to Purchase

During a training session, the projector stopped working, and instead of buying another projector, the buyer decided to replace it with a large-screen TV.[1]

The fact that there were trainees awaiting the rest of their course accelerated this buying cycle. It was not the usual decision of whether to buy a television that day, but which television would win a fast-paced battle of the brands.

Choosing a Product: Wooed by Big Brands

In an electronics store, looking at multiple models, the process is a little like speed-dating. You've got a tiny window to show your best features, then the buyer is on to the next candidate.

Communicating your brand is like speed-dating. You've got a tiny window to show your best features before the buyer moves on

The search for key features and benefits did not follow the manufacturers' recommended path through their websites. To paraphrase the popular television personality, Dr. Phil, the best indicator of future behavior is past behavior. In other words, you don't expect the company attitude to improve after the sale. What the buyer wanted was independent validation of the claims of each brand. Online reviews are a primary mechanism for this evaluation.

The buyer tapped brand and model numbers in the desired price range into his smartphone to look for star ratings and reviews online, first filtering by brand, with a preference for brands chosen on reputation.

Yet even among the choices he picked as best in class, the process was frustrating and disappointing. He found many online retailers vying for attention. The retailers are a third party, but they generally publish content provided by the manufacturer: feature lists, suggested retail pricing, product descriptions, product images, and so on.

---

[1] The rationale for replacing the projector with a television was twofold: replacing the projector would cost three times as much as a television, and a projector would sit in storage after the training session, while a television could be used on an ongoing basis.

However, manufacturers do not give retailers customer reviews. Manufacturers leave reviews to the retailers and trust retailers to do what's in the best interests of the brand. The retailers' sites make several mistakes, including:

- **Reviews only for one region:** Some sites would not only filter by language, but since they were local retailers, they would only show reviews from the local region. The buyer spoke three languages, and would have benefited from having access to more than just local reviews.
- **No reviews at all:** Many sites that rank highly for product names and models simply posted the manufacturer-supplied product description, product images, and price information, with no reviews at all.

Had manufacturers and retailers given any thought to what consumers need, particularly consumers accustomed to getting immediate answers online (which, today, is most of them), they would have understood the need to provide resources to improve the purchasing process. What the buyer wanted, but didn't get, was:

- **Similar model browsing:** Most manufacturers arrange products into product lines that share components. If there are no reviews on the specific model that interests me, where are the reviews of the closest model based on similar technology? Reading reviews of other products in a line would help potential buyers evaluate the post-sales experience of a particular model.
- **Similar model browsing across countries:** Manufacturers routinely assign different model numbers for essentially the same product. Because this isn't apparent to most consumers, looking for reviews for the same product in another country doesn't come to mind. This is a missed opportunity to provide more decision-making content to consumers.
- **Mobile-friendly views:** Zooming in and out of pages to switch between navigation, headings, and reviews is frustrating. The site with the easiest reading wins. Others were closed as soon as they loaded.
- **Reviews in other languages:** Over 56% of the European population speaks at least one foreign language, and for 38%, that language is English.[2] The other 18%

[2] See "Europeans and their Languages" [http://ec.europa.eu/education/languages/pdf/doc631_en.pdf], a Eurobarometer report, for more information.

speak one of these four common second languages: German, French, Spanish, and Russian. As a consumer, the buyer would always prefer to read consumer reviews in his native language, but he also wanted the option to read additional reviews in the second language of his choice.

Choosing a Brand

The buyer felt uneasy making the purchase, a bit like having a shotgun wedding after a speed-dating event. After as much on-the-spot research as could be managed, he decided on a brand. Price was a factor, but his history with the brand was also a strong consideration. Despite buying from a trusted brand, he felt annoyed at the manufacturer, mostly for not ensuring that its sites delivered the information he actually wanted.

The mistake most manufacturers make is assuming the job is done once the sale has been made.

As a consumer, he'd been trained to think that the brand itself has the least trustworthy content about its products. "Manufacturers have their own interests in mind, and they seem unable to put themselves in the shoes of their customers. Frankly, I spent little time reading the manufacturers' sites because of my opinion of their credibility." Despite his significant skepticism, he chose a television, paid, and took it home.

The First Disappointment: A Short Honeymoon

Before using the unit in a live training session, he decided to test-drive the television ahead of time. His first disappointment was that he couldn't turn it on.

Like many consumers, his first instinct was to (almost as a matter of principle) not "give in" and look in the manuals. The manuals were two gigantic print books, each with over 200 full-sized pages. They contained only the set-up instructions (no usage instructions), repeated in forty languages. Of the more than 400 pages, less than twenty were intended for any one person. Instead of opening the manuals, he turned to Google. But despite some very targeted search terms, all he found was commercial content about the unit, or user-generated content in discussion forums and on YouTube complaining about malfunctions. There was nothing applicable to the actual issue at hand.

Post-Sale Support: Where's the Love Now?

Now that the purchase had been made, the quality of the post-sale experience was up to the manufacturer. But their site turned out to be a study in how departmental silos and customer lifecycle segmentation can result in disjointed content.

The buyer said, "Potential customers are the clear and main focus of the site, and actual customers are definitely a secondary audience."

None of the manufacturer's pages lead to after-sale information. He said, "Support was not part of the product pages and was hard to find from the main site, which implies to me as a user that building brand loyalty matters only before a sale."

Karen Donoghue, in her book *Built for Use*[6], discusses the concept of "trust tokens." When users – in this case, customers – have a good experience, they give the company a trust token. When users have a bad experience, they take away a token. Brand loyalty ends up being the running total of trust tokens at any given time. In business-to-consumer commerce, where competitors abound and profit margins are being slashed, customers seem happy to take away multiple trust tokens for each one they give.

This was certainly the case for our buyer. As a savvy consumer, he wanted to be able to search by model number on his smartphone, get to the manufacturer's website, and search for mobile-friendly set-up instructions that could be read on a small screen.

After thirty minutes of frustration, he relented and read the manual. The illusive power button was hidden in a corner, covered by a flap of plastic. Out of sight, out of mind, the button was a perfect metaphor for how the after-sales content was treated.

Promoters: You Get Back the Love You Give

At the time of writing, many organizations are focused on their Net Promoter Score,[3] which Wikipedia calls an alternative to customer satisfaction measurements. The Net Promoter Score has a direct correlation to customer experience and is a general web success metric like time-on-page or conversions. Most web metrics track the effectiveness of the site in question. Although grouped with other web metrics, the Net

[3] http://en.wikipedia.org/wiki/Net_Promoter

Promoter Score is special because it specifically tracks satisfaction. A "promoter" is a satisfied customer who promotes your brand online.

Your website alone can't turn customers into promoters, it can only facilitate and motivate customers who are already happy.

Your website alone can't turn customers into promoters, it can only facilitate and motivate already satisfied customers to communicate. If you want people to publicize their opinions about your brand in a way that advances your strategic goals, you need to ensure that customer experiences are satisfying and engaging across the entire range of brand touch points. If any link in the value-chain is broken, then the customer will not feel the same level of support and care from the brand. Then, when called upon to be a Net Promoter, which is essentially returning support in a public way, the support given will be proportional to that originally received. Quid pro quo.

The True Test of Brand Loyalty

The morning after the buyer bought the television, it started to fail. The image display began to smear to one side, an abnormal behavior and a sign of a malfunction. He tried to reach out to the manufacturer, this time not just to avoid the printed manual, but because the television was having definite technical difficulties, and he needed more information: was this a simple fix or would it require some technical expertise?

There were few highly ranked search hits for common product problems – not helpful to consumers.

The manufacturer's commercial pages ranked high in search engine results when looking for models to buy, but were quite scarce when searching for common problems. When he added terms like "blurry," "smeared image," and "blurred picture" to the search, the manufacturer's pages were driven down to the third or fourth results page. The marketing department may have considered this a win – pre-sales customers would not see the common problems associated with a model – but the trade-off was that a post-sales customer was left feeling neglected.

The focus on pre-sales content effectively abandoned the buyer at the transition from pre- to post-sales in the customer lifecycle. When post-sales content was really needed and the relationship was at a critical early stage, the manufacturer's presence as far as the buyer's interests were concerned – value-added content – was nowhere to be found. Instead of representing the brand directly to a frustrated customer, all the high-ranking search results were forums and other third-party sites, leaving the buyer to pick through an array of unrelated topics to find an answer.

Post-Sale Terms Need SEO, Too

After hearing about the buyer's frustration, we decided to analyze how common his situation was. Did users frequently want post-sale content – manuals, calibration information, and trouble-shooting guides – for products as simple as a television, camera, or stereo? Some simple guerrilla research using Google was revealing. Here's what we did:

1. Enter the product line name or prefix from a manufacturer (For a Canon compact camera for example this might be "Canon IXUS" in Europe, "Canon ELPH" in US and Canada. For a Sony TV, it could be "Sony KDL"). Google will show the most searched for models in a drop-down.
2. Select one of the model numbers from the drop-down.
3. Press the space bar to see the most common search terms for that model

We tried this for Sony TVs, Canon compact cameras, and several other business-to-consumer electronics. The results were even more pronounced than we had expected. The term "manual" was consistently the second most searched term – the most searched term was "review." This meant that "manual" was the most highly ranked search for something tangible created and published by the brand. (Reviews are generated by the community, not the brand.)

Search behavior clearly shows what consumers want to know.

Right Content, Wrong Format

"Manual" was the most highly ranked search term that matched something tangible created and published by the brand.

Manufacturers might recognize that manuals and post-sales content are important, but are they taking appropriate action? It was clear from the manufacturer sites we analyzed that they were leveraging the term "manual" to drive up page views. On the surface, this is fine. We tell companies that potential customers now commonly use what was traditionally post-sales content during their pre-sales evaluation.

However, for the majority of manufacturers we surveyed, the manuals the users were searching for were in PDF files. This means that customers – pre- or post-sale – who were operating in a "web modality," arrived at the information they needed, only to be forced to switch modes to the print paradigm in order to actually consume the content they were after. Manuals and post-sales content were linked from the landing pages, but they clearly were second-class citizens.

From our client experience, we know that this inconsistency isn't usually an intentional choice by the brand; rather it's a by-product of a legacy situation, organizational silos, or the perceived complexity, cost, or difficulty in moving content across formats and channels. The result of avoiding this perceived cost is that customers have to download dozens, and in some cases hundreds, of pages of PDF material to get the answer to a single question.

It also raises an important question. Does this tactic drive customers to use expensive-to-supply and slow-to-consume support channels such as telephone support or resort to third-parties or social media rather than consume content that is not optimized for online or mobile consumption? Or do they just "take back their trust tokens" and find another product?

The Role of Content in the Customer Experience

The buyer eventually had to take the television back to the retailer to exchange it. At this point, his loyalty had waned. The buyer said, "While I could have forgiven a manufacturing flaw, I felt a lack of regard for me as a customer that grated on me." The pre-sales phase lasted a mere 24 hours; the post-sales phase could last for years and potentially involve repeat sales. Yet, the overall feeling of quality and post-sales support dropped off sharply. The buyer was annoyed with the manufacturer, who lost the sale.

The buyer wandered around the store looking more closely at other televisions and eventually decided to buy two from a competitor – one replacement and another that was needed for a spare room. It didn't matter much who the competitor was, or how their content compared. By that point, the first manufacturer had let a customer down and opened the door to competition.

ROI and the Long View

Your return on investment depends as much on not breaking the sale as it does on making the sale. And if a transaction is not about the current sale, then it's about subsequent sales. We see in this case study that short-term content strategies that do not account for the entire customer lifecycle can lead to disaffected, unhappy customers. It is also an example of how the difficulty of integrating a content strategy across departmental boundaries and making content multi-channel ready (in this case, print, desktop web and mobile) can hurt sales.

Short-term content strategies that do not account for the entire customer lifecycle can lead to disaffected, unhappy customers.

In the business-to-consumer transaction recounted here, the entire experience took place within just 24 hours. Yet, it was a typical consumer experience, and it exposed the importance of content in supporting a sales decision. Many consumer product returns fall into the "No Fault Found (NFF)" category, where the device is fully functional, but the user can't make it work. Mobile solutions provider WDL Global estimates that product returns in the NFF category cost the mobile industry $4.5 billion annually.[4]

From consumer electronics to industrial equipment, a high percentage of returns are considered "No Fault Found," often due to inadequate documentation that leads users to believe the unit is faulty when it actually isn't. Yet, this same documentation is a well known cost avoidance point for many manufacturers.

A high percentage of returns are considered "No Fault Found," often due to inadequate documentation that leads users to believe the unit is faulty.

Anticipating user need can be daunting because it involves multiple publishing channels, output in multiple formats, and cross-departmental cooperation; it requires you to think of content strategy in an integrated way to support the brand. The benefits of overcoming these challenges are tied to your organization's long-term success.

Here are a few of the lessons we can learn:

- Underestimating the need for strong post-sales content can affect the customer experience, which in turn can affect repeat business.

---

[4] Statistics are from "Investigating the No Fault Found Phenomenon" [http://www.wds.co/news/-whitepapers/20060717/MediaBulletinNFF.pdf], from WDS Global.

- If you want to maximize marketing ROI with customer advocates – and judging by the placement of "review" on search engine results pages, you should – you need to give your customers a solid, holistic, cross-platform experience. The website itself is not enough; all your communications channels play their respective parts in shaping the user experience.
- Relationships and brand are hard to build and easy to damage. It's easier to retain customers than acquire them.
- As customers become more interconnected and digitally savvy, you need to start bringing a business-to-business mentality into the business-to-consumer space to keep driving revenues. The Internet means consumers are now better equipped than ever to evaluate the post-sales experience before investing – a type of "due diligence" that was once only a feature of B2B purchasing.

So if shoddy content loses business, why do we still need to make this case? The reason is captured in the concept of *multiplicity,* which we discuss in detail in Chapter 16, *The Nature of Content*. Multiplicity is a term for the reality that modern content delivery involves multiple content stakeholders, who have multiple audiences, multiple deliverables, multiple formats, and so forth. And the goals of these multiple stakeholders do not always align, even in one organization. It takes a comprehensive content strategy, support from upper-level management, and a strong governance plan to break out of the problems illustrated by this case study.

CHAPTER 14

Content Strategy in Business to Business

> When I worked at a multinational company, I had a boss who had risen from technical writer to director quickly, but who really didn't know how to think strategically about content. When my internal client, the Director of Professional Services, decided to streamline content production by extracting instructions from data models, I became quite excited. The idea that the content could live in a central place and be edited once meant our team would have more time for high-value activities associated with content creation. My boss, on the other hand, expressed her dismay that the team would become glorified proofreaders. It was an unfortunate disconnect: was the organization better served by a large team creating one-off content on an ongoing basis, or by fewer staff doing higher-level tasks, leaving the rote work to the software? The internal client, proficient in calculating ROI, definitely favored the latter approach.
>
> —Rahel Bailie

At the other end of the spectrum from business-to-consumer sites, in the business-to-business world, user-facing content comes in varieties that have nothing to do with website home pages and marketing.

Case Study: A Start-up Treats its Content Right

Over a decade ago, an extremely smart and talented software developer, Dean, became the Director of Professional Services for a Fortune 500 company. Today, he is the founder of a start-up, Malaspina Labs, poised to revolutionize a niche market that could affect an entire industry. Their market is not consumers or even retailers. They sell middleware to component manufacturers – companies that build components that become part of another manufacturer's product.

The Organization and the Product

Malaspina Labs sells meticulously documented audio-processing and speech-isolation source code. When complex source code is a product, the accompanying documentation is critical. Each function must be documented as to what it does, how it works, and what constraints it has. Malaspina's products comprise hundreds of files and tens of thousands of lines of source code. Customers need precise, comprehensive documentation to seamlessly integrate the code into their products.

The Problem

The client receives several sets of files:

- A set of files containing the source code to be incorporated into the client's product
- A set of files containing a test suite, which validates that the source code still produces correct output after the client has modified and configured it
- A set of documents that describe the source code, its functions, the configuration and modification instructions, the theory of operation, and the expected results from the test suite

Every time an engineer handed over a specification, the original mistakes would be re-introduced into the new document.

The traditional way of handling this is to create a lengthy document that itemizes each function. Each time a software function is updated, an engineer updates the corresponding section of the main document, and then a writer examines the other documents for where it would be appropriate to cut and paste that description and includes it in those documents.

Ten years ago, in Dean's previous company, that's the way it worked. In that case, the engineers came from many countries. While English is the de facto standard of engineering, the various flavors of English spoken by the engineers differed quite a bit. Therefore, the documentation needed to be edited to a standard form that would be intelligible to clients, who were also engineers and also from many countries. However, no matter how many times the writers corrected the English, every time an engineer handed over a specification, the original mistakes would be re-introduced into the document. Not only was the output an unprofessional-looking document, it was inefficient and a waste of resources.

The Goal

Dean decided that in his start-up, he was going to eliminate as much wasted effort as he could. His developers didn't have time to ensure that they had found all the instances that need to be updated. And they certainly didn't have the resources to cut and paste information from one place to another. Instead, Dean wanted a system in which his developers could author once and then generate all of the combinations needed by multiple customers from a single superset of content.

The goal was to generate all combinations of files needed by multiple customers from a single superset of content.

The Strategy

Dean's strategy was to have a "single source of truth" for each type of information and to build the output documents they needed by combining information from that single source. In their Programmer's Reference Guide, for example, each code function is listed, followed by an explanation of what the function does. The code function comes from the code file, and the explanation comes from the Architectural Specification. Without going into too much detail about the mechanics of how this happens, the content gets combined to look like Figure 14.1.

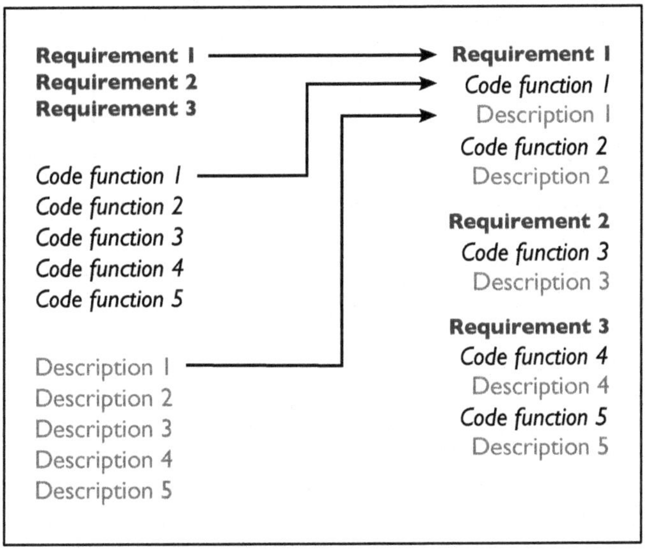

Figure 14.1. Content combinations

Every time information is updated from any source document, a simple "generate" command combines the output into a document that can be delivered to the customer.

Aside from the actual source code, the product includes the following suite of documents, as shown in Figure 14.2:

- Architectural Specification, which describes how the code is structured.
- Programmer's Reference Guide, which details the function of each piece of code.
- "Portation" Guide, used by customers to figure out how to integrate the content into their products.
- Verification results, which developers use to test the integrity of the code.

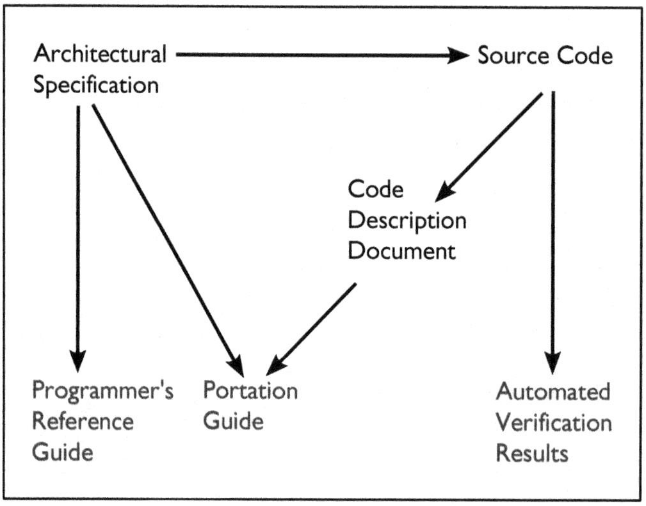

Figure 14.2. Generated suite of documents

But wait, there's more. Customers need to know how to integrate the code into their products. They receive these documents in an editable format, and as they modify the code, they *must* update the documentation so it continues to accurately reflect the source code. Integrating code into a generated document allows you not only to capitalize on the technology, but also to retain an audit trail that will satisfy the regulatory agencies, should you be audited.

The Results

Content reuse may not be terribly sexy, but it brings incredible value to the organization.

The advantages of this content strategy can be measured in several ways:

- The time and effort saved by the developers allows the organization to maintain a complex set of documentation using subject matter experts, in this case developers, as the sole content authors.
- Process automation avoids manual maintenance of the documentation suite during the many iterations of source code change and test suite changes.
- Automation reduces human error.
- Customers have procedurally reproducible documentation.
- The organization has well-defined and documented processes to ensure that their technologies are acceptable for use in ISO 9001 development environments and meet FDA or other applicable requirements for Commercial Off The Shelf software use in medical devices.

This may not be terribly sexy stuff, but it brings incredible value to the organization, and it is a model for how to move up the content strategy maturity model at a rapid rate, even as a start-up.

Content Under the Hood

This section of the book looks more deeply into content and how to turn it into a valuable corporate asset. At first glance, this section might appear to be too technical for many in our audience, but our experience has shown that to make informed decisions, you must know something about the technical side of content strategy.

We know our audience comes from varied backgrounds, but we have found that many who do not have a technical background still want to know about these concepts. In fact, we've been asked to run workshops for directors, developers, and technical and project leads to explain these concepts.

As a final reassurance, early reviewers of this book told us we've done a good job of shedding light on concepts that were vague or overwhelming. We address the following topics:

- Breaking content out of silos and format lock-in, and readying it for reuse.
- Using adaptive content and responsive design.
- Labeling content semantically to future-proof your content.

However, if the technicalities of content really bore you to tears, read Chapter 15, *What Exactly Is Content?* and Chapter 19, *Making Content User-centric Using Modular Building Blocks*, and then enlist the technical people on your team to synthesize the rest and tell you if there's anything you need to go back and read.

CHAPTER 15

What Exactly Is Content?

> I have a t-shirt that sports a message about content strategy marked-up using XML tags. I wore it when I went to visit my accountant and his database administrator wife. When I arrived, they both studied the t-shirt intently for a minute. The database administrator's reaction was, "yep, you wrote valid code." Her husband's reaction was, "tell me about content strategy."
>
> I realized there are two types of people: those who read the tags, and those who read the content between the tags. Until recently, it's been the tag-readers who have been running the industry.
>
> —Rahel Bailie

In a technology-enabled world, content is "the stuff" inside the container. Content means all the text, graphics, audio files, video files, metadata, and a whole bunch of other information that is part of the wayfinding exercise, but not actually the driver behind the wayfinding. Technically, all of this material is still "content" because it is "contained" by the deliverable, whether that deliverable is a website, app, brochure, guidebook or some other container.

Copy and Content

However, much of the content used in wayfinding is not what the end user – the content consumer – is looking for. In other words, a reader who wants to find an article on photographic techniques may use the navigation bar on a website to find the article, and that navigation bar may be critical to get to the article, but the navigation bar is not the end goal, and the reader derives no meaning about photographic techniques from the menu item. What the reader wants – and for purposes of this example, we will confine ourselves to text – is copy. Copy is the message. It's what content consumers read; it conveys meaning.

When practitioners ask "What do you mean by content," they are often trying to figure out which content they are responsible for. Content outside of their purview is often discounted.

To create copy, writers need to understand some basic elements, starting with the notion of "genre." Genres are a way to classify works into groups that share common characteristics. For example, two popular genres of novels are murder mysteries and romance novels. The common aspects of each genre – a body, a detective, suspicious characters for murder mysteries; a couple, a courtship, a happy ending for romance novels – cue users to understand what to expect when they pick up a book.

There are two basic genres of copy used in business.

Persuasive

Persuasive copy tries to convince users to do a certain thing or think in a certain way. The most common characteristic is the call to action. Persuasive copy has a built-in message meant to convert a "looker" into a "buyer." It is the written equivalent of "buy now" text or a link to click. Persuasive copy includes messages like an invitation to register for a free account, receive a white paper, or contact your local politician.

Writers who create persuasive copy need to know what the appropriate rhythm is for what they are creating. They should know how much copy readers will tolerate before they lose interest and potentially miss the call to action. When presented with an unfocused block of writing, the first question should be: "What is the call to action here?" And the next question should be: "How do you see the conversion happening?"

Within the genre of persuasive copy, there are sub-genres such as news releases, marketing-oriented product overviews, and ads. While not the most exciting of genres, we'll use news releases as an example here because they belong to an established genre. Later we will use them to illustrate the difference between copy and content.

A typical news release begins with the line, FOR IMMEDIATE RELEASE, followed by a release date and location. The writing follows the "pyramid" style:

- The most important content is contained in the first sentence.
- The middle section elaborates on the summary and includes the call to action.
- The end contains "boilerplate" – company description and contact information.

The call to action in the middle section should be subtle. A typical news release reports on some upcoming event, product release, or initiative with information on how to answer the call to action – where to buy tickets, when the product will become available, or how to get involved. It's all about the editorial qualities leading to a "conversion," where the content consumer goes from just consuming content to taking the action called for in the copy.

In the public sector, conversion means a change in behavior or attitude; for example, supporting a new initiative or voting for a particular candidate. In the private sector, conversion means taking a step toward a purchase.

Enabling

Enabling copy helps you complete a process or task. It explains "how to" – from setting up a piece of equipment to registering for an account to paying your taxes to ordering a passport. It's also the text within a software application that describes menu items, the knowledge-base files that demonstrate how something works, or the training materials that help customers use your products or services.

Within this genre, too, we have many sub-genres. The most recognizable genre is the procedure. This has a well-defined structure, or "schema", to use the industry term. This structure includes: a heading, a contextual introduction, numbered steps, and a conclusion that explains the success or failure state. Each numbered step begins with an active verb and uses a technique that writers refer to as the "given-new contract,"[1] and when appropriate, is followed by a feedback statement to demonstrate the expected result. It's all about guiding users to the desired outcome.

Writers, whether they write enabling material or persuasive material, apply a combination of training, experience, and skill as they create copy. Their training is what gives professional writers their strong understanding of their craft. But that craft is creating messages. This is copy because it pays attention to the message.

---

[1] The given-new contract is a writing technique used in learning material to connect new material to that already stated. This technique is explained in "The Given/New Contract and Cohesion: Some Suggestions for Classroom Practice"[22].

Turning Copy into Content

If copy is the message, then what makes copy into content? At the risk of oversimplification: semantics turns copy into content. The topic of semantics will be discussed in more detail later in the book, but for the moment, we'll define semantics as giving content extra meaning by attaching metadata. Metadata allows computers to sort, filter, and combine content based.

Computers don't understand information so they can't support any of the complex ways you want to use information.

In a day when virtually all content gets processed by some sort of technology, the union of editorial structure – that is, the structure that allows people to understand what to do with copy – and semantic structure – the structure that allows computers to understand what to do with copy – is the combination that creates content.

A basic example of marrying editorial and semantic structures is using a stylesheet when creating a document in a word processor. A stylesheet lets you apply the right styles and structural information to headings, subheadings, various list types, and so on. Why is this important? Once you save your document as a PDF, this information allows a Table of Contents to be created that links to the appropriate headings, and an index to be generated with entries that link to the right pages. It also allows headers and footers to be automatically generated with the appropriate heading names, and major sections to start automatically on odd-numbered pages.

At the risk of oversimplifying: semantics turns copy into content

When content is created in a semantically structured format – that is, with structure that allows other systems to understand and programmatically process the content – then it's possible to leverage that content to get better value from it. Although our example used news releases, the important point is how to get the best use from whatever content you create. In other words, no matter what the message is, it needs to be created, stored, and prepared for use in a modern content system. How it is stored will be critical to putting some *technopower* behind your copy to make it go farther and turn into content.

We explore how and why storage format and structures enable new functionality, accessibility compliance, and more agile publishing in Chapter 17, *Planning for Power Publishing*. For now, what is important is the benefit such technopower can deliver.

Defining Content in the Age of Technology

To look further into technopower, we'll borrow the term "asset *amplification*" from the financial industry. In the context of financial markets, asset amplification describes how changes in financial markets can be amplified because of follow-on consequences. Similarly, the power of copy can be amplified if it is placed into a robust technology framework. Once copy is placed inside of a framework, it becomes the content of that framework.

Just as coffee is the content of a cup, copy is the content within a technology framework. And like a super-hero with the appropriate gear, copy, with the appropriate framework, gets super-powers, too.

Like coffee is the content of a cup, copy is the content within a technology framework.

One example of amplification started with a letter by Dave Carroll to United Airlines. Perhaps you've heard of it? Dave Carroll had a complaint about United Airlines breaking his guitar. After nine months trying to work one-on-one with United, Carroll had gotten nowhere. There was no amplification. So, he wrote a protest song and posted it on YouTube. The technopower that YouTube provided – the ability to "like," share on social media, add to a playlist, and so on – amplified his message. In fact, the video was viewed over 10 million times, leading to a belated, but ultimately satisfactory, resolution from United – and significantly helping Carroll's musical career.[2]

Another example is how municipalities advise residents of new development in a city. The traditional notification involves putting up signs on the property and sending postcards to residents within a certain number of blocks of the proposed development. Turning that posted *copy* into *content,* the city could take advantage of technology to amplify the notification process; the proposed development could have a page on the municipal website, with the ability to subscribe to, or share, news about the project. The technology would give residents the power to amplify the message through a syndication feed or share the news with other residents through social media.

Reuters provides yet another example. It uses a variety of techniques to ensure its content is easy to access and consume. However, this didn't just happen through the

[2] A synopsis of the incident that led to Dave Carroll writing the song is available on Wikipedia: United Breaks Guitars [http://en.wikipedia.org/wiki/United_Breaks_Guitars].

underlying technopower. Reuters invested significantly to achieve the goal of providing content that is timely and relevant.

Until recently, communications coordinators who organized events would type out the event details: event name, start and time, place, cost, and so on, and then spend hours copying and pasting that copy into website text boxes or filling in forms. Each site had different requirements and had to be handled manually and individually. Today, we use content feeds that allow event information – in other words, content assets – to be amplified without manual intervention.

In the end, content may be nothing without copy, but in a post-paper world, copy is nothing without content.

As we evolve from online brochures and "brochure-ware" toward robust interactivity, the need for content that can be understood and processed by computers has dramatically increased. (we discuss this type of content in Chapter 20, *The Power of Semantic Content*). For now, what is important is the benefit such technopower can deliver.

Again, copy multiplied by technopower makes content that can be processed by other systems. The event example is a simple one, but there are other more complex examples, from straightforward publishing to interactive deliverables that require complex transformations of content.

If you subscribe to a content feed on the Web, you have seen syndicated content, but you might be surprised at how extensively content is manipulated and transformed within such a system. Each transformation provides the potential for additional amplification and eventually provides a richer user experience for the content consumer. In the end, content may be nothing without copy, but in a post-paper world, copy is nothing without content.

Why do you need to know this? As a manager, you may not be that interested in the technical aspects of content, but you are interested in meeting your business objectives, and you know your content plays a role in meeting those objectives. The heart of the matter lies in transforming your copy into content. Once you understand the basic mechanics behind how to make content work for you, then you understand how powerful a tool you have in your arsenal.

CHAPTER 16

The Nature of Content

> When I started working for a medical device company, I went in assuming that all the deliverables would be very formal: detailed technical manuals, context-linked online help files, and so on. In the end, one of the deliverables the end users liked best was not one of these more complex deliverables, it was a simple, color-coded wall chart with quick-reference information. It underlined the importance of designing and testing content in various forms, for various contexts.
>
> —Noz Urbina

In the enthusiasm that exists around the Internet, it is tempting to say that content is "going online." While that is true, the statement needs context. Just because content is online does not mean that content is not alive and well in other places. A more complete statement would be that content is going multi-modal. That is, there are various ways – or "modalities," to use a term from user experience professionals – in which we can interact with the same content. Many are online including, of course, the newest. But when brand is at stake, it pays to make sure you're aware of the full customer journey and all customer interactions.

The Multiplicity of Content

Each scope or modality, each format and channel, and even each language and audience has a multiplying effect on the content and issues around managing it. We call this the *multiplicity* of modern content. Our premise, in both Chapter 5, *Content as Part of a Complex System* and this chapter, is that both content strategy and infrastructure are required to deliver effective content in the face of multiplicity. Done well, multiple discrete working parts under unified direction can create something that people want to consume and engage with.

Done well, multiple discrete working parts under unified direction can create something that people want to consume and engage with.

Modern content delivery often involves multiple content stakeholders who create, review, approve, translate, and curate a multitude of documents, sites and deliverables. There are also multiple audiences to address with all this content, including internal consumers and multiple segments and personas in the outside world. And these multiple deliverables, created by multiple participants, and designed for multiple consumers, must also be available in multiple presentation formats and devices (mobile, desktop web, print, and more).

We can call this state *multiplicity*.

Across many projects over the last 20 years, we have seen that managing multiple moving parts overwhelms many companies.

Multiplicity in Creation

Today's enterprises must wrangle content coming in from multiple sources, which we've divided into groups, to make them less overwhelming:

Product sales and marketing: Product sales and marketing content is traditionally seen as pre-sales, persuasive content. This is because this type of content is intended to persuade the consumer to take a particular action. Because of this, the content developers who create sales and marketing content are usually located in areas of the organization credited with generating revenue. Their content includes the following:

- Brand guidelines
- Brochures, advertisements, and marketing copy
- Product and feature overviews
- Preliminary product data such as functional specs and process descriptions
- Pre-sales "how to" content
- Product announcements for prospective customers
- Sales proposals

Product services and documentation content: Typically seen as post-sales, this is generally "enabling content" that helps consumers directly, rather than convincing them to take an action the company might want. Although suppliers want their products to be used, developing this content is typically considered a cost-center. The content developers for these genres include product engineers, software developers, field service staff, customer support engineers, technical communicators, trainers, and product managers. And we should not forget lawyers, who vet content and often contribute content of their own. This category of content includes the following:

- Troubleshooting content
- User guides, quick start guides, and cheat sheets
- Maintenance and technical manuals
- Online or embedded help, also known as Embedded User Assistance
- User interface and embedded content
- Training material
- Knowledge-base articles
- Product announcements for existing customers
- Release notes
- Technical bulletins, field and engineering change requests, health and safety bulletins, disclaimers, terms and conditions, and warnings

Third-party contributions. This content is usually produced post-sales, or at least post-launch, and is outside the control and governance of internal content teams. These content developers vary wildly in their levels of product and publishing expertise. They include sales partners, outside equipment manufacturers (also known as "white label" partners), staff remote offices, industry analysts, and customers. Their content – which could be revenue-generating, a cost, or neither – includes the following:

- Translated marketing, product, and user assistance material
- User contributions to forums and knowledge bases
- User-contributed product content, such as procedures and tips
- Social media content like reviews

Multiplicity in Delivery

It's already a challenge that all the content produced by these groups has to coalesce on the website; but in addition, all this content needs to be delivered to:

- Multiple audiences and audience sub-segments
- Multiple deliverables such as:
  - Traditional websites – desktop (large screen)
  - Mobile websites – tablets and smartphones
  - Native apps on multiple operating systems and device platforms
  - Print
  - White-label content for use by third-parties and channel partners
  - Social channels on organizational and third-party websites
  - Other more exotic formats, such as large-surface touch-enabled devices or gesture-controlled devices
- Multiple other enterprise systems, such as:
  - Extranets/intranets
  - Client Relationship Management and Client Lifecycle Management Systems
  - Learning Management Systems
- All of the above for multiple language and geographical segments

Multiplicity in Engagement

In today's market, customers also expect the organization to be listening on multiple channels and to provide engagement and social interaction. As content goes online and social, the audience is now a publisher, and the brand must learn to be the audience. Content consumers and customers are themselves stakeholders and part of the content lifecycle.

When looked at in its totality, what we can see here is an interconnected ecosystem of content production and consumption. The various audience profiles and personas that we previously labelled "consumers" – whether they were internal or external to the brand – are now becoming contributors who also create content that must be managed.

To bring the gravity of multiplicity to light, Figure 16.1 shows how a relatively small number of products, deliverables, formats, languages, and audiences can quickly multiply into a huge number of distinct deliverables. Multiplicity is significant.

As content goes online and social, an alternate channel has been created, where the audience has become the publisher, and the brand must learn to be the audience.

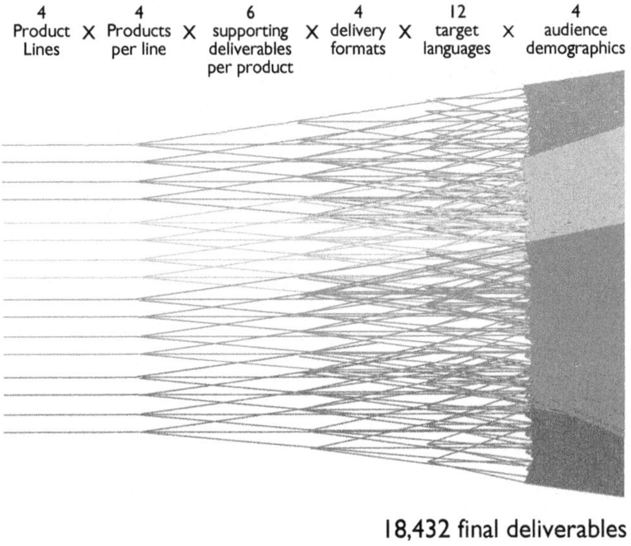

Figure 16.1. Multiplicity of deliverables for a small company

Identifying the multiplicity in an organization allows us to demonstrate that what the budget holders and the executive team often dismissively summarize as "a project" is really thousands, if not tens or hundreds of thousands, of individual deliverables all inextricably tied to the organization's products and services.

Business-Critical Content

When talking about content, we're referring to business-critical content. To illustrate what that means in the context of this book, we've decided to pack a few thousand words worth of meaning into an illustration. Business-critical content affects users and their experience. But how directly? In Figure 16.2 we've scatter-graphed some of the multiple types of business-critical content across the spectrum from persuasive to enabling and from purely internal enterprise content to the content that most intimately impacts user experience, the content generated by the user themselves.

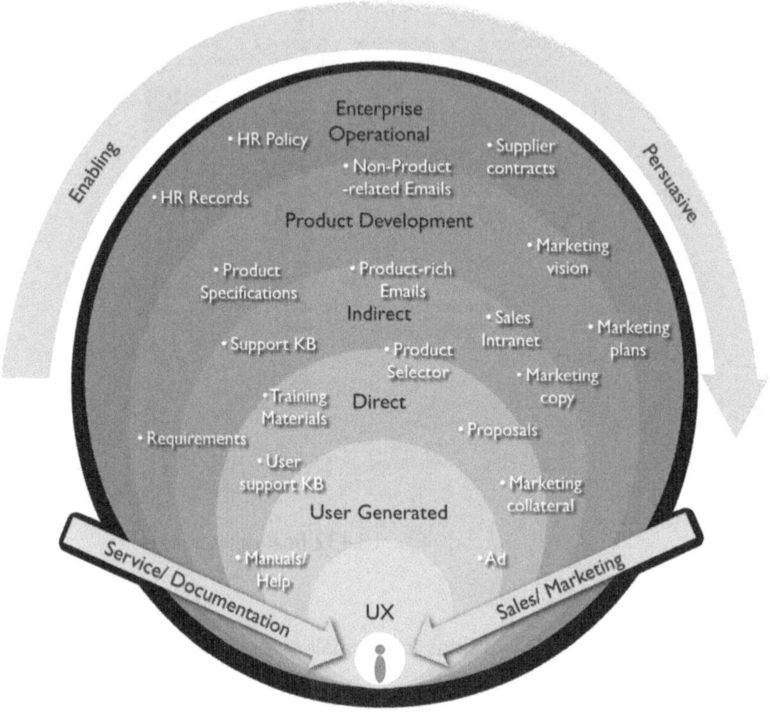

Figure 16.2. Types of content and how they affect user experience

At the bottom-center of the graphic sits the user and the user experience. On the lower right, we have persuasive content: marketing copy, ads, proposals, marketing collateral, and so on. This is, unfortunately, often the full scope of content strategy for some practitioners. On the lower left, we have content that has high brand-impact but is not created to persuade. This content enables the customer to use or evaluate the product. Here we find manuals, help, and other content that fits the larger category of user assistance.

The circles further away from the user indicate content that has less effect on the user; closest is the content that users generate. The impact of content generated by the user community depends on the market and the product. Some markets find that user-community buzz and feedback can make or break a sale. However, the greatest impact comes from how a user's content is handled by the organization. If a user writes to the organization, what happens to the content the user creates will be very significant to that user's personal customer experience.

As we get further from the user, we get deeper into the organization and its operational content. Internal policies are of little interest to customers, unless those policies spill over into the user experience. While some companies have been the target of customer protests over policies that were found to be discriminatory, this is rare.

In the middle is where we see an interesting blend of persuasive and enabling content. Although we'd like to make clean lines between departments and the pre- and post-sale process, customers don't care.

When customers are evaluating a product, they may do research on the website, but they may also talk to sales people. Those sales people get information from various channels, possibly including a sales intranet, a shared folder on a corporate server, or very commonly, a personal store of content that the sales person has collected, indexed, and annotated. What the salesperson says must match what the customer has seen.

Although we'd like to make clean lines between departments and the pre- and post-sale process, customers don't care.

When customers get stuck and can't find the right information in the available manuals, they're likely to call a support center and talk to representatives who have a different, but overlapping, set of content at their disposal. That makes the support knowledge base business-critical content, too.

The customer who has a notable experience, either good or bad, might comment about it or write a user review in a social media channel, amplifying the comment into the realm of pre-sales content for potential customers.

Business-Critical Content in the Semiconductor Industry

Semiconductor and microchip manufacturing is not a particularly sexy industry – at least to those outside the industry. Most people would consider the cutting edge of web delivery to be consumer electronics, retail, automotive, and so on – industry verticals that deliver in a business-to-consumer sales model. Business-to-consumer is definitely an interesting model, and we'll be looking at a business-to-consumer case study in Chapter 13. But for this example, we've chosen a business-to-business organization to highlight the importance of thinking about content differently from the way most industry practitioners do today.

It's so competitive that teams must handle products designed on the fly, and are just told to "make [content] happen."

Customer relationships and brand management might not seem to be a major factor for the semiconductor industry. The chip makers design some microchips, and the best, cheapest, fastest microchips get bought by those who want to use them in their products, right? True and false. This market is one of the most fast-paced and volatile around. There are few industries that can be matched for fickle customers and lighting-fast market upturns and downturns. Only the fittest survive, and if one organization stumbles, several others will dive in for the kill.

However, it is also a market with extremely close and interactive customer relations and management. It is so competitive, and the customer is so definitively king, that rival organizations will often partner to meet a new unexpected demand or provide the buyer multiple supply options.[1]

Teams must be ready to handle new product designs hatched by product managers on the way to or from client meetings. When the product managers get back to the office, they hand over instructions and customer feedback to the technical teams and tell them to "make it happen."

[1] Why would they do this? Because to the buyers, the reliability of supply is so important that if only one organization is supplying a certain technology, it can be considered too risky to buy. A manufacturer that invents something might be forced to partner with a competitor so there can be more than one supplier.

Although a product may be created for a specific client, the company will want to sell it to as many other clients as possible. With every product comes a raft of content, and because of intense product release schedules, marketing content managers and technical content teams must work very closely. Table 16.1 shows a typical product breakdown.

Table 16.1 – Content reuse in the semiconductor industry

	Print Deliverables			Web Deliverables		
Component	Datasheet	Leaflet	Brochure	Landing Page	Selector	Documentation
Product Image	■	■	■	■	■	■
Product Name	■	■	■	■	■	■
Product Number	■	■	■	■	■	■
Product Feature List – Short			■	■		

The various content components, each indicated by a row in Table 16.1, are often created in different departments. Research and development groups are usually in charge of long feature lists and the detail in the product feature sections of the documentation. Marketing staff are responsible for turning that content into short, snappy lists of the most attractive features and creating the "spin" versions of the overviews that describe the product in the most attractive light.

Technical documentation teams are responsible for rendering content into a printable format (PDF) and marketing teams into web format (HTML). Both formats are available from the website. When selling technical products in a business-to-business environment, all documents have a "sliding scale of technical content" from R&D content to Marketing. This is illustrated in Figure 16.3.

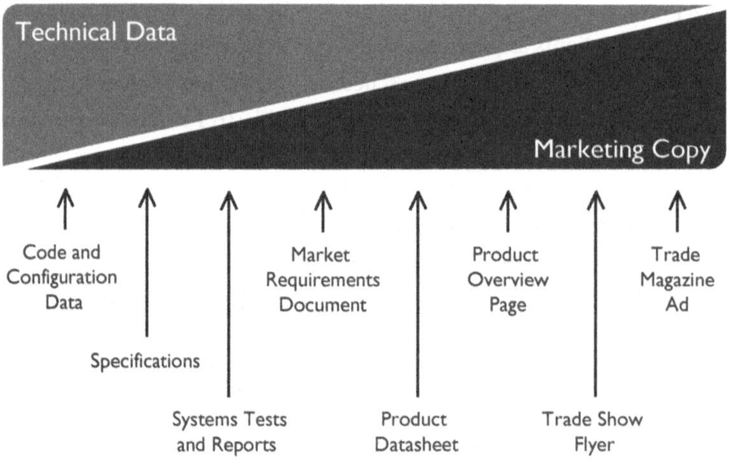

Figure 16.3. Deliverables as a blend of technical and marketing content

The difficulty of managing the multitude of document types is compounded because features can be shared across multiple products. Two products might even be so similar that the overviews and much of the rest of the documentation are the same except for a few details. Some organizations still copy-and-paste content from one variant of a product to its sibling products.

Many organizations deliver content online as downloadable PDFs in addition to printing hard-copy documents. Since everything in the print needs to match the Web, the result, as you can imagine, is an update nightmare. One feature update from engineering could update multiple products, causing a cascade of update requirements across multiple deliverables. Someone in marketing might decide that a feature needs renaming, even if it has not actually changed, because a competitor has a zippy name they need to match in order to move units. As you can imagine, the number of changes required on a monthly basis is huge, and so is the associated effort in making it happen on time, time after time.

Organizational divisions and lack of integrated process often mean that this already complex work simply never gets done, and the client suffers because of the manufacturer's problems.

Your Customer Doesn't Care about Your Org Chart

Content is a critical part of a product or service. It doesn't matter whether you are marketing a product or service or whether your target audience is consumers or business. Potential customers want enough information to make informed decisions, regardless of where on the organizational chart it came from.

Potential customers want enough information to make informed decisions, regardless of where on the organizational chart it came from.

However you subdivide content – pre-sales or post-sales, internal or external, persuasive or enabling – organizations have more content than they realize, or than they'd like to think about, and that impacts customer experience. The problem is more obvious in industries like semiconductors, but the principles apply to any organization that needs to handle product information across a multitude of deliverables.

Companies have more content than they realize or than they'd like to think about.

The issues around content cannot be neatly labelled as "the website," "technical documentation," or "marketing collateral," nor do the organizational divisions of marketing, sales, support, or R&D encapsulate the whole issue. All of these are touch points with the customer or sources of content that underpin customer touch points with staff. Because many of the deliverables describe the same products, content must be able to be shared across formats and organizational silos to ensure consistency and quality.

This means that any efficient assessment of the "what is content?" question cannot apply only to external content or content in one delivery channel, but must address all business-critical content that is part of the customer lifecycle, extending into the organization as well as out into the market.

Multimodal, Customer-centric Content Strategy

On a mobile device with a small visual interface and keypad, a word may be quite difficult to type but very easy to say (e.g. Poughkeepsie). Consider how you would access and search through digital media catalogs from these same devices or set-top boxes. And in one real-world example, patient information in an operating room environment is accessed verbally by members of the surgical team to maintain an antiseptic environment and presented, in near real-time, aurally – and visually – to maximize comprehension.

An advantage of multiple input modalities is increased usability. The weaknesses of one modality are offset by the strengths of another.

If everything is content, does a content strategist need to worry about everything on a printed page, in a PDF, in a mobile device app, or on a website? In one sense, yes. A content strategist is responsible for all elements of content and for deciding whether the various types of content make sense in terms of comprehension. The strategist needs to determine whether the colors on a button affect the comprehension of the text on the button or whether other elements interfere with how a user understands the text. A strategist would know whether cross-references work better than repeated text or whether an animation is needed instead of an explanation.

Customers are not concerned that it's the engineering department that produces the specifications in a brochure, they're concerned that the brochure is accurate and allows them to evaluate the product. Similarly, if they've already bought the product, but have received poor training, they'll be unhappy. If they call in an engineer to repair the product, they don't care if the engineer doesn't have the right tools or the maintenance instructions are wrong or the diagnostic procedures in the manual haven't been updated for that model. Customers want what they want, and when they don't get what they want, the relationship suffers. And the moment a customer shares a bad experience, the brand will suffer, too.

Most organizations do not optimize for many of the modalities we've described, and their content strategy, if they've ever developed one, is to bury their heads at varying depths in the sand. Some content strategies prioritize the Web and web-formatted content, ignoring a large portion of the content that goes in between the lines and is behind the buttons.

A good web content strategist will tell you that you need to map the whole customer lifecycle. You can't expect customers to "walk a path of breadcrumbs" from your home page to find relevant content. Search and offsite inbound links bypass our navigational structures, and multichannel publishing gives users even more paths to our information. These changes mean that having a single "home page" is less important than it was previously.[2]

---

[2] Around 2010, there was frequent discussion of the declining importance, or even "death," of the home page. See "Myth #17: The homepage is your most important page" [http://uxmyths.com/post/717779908/-myth-the-homepage-is-your-most-important-page?8f6dfd00]

A better content strategist will remind the client that social media is a major factor in brand management and lead acquisition.

A multimodal content strategist will tell you that you need to do all that, and map it across the entire interaction lifecycle for all modalities of interaction, not only web or print, but any interaction that affects the user or customer experience. That includes the support knowledge base, the sales intranet, or the knowledge assets that field or customer services staff use.

Consumer Products Manufacturer Gets It Wrong

One of the most striking examples of the importance of multimodal content strategy we have seen concerns a consumer products company. Its marketing department had a reasonable website and did a good job on events and brochures. This, along with a strong product line, helped make the organization a relative leader in its niche.

However, the company was concerned about escalating documentation and translation costs. In addition, analysis showed that the organization suffered from a costly, higher-than-industry-standard number of No Fault Found (NFF) returns. An NFF return occurs when a customer returns a product thinking it has a flaw, but on investigation, the product turns out to be in perfect working order. NFF returns are costly not only because of the unnecessary shipping, testing, and re-stocking costs, but also because frustrated customers breed distrust and may switch brands.

The maintenance teams were being bombarded with hundreds of NFF returns annually on products that were worth less than what it cost (time plus postage) to return and test a unit. They were given such poor content that the field service centers around the world were generating their own quarterly DVD of technical tips, reference charts, and other documentation. Every quarter, a staff member would collate the updates and re-issue the DVD to the internal community of content consumers.

The technical communications, engineering, and marketing teams were unaware that this useful content and hands-on learning existed. Worse, this content was only available to the internal maintenance team and only in English.

Clearly, they had a major problem with their content. They needed a content strategy that would address their NFF return problem, give their maintenance team better information, and make the field service center information broadly available. Unfortunately, they chose to address only a small part of their problem; they bought a system focused exclusively on technical manuals and did not address the broader issues. And rather than looking at their specific requirements, they took a shortcut and purchased a system that the CIO had used in a previous company.

Unfortunately this is not uncommon. This company made two critical mistakes that turn up again and again in our experience as consultants.

- They failed to look at their complete content situation.
- They failed to select a content management system based on their needs, instead selecting one based on anecdotal past experience.

Since then, this company's success in the market has declined. While it is impossible to say to what degree the lack of a content strategy has contributed to its current situation, it is fair to say that this company's short-sighted approach to managing their multimodal content assets could not have helped.

The Nature of Content is Cyclical

Multiplicity, if ignored, will come back to haunt you. The lesson of multiplicity is that although each participant in a content strategy may be tempted to look only at a single view of the world, together they are multiple agents in multiple departments interacting in a complex system. Marketing communicators may see the scope of their content work as limited to generating leads or increasing downloads. Technical communicator may see their job as creating the manual or the help files. Support engineers may only be focused on answering this week's queries as fast as they can. The content strategist must embrace the objectives, policies, processes, and content assets of all of these agents and ensure that the overall content strategy supports the organization's goals.

In commercial organizations, content is not only about directly persuading users or moving units. Content must continue persuading users and moving units over the course of a customer relationship and the life of the brand. In not-for-profits, the job is not done when content has been made available to users. It has to be actively delivered in a way that engages users and makes them take the desired actions and understand the intended messages.

Multiplicity, if ignored, will come back to haunt you.

If the round pegs of content strategy get hammered into the square holes of departmental silos, this multiplicity of assets and agents won't be working toward common goals, and you will end up with inconsistent messages, language, structures and even facts. That diminishes your customer experience, affecting brand and the top line.

If you don't have a strategy for efficiently handling multiplicity, you will spend too much and undermine your staff's ability to serve the customer efficiently. That affects the bottom line. Each action by each agent feeds multiple assets into a cyclical exchange with users in and outside of the organization. Without a strategy that takes the full range of multiplicity into account, the wheels will grind to a halt.

CHAPTER 17

Planning for Power Publishing

> All media work us over completely. They are so pervasive in their personal, political, economic, aesthetic, psychological, moral, ethical, and social consequences that they leave no part of us untouched, unaffected, unaltered.
>
> —Marshall McLuhan, *The Medium is the Massage*[14]

Planning for *power publishing* is a little like buying insurance: it costs a bit extra up front to avoid locking in your content; but when you later need to leverage that content, the investment is definitely worth the effort.

Marshall McLuhan predicted the impact of technology, coining the term "global village" long before the World-Wide Web and personal computing.

The quote that opens this chapter is from one of the leading lights in the history of communications, Marshall McLuhan. For professionals like us, who spend each day with today's content systems, it's almost eerie reading his words. McLuhan posited that electronic communication shrinks distances while simultaneously increasing opportunities for cross-cultural discussion and sharing, and he coined the term global village[1] to describe this phenomenon. Had he not been several decades too early, McLuhan could have easily been alluding to the Web.

McLuhan was writing during the five-hundred-fifty-plus year period during which text-based mass communication enjoyed an unchallenged, single-format paradigm: the printed page. Technology moves faster now, and just over twenty years after the very first web page was served between two computers, the desktop web's period of "dominance" has ended and we now have to plan for new modes of publishing that are more powerful, but also more complex, than anything the world has seen.

1 http://www.collectionscanada.gc.ca/innis-mcluhan/030003-2060-e.html

Mobile, the Game Changer

Only about a decade after the popularization of the mobile web, the paradigm of the desktop-web has shifted to mobile. Mobile took prominence at a truly breathtaking rate, reaching a 50% adoption rate in just five years. In the United States, it took about 25 years to reach a similar adoption rate for home computers.[2] This is largely attributable to Apple's iPhone, which moved smartphones from being early adopter, niche products to the ubiquitous, mass-market products they are today.[3] In roughly one fifth the time it took desktop computers, mobile devices have established themselves as a driving force in communications globally.[4]

In roughly one fifth the time it took desktop computers, mobile devices have established themselves as a driving force in communications globally.

According to industry analyst comScore, desktop-web publishers have seen enormous change in mobile use. For example, in August 2011, mobile and connected devices accounted for more than half of Pandora's audience.[5] According to The Gartner Group, the majority of new web-enabled devices are mobile,[6] and the percentage of web traffic coming from mobile devices continues to increase.[7]

Online publishers are being pushed to adapt, just as print publishers before them. In line with McLuhan's prediction forty years before the fact, new technology has opened up new ways of communicating and consuming content, and user expectations are changing. Old methods and tools will no longer satisfy consumer expectations. Mobile helped us see that a "single-web" paradigm was not going to last forever. And the future will bring more devices and formats to contend with.

---

[2] "Home Computers and Internet Use in the United States: August 2000" [http://www.census.gov/prod/-2001pubs/p23-207.pdf].

[3] "How the iPhone Blew Up the Wireless Industry" [http://www.wired.com/gadgets/wireless/magazine/-16-02/ff_iphone], Wired Magazine.

[4] "America's New Mobile Majority: a Look at Smartphone Owners in the U.S." [http://blog.nielsen.com/-nielsenwire/online_mobile/who-owns-smartphones-in-the-us/], NielsenWire.

[5] "Digital Omnivores: How Tablets, Smartphones and Connected Devices are Changing U.S. Digital Media Consumption Habits" [http://www.comscore.com/content/download/10633/180227/file/-Digital_Omnivores.pdf].

[6] "Gartner Identifies Top 10 Commercial Business Applications for Tablet Devices" [http://-www.gartner.com/it/page.jsp?id=1849621].

[7] "Smartphones and Tablets Drive Nearly 7 Percent of Total U.S. Digital Traffic" [http://www.comscore.com/-Press_Events/Press_Releases/2011/10/-Smartphones_and_Tablets_Drive_Nearly_7_Percent_of_Total_U.S._Digital_Traffic].

Considering the speed with which new technologies, new devices, and new expectations arise, you need new ways of creating, structuring, and managing content – in other words, you need a strategy to deal with tomorrow's formats today. We call this "power publishing." To help you develop a plan for power publishing, we will look at:

- Why mastering the next new thing is not enough.
- Why designing for any single format is a problem.
- Why not separating content and deliverables lowers content ROI.

Mastering the Next New Thing is Not Enough

Between 2010 and 2012, the mobile internet was a primary catalyst for change in the world of mass communications. Yet it is only one step in a long series of changes that have altered how we exchange content. Each change has caused content professionals to rethink their approach, methods, and tools. And keep in mind that these changes will continue. Smartphones that seemed like science fiction at the turn of this century were commonplace within a decade, and tablets followed soon after. So, while mobile is the hot topic as we write this, it is already evolving and will continue to evolve.

To align content and processes with organizational goals, content strategists must take into account the entire lifespan of the content and its role in the life of the organization. We need to think long-term and act short term.

Designing for Any Format is a Problem

The word "format" is a somewhat loaded term, with multiple valid, yet dissimilar meanings. We are primarily concerned with the following two meanings of format.

- **Technical:** A format is a file type, for example, .PDF or .HTML.
- **Visual:** A format describes how to display and lay out content visually.[8]

---

[8] We will not be addressing formats for delivering content to the visually impaired. Not because they are not important, but precisely because it's the (excessive) focus on the visual aspects of formatting over content that make delivery to the visually impaired – among other power publishing scenarios – difficult.

Formats that are designed for storing and representing content visually are generally not designed around the content itself.

Formats that are designed for storing and representing content visually are generally not designed around the content itself. Although McLuhan was correct in saying that new media and methods of communication have changed expectations, it is still the content that addresses the user's actual need. Those needs are often common across various devices; the device is simply a way to access and consume the content. We might say that no individual device – phone, tablet, or desktop computer – should be considered a medium, but rather that the medium is all the devices and the network that connects them.

Consumers' expectations are not shaped by their history with any one organization, but by the aggregate of all their content experiences. Consumers' expectations about your content are being formed by their interactions with companies such as Evernote, Facebook, Dropbox, and Google, where content lives in various incarnations across multiple networked devices and platforms. Having your content only available on one platform or in one format is no longer acceptable.

Separating Content from Deliverables

You can get locked into a format by focusing on a single set of deliverables and losing sight of the overall content strategy. Content is not a set of project deliverables.

Content is not a set of project deliverables.

- **Deliverables:** encapsulate a specific set of content assets for one context, time, and audience – for example, a print brochure in PDF or a site in HTML designed for the desktop web. A deliverable is the content, in a formatted container, ready for consumption.
- **Content:** is a business asset that persists across projects, crosses format and deliverable boundaries, and can be leveraged for various strategic goals.

Under the pressure of publishing deadlines, it is easy for a team to focus on their to-do list of formatted deliverables and to de-prioritize planning that would benefit the organization and content in the longer term.

Content as a Service (CaaS), Not a Deliverable

If taken to its logical conclusion, separating content from deliverables means we could have a centralized pool of content that could be drawn on by whoever needs it and made into multiple deliverables as an on-demand service. This is not necessarily a service in the sense of a commercial, leasing relationship – although some organizations are taking this approach[9] – but more of a service model and mentality between suppliers and consumers that could be either internal or external to the organization.

Separating content from deliverables means having a centralized pool of content that can be drawn on and made into multiple deliverables as an on-demand service.

The service providers could be content teams, in any organization, working on a CaaS model and serving content assets to the rest of their organizations or external users. Departments could serve content to and share content with each other so the best, most up-to-date content gets to where it needs to go in all the multiple contexts, departmental silos and formats. This is a different publishing paradigm from static, hand-crafted deliverables that are uniquely created for each device, site, platform, and time.

This is the most sophisticated implementation of power publishing. Sadly, in our experience, few organizations achieve this type of sharing, and most of them only share content between a few closely aligned departments. Still, leveraging content to its full potential is an excellent goal. Every step in this direction aligns content strategies towards longevity and best practices in power publishing. Even if your organization never reaches this level of power publishing, establishing the vision and taking steps towards it can improve content processes.

The Risks of Binding Content to Format

Some formats, such as Amazon's .azw and Apple's .ibook, have specific visual layouts and formatting built in. Using such formats creates long-term risks. The device your audience uses may change after a publication has been released. It's the Betamax vs VHS format war of the 1970s all over again. Choosing any side in a format war can be costly.

---

9 See "How Content-as-a-Service Is Forever Changing the Learning Content Industry" [http://-www.webcitation.org/6Br5sOQos]

Proprietary formats – it's the Betamax vs VHS format war of the 1970s all over again.

In the American Economic Association's *Journal of Economic Perspectives*[2], Stanley M. Besen and Joseph Farrell state that several properties of what are called "network markets" – markets where users want to buy products compatible with products bought by others – distinguish those markets from more conventional ones and affect the strategies that firms pursue.

For example, network markets are "tippy." That is, the coexistence of incompatible products may be unstable, leading to a single winning standard quickly dominating a market. The triumph of VHS over Betamax is a classic case. Moreover, tipping can happen very rapidly.

Applied to content, processes that focus on the creation and delivery of content for a specific device or format or a narrowly defined set of formats are dangerous. Content that depends on a particular format can become "locked in" and fall out of favor with your target audience. The videotape format war is one of the earlier examples, and there are other recent cases – iTunes vs non-Apple formats and Blu-ray vs HD DVD come to mind.

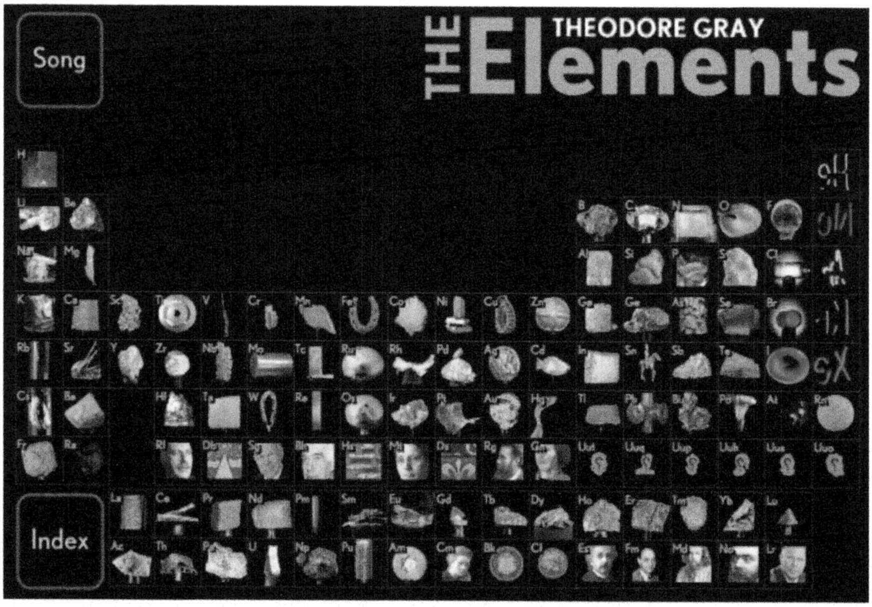

Figure 17.1. Home page of *Elements: A Visual Exploration*

Another example is the ebook, *Elements: A Visual Exploration,*[10] which was created exclusively for the iPad (see Figure 17.1). Although it is a stunning eBook, the format limitation excludes anyone who doesn't have an iPad.

Even when one format is a clear winner and the only marketable choice for some period of time – for example, VHS – tying content exclusively to that format will lock you in when that format is superseded – as has happened with DVDs and now Blu-ray superseding VHS. It then becomes difficult and costly to deliver the desired experience across the new channels as older formats reach obsolescence. Content technologies change so quickly today that it is unwise to predict how long a format will dominate.

Content technologies change so quickly today that it is unwise to predict how long a format will dominate.

Here are some tell-tale signs that you may be locked into one format.

- Your print deliverables don't work online or on smaller screens.
- You regularly copy and paste content between mobile and desktop versions of your website.
- You developed a smartphone application, but your content isn't ready to flow into the app.
- You have content pre-loaded in an app in a manner that doesn't support automatic updates.
- You repeatedly incur high costs for content migration initiatives.
- You are forced to prioritize which content gets converted and which gets left behind for purely financial reasons rather than the users' needs.
- You are trying to change content management tools and when you export the content, you lose structure, links, and flows.

If none of these signs sound familiar, that is probably a good thing. It could mean you have not, or at least not yet, had to contend with some of the challenges of multichannel publishing. Or these issues might be occurring in your organization, but under your radar. Staff may be treating these issues as a matter of logistics, technology, or resourcing and not escalating them to a strategic level. We often find that team members do not view publishing complexity as a strategic issue.

[10] http://periodictable.com/ipad/

Other reasons we've heard for sticking with an existing, but locked-in, method of producing content include the following:

- The alternative sounds too good to be true.
- I don't know how to evaluate whether it will work.
- I'm close to retirement, and I don't want to spend my last few years working that hard; my successor can worry about it.
- Let another group be the guinea pigs.
- I don't want to risk changing methods for a new one that doesn't have the kinks worked out.
- We track everything using an Excel spreadsheet, and that's good enough for our needs.
- Management will never fund something like that; they'll say: why fix what's not broken?

So how can a team be expected to propose a new methodology when they don't understand that a different way of working even exists, or they have never had the benefits explained to them? And when the benefits are explained, how can you be confident that the new methodology will be implemented effectively? Understanding both the problem and the solution is critical, both at the decision-making level and the operational level.[11]

Formats and Silos

When planning for power publishing, many teams still hold onto both departmental and format silos. Organizational teams and agencies that have become specialized in either web-based or print-based processes and tools can feel reluctant to bridge the chasms that seem to separate them.

Although many organizations and practitioners in the community of web professionals are already fully immersed in a web-based world, power publishing is not restricted

[11] Best practices and principles for overcoming resistance to change fill several books, including, *E-Business Innovation and Change Management*[21].

to the Web or any other format. The techniques that constitute power publishing, as we define it, apply across formats and channels and allow print and web deliverables to share content more effectively.

With the ubiquity of the Internet, it is easy to forget that individuals and organizations are still adapting to web publishing. Not all departments of an organization adapt at the same time. The result is that many websites, even some published by large, household-name organizations, still serve vital content only in page-oriented formats (for example, PDF, MS Word, or other lesser-known paginated electronic formats).

We often find that the IT and marketing departments that manage the organization's web presence are siloed off from departments like technical communications, support, and product management. Although product management and technical communications may create content that is of primary importance to users, these departments' print content can become secondary to other content on the website.

Anything in a format like PDF is often treated as a fixed quantity during a web project, as if it is some other team's problem and responsibility. Instead of being modeled and audited like the rest of the content, thousands of pages are simply dumped on the site under links like, "PDF download."

Format Silos are Bad for Users

Users looking at content on the Internet can feel frustrated, confused, or disoriented when they are forced to switch modes from web to print.[12] This happens for several reasons, including, but not limited to the following.

Users looking at content on the Internet can feel frustrated, confused, or disoriented when they have to switch modes from web to print.

- **Loss of web features:** Page-oriented files generally lack web features such as the ability to manipulate, sort, and filter content. Users also lose the ability to bookmark or socially share individual pieces of content because page-oriented formats bind any number of pages into a single object.
- **Search disconnect:** Users often feel frustrated with the separation between search inside and outside page-oriented files. Web search engines can index PDF and most other page-oriented files. Therefore, searches on the Web will return

[12] This is discussed in Chapter 13, *Content Strategy in Business to Consumer.*

page-oriented files as hits, but the user is then presented with the first page of a potentially very long file. The user then needs to search again, within the file, using what may be a significantly different search interface. If the original search started inside another page-oriented file, – as is often the case – the user may end up jumping back and forth between multiple page-oriented files and the website. Only the most determined users will persist for long.

- **File size:** Page-oriented files are generally much larger than web-oriented files. Users must wait for them to download, and they can't skim and scan them in the same way they can online.
- **Inconsistency:** Because of the same silos that preserved format separation in the first place, visual display, editorial standards, and content processes are often not shared across web and print deliverables. This ranges from rather innocuous color or styling differences to substantive conflicts in the actual content. Many organizations have told us, "That content got updated in the PDF months ago, but the website is still out of date," or vice-versa.
- **Display inflexibility:** Page-oriented files are excellent at preserving layouts, which can make them very difficult to read on smaller screens.

Format Silos are Bad for Organizations

Because dozens, hundreds, or even thousands of pages can end up bound together in a single unit, page-oriented content limits the effectiveness of analytics and metrics tools. This makes it difficult, if not impossible, to track, analyze, measure, and govern the actual content contained in a page-oriented file.

Not knowing what is happening with your content means you can't make strategic decisions about it. Many people in departments such as technical communications have told us that they have to strategize about their content "in the dark," without having any view into who, if anyone, is deriving value from it. This lack of knowledge invariably translates into lost opportunity, increased costs, and lost profits.

Competitors that offer an integrated and seamless content experience will have an advantage over organizations that offer a disjointed experience. To derive maximum strategic benefit from your content assets, you must enable your customer-facing content for ongoing assessment, governance, and of course, power publishing.

CHAPTER 18

Right Content, Right Context

> During a *content strategy audit,* a client once showed me their new Client Relationship Management system (CRM). The CRM data showed which users had which interests, and (theoretically) enabled highly tailored content experiences. The problem: the content was in non-modular, print-oriented Word and PDF files, which held content for various interest groups together. So they knew who wanted what, but had no way of extracting or delivering it.
>
> —Noz Urbina

A user's experience is formed by the content and the context in which that content is delivered. When content is locked into a single format or inflexible structure, it is hard to leverage it to deliver a new experience in another context. When we talk about context, we mean the combination of the following:

- The right content (and the right version)
- At a certain time or in a particular scenario
- On a certain device
- In a certain format
- In the right language

Different content consumers might need enabling content in several contexts.

As content strategists, we're trying to tune the user experience to align user and organizational goals. To do this successfully, we need our content to work in a wide variety of contexts. Here are some examples of possible new contexts:

- A new campaign site or microsite that uses elements of your existing content, but not all of it and not in the same order or structure
- A new campaign that reuses various elements of related or previous campaigns
- An advanced-features manual or a quick-start guide
- In-context instructions embedded in the interface of your product or site
- Content variations for online stores in different countries

Context is an important aspect of both enabling and persuasive content. As discussed in Chapter 16, *The Nature of Content*, enabling content should not be considered only post-sales. How users feel supported, and in many industries, their access to product reference content, is important throughout the relationship. Different content consumers might need enabling content in several contexts. Here are a few content consumers, and possible contexts, to consider:

- **A user:** I'm learning about my new product … while on the bus to work, or I'm using a product right now and need information to finish my task.
- **An employee:** I need access to legal information by region because we're announcing a product's availability in multiple countries with simultaneous launches.
- **A potential buyer:** We're evaluating a product or service to make sure it lives up to the pre-sales promises.
- **A user-stakeholder:** I'm an internal user (or partner, retailer, or value-added service provider) and I'm answering someone else's questions about a product.

Each context might require different subsets of a core content pool, along with different relationships, or navigational pathways, through the content. For example, new customers might need all the guidance available for their demographic, whereas users upgrading their product or service might need guidance only on changed features and be interested only in new related offers.

Adaptive Content

The industry term for this type of *modular content* is *adaptive content.*[1] You may also hear terms such as "content with agility," "intelligent content," "smart documents," "nimble content," and so forth. Ann Rockley defines adaptive content as follows: "Adaptive content is format-free, device-independent, scalable, and filterable content that is transformable for display in different environments and on different devices in an automated or dynamic fashion."[2] In other words, content with building-block

1 The earliest reference we could find to adaptive content is a 2000 article by a Microsoft researcher, HongJiang Zhang, titled "Adaptive Content Delivery: A New Application Area for Media Computing Research"[25].

2 *Managing Enterprise Content: A Unified Content Strategy*[19], p. 134

qualities can be adapted from a single source and be read on the smallest to the largest of screens or even hard-copy – all without having to be rewritten or reformatted.

Adaptive content lets a given piece of content live multiple lives for different users and be delivered appropriately for each user's context. It is the content-side corollary to the design-side industry term *responsive design*.

Responsive Design

Content can only be as flexible as the design framework in which it lives.

Content can only be as flexible as the design framework in which it lives. When content or content containers are riddled with design controls or formatting that constrain the look and feel, the content becomes constrained as well. Ethan Marcotte describes responsive design as a way to "design for the ebb and flow of things."[3] Responsive design allows visual layout to respond to display contexts in the same the way that adaptive content can respond to different user contexts. Display contexts could include the following:

- **Different display sizes:** Everything from a few square centimeters to tablets to the size of a billboard, all with a variety of resolutions
- **Different display and delivery types:** Black and white, tactile, gesture-interactive, text-to-speech, and so forth

The ideal marriage is adaptive content and responsive design.

The best marriage, then, is between adaptive content and responsive design. Responsive design, working with adaptive content, seamlessly displays content on whatever device the user chooses to view it on. A discussion of responsive design is beyond the scope of this book. For more information, we recommend Ethan Marcotte's *Responsive Web Design*[13].

---

[3] From a May 25, 2010 article titled, "Responsive Web Design" [http://www.alistapart.com/articles/-responsive-web-design/].

Modular, Format-free Content

It is possible to write for one anticipated flow of information, and if we structure the content properly, we can create different arrangements, navigation, and deliverables easily, if not 100% automatically, from the content superset.

Early in Chapter 15, *What Exactly Is Content?*, we discussed genres and sub-genres. A genre might be marketing material with sub-genres of white papers and data sheets. Each of the sub-genres is made up of smaller pieces that separately may not be particularly helpful but, much like building blocks, get combined into a recognizable object that a user would want to consume. Figure 18.1 is an example of how this can work.

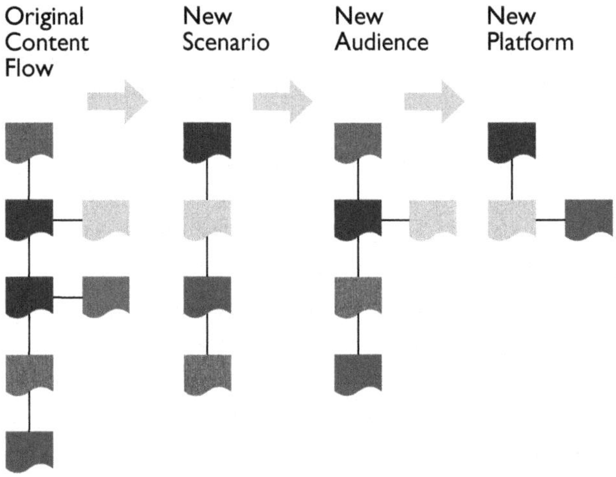

Figure 18.1. Modular, component-based deliverables

Modules are the building blocks that form new objects and new contexts. The size of modules is critical. Sometimes an entire piece of content – an article, brochure, or procedure – has too much information to be reused effectively. When that happens, the module becomes hard to reuse and probably hard to consume because of its bloat.

Modular content, on the other hand, consists of small building blocks that can be assembled to create deliverables to meet the needs of different users, groups, contexts, or formats.[4]

When properly implemented, modular content can deliver the best of both worlds for an organization and its content consumers. The key phrase here is "when properly implemented." Modules are content assets, much like building blocks are physical assets. And just as the quality of building blocks affects the quality of the finished building, the quality of the modules affects the quality of the finished content assembly.

Modular content consists of small building blocks that can be assembled to create different configurations.

If a content asset loses accuracy or relevance when placed in a different context, or if the content becomes harder to consume, then it has lost some of its value. There are several ways that this might happen. For example, in a printed book, content is presented in a predictable, linear narrative. The user is expected to understand the relative location of references that use the words "earlier" and "later." Consider the following scenarios:

- **Linear content descriptions:** "Later in this manual, we will talk in more detail about ____." This type of reference implies not only a relationship between two sections, but the order in which they are presented. On the Web or a small-screen device such as a smartphone, these "soft" references prevent sections from being easily separated or presented in a different order. When a user arrives in the middle of a linear narrative from a search engine result, the idea of "later" becomes irrelevant and confusing. And because there is no "hard" reference for production software to follow, there is no easy way to avoid a broken reference if a "later" section doesn't exist in a particular deliverable.
- **Misplaced content references:** "The platform for L10N professionals, writers, SGML wizards, XSLT scripters, and everybody involved with I18N ..." Content creators accustomed to writing for linear texts are taught to define acronyms the first time they are used. When content is broken apart and used in multiple online contexts, the concept of a "first time" is lost. Each page where the acronym is shown could be a reader's first time.

[4] For example, the format for a printed book requires specific text assets for things like the cover, spine, headers and footers that wouldn't be required or relevant for other formats.

- **Static layout references:** "To the right, the two-way table shows..." Similarly, conventions that read smoothly in print, such as "in the illustration below," may not work in mobile device layouts. For example, in print or on a large screen, the table may, indeed, be "to the right," as shown in Figure 18.2

Two-Way Frequency Tables

To the right, the two-way table shows the favorite leisure activities for 50 adults - 20 men and 30 women. Because entries in the table are frequency counts, the table is a **frequency table**.

Entries in the "Total" row and "Total" column are called **marginal frequencies** or the **marginal distribution.** Entries in the body of the table are **joint frequencies.**

	Dance	Sports	TV	Total
Men	2	10	8	20
Women	16	6	8	30
Total	18	16	16	50

Figure 18.2. Table meant for print layout[5]

However, on some devices, the table might be moved below or above the text. The table may not even be visible. For example, it may be on the next page of a paged device, leaving the user to wonder what should be showing "in the table below."

Finally, writing inconsistencies become more obvious when content is reused. Combining content from multiple creators can result in a Frankendoc – a deliverable that has clearly been stitched together from disparate parts. Issues that can lead to Frankendocs include:

- Heading/title length
- Capitalization anomalies
- Spelling differences (e.g., UK vs. US English)
- Heading/title conjugation discrepancies
- Stylistic differences
- Tone variances
- Grammatical conventions
- Terminology inconsistencies

[5] http://stattrek.com/statistics/two-way-table.aspx

Right Place, Wrong Content

Inappropriate soft references can have serious consequences. In a complex layout, there actually may be something "to the right," but that something might be different from what you intended. At best, this is confusing, but in some situations, such as a medication dosage chart, the consequences can be dangerous.[6]

When factual content is reused improperly, it can create errors that mislead the user. For example, if you duplicate a section across two related product descriptions and the feature list is not exactly the same, the user could be reading something about your product that is simply wrong. In public policy, procedures, and governmental content, this means the public is being misinformed. In marketing or sales materials this can lead to unhappy customers, which can lead to returns, support calls, and complaints. In sales contracts, legal content, technical information, or operating instructions, this can increase support costs and expose you to liability, litigation, or safety risks.

Reusing content can result in higher ROI, but that content must be reused intelligently.

Creating and managing content for reuse can result in a higher return on investment, but that content must be accurate, complete, and reused intelligently; anything else is at best a distraction that will reduce the value of your content, and at worst a catastrophe for your customers and your company.

Defining Module Types

To help explain the concept of modular structure, here is a simple example, the IMRAD report structure. IMRAD[7] stands for Introduction, Methods, Results, and Discussion:

- **Introduction:** The hypothesis and main drivers of the report along with contextual information like reasons for writing the report.
- **Methods:** How, where, and when information was gathered.

---

[6] This is one reason academic and technical texts often use a strict numbering system and refer to items by number, for example "See table 4.1." The numbering system must also be reuse-ready, because if the same table is used in various places, it may not always be table "4.1" in every context.

[7] This is also referred to as AIMRAD, where the initial A is for Abstract. See IMRAD Research Paper Format [http://www.webcitation.org/69OygwWZP] http://www.webcitation.org/69OygwWZP

- **Results:** The main body of the report. What was found? Was the hypothesis supported?
- **Discussion:** Implications of the results and how they support the hypothesis. Description of any follow-up recommendations.

Having a clearly defined structure like IMRAD helps authors organize their content. Most professionals have worked with defined section types in their career – a document overview, a statement of work, an assumptions and risks section, a disclaimer, a conclusion, and more. Each section has a structure, and there are expectations as to the content of each.

Left to their own devices, writers will create content in a way that makes sense to them individually, but which may not actually be fit for the context. Editorial and authoring guidelines help people write consistently and create consistent structures. And readers benefit because consistently edited and structured content is easier to comprehend.

Reusing Modules

Having defined module types means we can reuse content much more effectively. Using the IMRAD report as an example, we will look at the most common types of reuse: within a deliverable, across similar deliverables, in the context of *progressive disclosure,* and across the organization.

Reuse Within a Deliverable

Large and potentially complex deliverables such as reports may provide an opportunity to reuse content within a single deliverable. For example, an abstract could be written by hand. However, with the right authoring guidelines, you could use the first paragraph of key sections – the paragraph introducing the key findings and concepts of the section – to automatically compile the abstract when the report is finished. Or if you make the first paragraph of every section an introduction, you can automatically generate an executive summary.

Reuse Across Similar Deliverables

When you develop content using standard processes and guidelines, it can be reused in other deliverables. This holds true regardless of the type of content – branding guidelines, research methods, manufacturing processes, the possibilities are endless. For example, you could create internal reports in several flavors, each tailored to the needs of a particular audience: for example CFO, CIO, CEO, and middle managers. Each audience wants a different view, tailored to its needs.[8]

Some sections in an IMRAD report lend themselves to reuse and are similar to what we've defined as a module, whereas other sections are unique and not very reusable. The methods section is an example of the former – assuming your organization uses standard methods – whereas the report introduction and the preamble to the discussion section are examples of the latter.

That said, IMRAD is very simple. The sections are very large, and there is not a lot of detailed substructure. The large sections make tailoring output difficult. You could pull out components from inside your modules, but you may need to break down your content to smaller modules to take full advantage of reuse opportunities.

Reuse for Progressive Disclosure

"Progressive disclosure" is a technique that breaks down a body of content into stages, so that a user can read a portion, then decide whether to read more. This technique is common in modular systems. The optional abstract section in IMRAD is an example. In organizations such as medical device manufacturers or pharmaceutical research companies, abstracts are meant to be extracted and used in catalogs and other documents. A reader can view the abstract and then decide whether to continue.

Progressive disclosure is particularly useful when reading time and screen real-estate are at a premium – for example on smartphones and other small-screen devices – and you want to avoid scrolling or transferring data unnecessarily. Adaptive content and responsive design (see the section titled "Responsive Design and Reuse with Semantics" (p. 202)) provide the technical underpinnings for progressive disclosure.

---

[8] Different stakeholders might also want the report in different formats, like PowerPoint or HTML. We'll leave formatting issues to the side for the moment.

Reuse Across the Organization

Once you create content *modules,* you can use them across your organization, not just in similar deliverables, but in widely varying contexts. Some types of modules, such as glossary definitions and legal disclaimers, are commonly reused.

The savings in writing time is not always the driving factor. After all, once a glossary definition or legal disclaimer is written, it is not normally updated for every deliverable. Instead, the biggest benefits come from manageability, consistency, and the significant savings you get when a widely reused module does get the occasional update.

Benefiting from Modular Reuse

The labor saved, and therefore the amplification of the asset value, when content is reused means that certain modules increase in value as they are leveraged. If you publish multiple reports, with high reuse, then you can get a great deal of leverage and asset amplification, especially if you have common features like legal texts, instructions, corporate boilerplate, and other repeatable content.

In many projects, actual module reuse potential is far higher than originally perceived.

In enabling genres, like technical information or user assistance, content reuse could be focused on leveraging unique, discrete FAQs or how-to procedures. The content must first be separated into info-typed, reuse-ready modules. Overly complex tasks that address too many product or user scenarios reduce re-usability, as does mixing conceptual and reference material in the flow of a task. Similarly you will get less reuse when the steps needed to complete a task are mixed up with concepts that the user must understand and the data needed during the task. If you do that, the different types of information can be difficult to separate, making reuse more difficult.

In many projects, the actual reuse potential is far higher than originally perceived. This is usually because in a non-modular, unstructured content world, it is so difficult to reuse content that most people don't try unless they are forced to. When reuse is attempted in that environment, it usually gets done through copy-and-paste, which is inefficient and error-prone. When good reuse practices are implemented, the improvement can be dramatic and well worth the implementation effort

CHAPTER 19

Making Content User-centric Using Modular Building Blocks

> One of my favorite projects was working with a medical devices manufacturer that wanted to structure and reuse content to lower translation costs. The strategic content vision we took to the executive level offered savings from structure, reuse, silo-busting, efficiency, and improved customer experience. The principle was simple: use content to improve the customer experience, and you strengthen the brand. If only every executive team "got it".
>
> —Noz Urbina

Creating modular, format-free content in appropriately sized and structured building blocks allows organizations to deliver content that is more directly adapted to their users' interests. While content can be written in user-centric ways, not all users will be interested in the same information.

No matter how user-centric the writing, one user can have a good experience, while another user looking at the same content will find it irrelevant or distracting.

This leads to a paradox: no matter how user-centric the writing, one user can have a good experience, while another user looking at the same content will find it irrelevant or distracting. A classic example is the car website that tells you about optional features that your car doesn't have and that you can't buy as an after-sale upgrade. Reading about those features is a distraction from content that is relevant to you, and possibly even generates negative feelings.

User-centric experiences must have user- or profile-specific content living side-by-side with the core, common messages. If content is not stored in modular components, then reusing shared content alongside user-specific content becomes prohibitively labor-intensive. The increased effort often means the organization has to compromise on the user experience. With *modules,* the organization can leverage its assets more flexibly and build deliverables that are truly user-centric.

If content is not stored in modular components, then reusing shared content with user-specific content becomes prohibitively labor-intensive.

Modular Content is More Adaptive

To deliver new experiences for new contexts, users, and devices, your content needs to have the following characteristics:

- Be structured as discrete *modules*
- Have the right level of granularity (size)
- Have clearly defined structures within each module
- Be tagged (labelled) to identify the content relationships

Even if you don't plan to reuse content modules initially, starting with a defined standard for consistent content enables a level of reuse, because standardization is the first step toward enabling adaptive content.

Standardization can be considered a type of reuse; even if the content is not reused, the structure, metadata, and presentation can be.

Standardization of almost any kind can, in fact, be considered a type of reuse. Even if the content – words, images, video streams – is not reused, the structure, metadata, and presentation can be. Every consistent aspect, from stylesheets to templates to standard file names to title conventions, helps support future reuse. However, if you stop with presentation and styling or choose to simply implement responsive design – the easiest type of standardization – you will miss a large opportunity both for users and the organization.

Component Content on Municipal Websites

The following example comes from the City of Vancouver municipal government website. It shows how designing content in building blocks allows technology and web design to deliver content from a single source to multiple destinations. Not only do these adaptive qualities allow the organization to efficiently provide content to the public, it also makes it easier for users to get information by aggregating content in convenient ways.

Every municipality, at some point, proposes to undertake projects or initiatives, which then go to the city council or equivalent body to be voted on. If approved, they become part of the overall plan for how the municipality operates. To gather input and keep the public informed, the initiatives are publicized beforehand and published after being approved.

Some municipalities, for example, Toronto, publish their initiatives as an alphabetical list of PDF documents (see Figure 19.1):

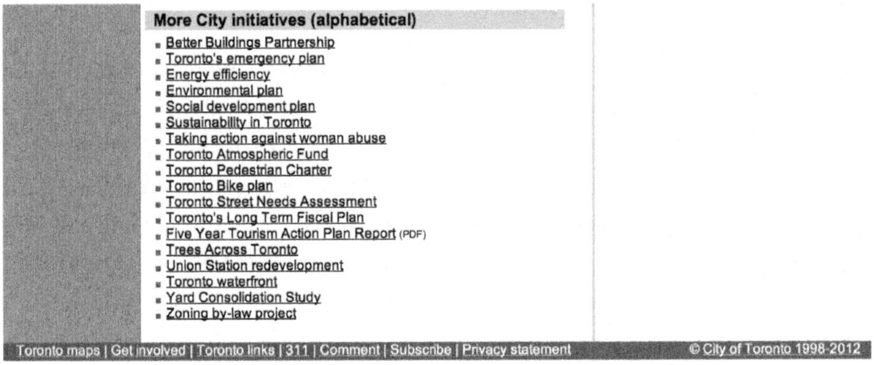

Figure 19.1. Initiatives published by the City of Toronto

Other municipalities publish their initiatives in HTML format, organized according to departmental silos, as Portland, Oregon, does (see Figure 19.2):

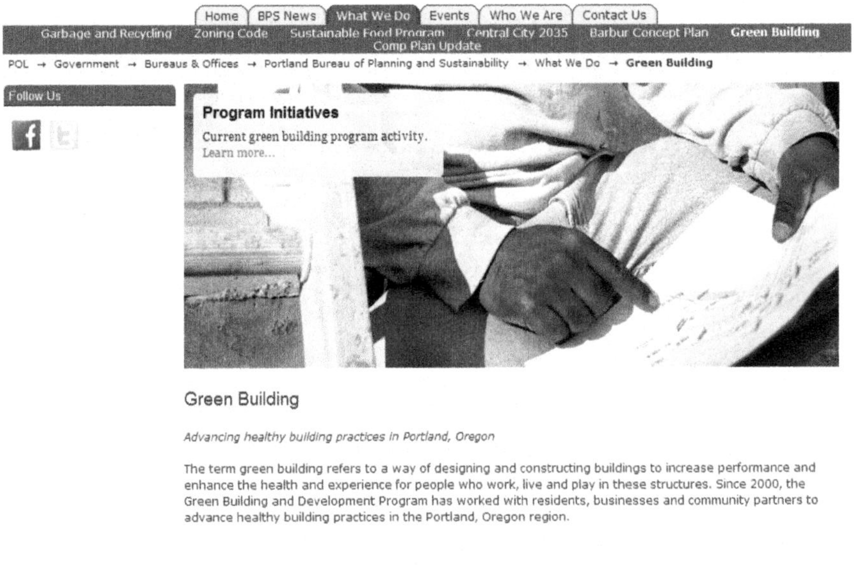

Figure 19.2. Initiatives published by the City of Portland

The City of Vancouver, British Columbia, decided to take the publication of initiatives a step further and make adaptability the core of its content strategy. The strategy addressed the following requirements:

- **User requirements:** Research showed that residents tend to care more about what happens in their area, so the website was designed to give each major city area a page containing information relevant to that area, including initiatives.
- **Business requirements:** The city wanted to publish its initiatives by topic as well – for example, an initiative regarding new bicycle lanes would be published with other information about transportation or greening the city. Initiatives would be published by topic and also on the community pages.
- **System and content requirements:** The city wanted a content management system that would understand which content goes on which page and automatically populate pages with appropriate content. To automate this, each initiative would have a content module – a description of the initiative – that could be pulled into any community page.

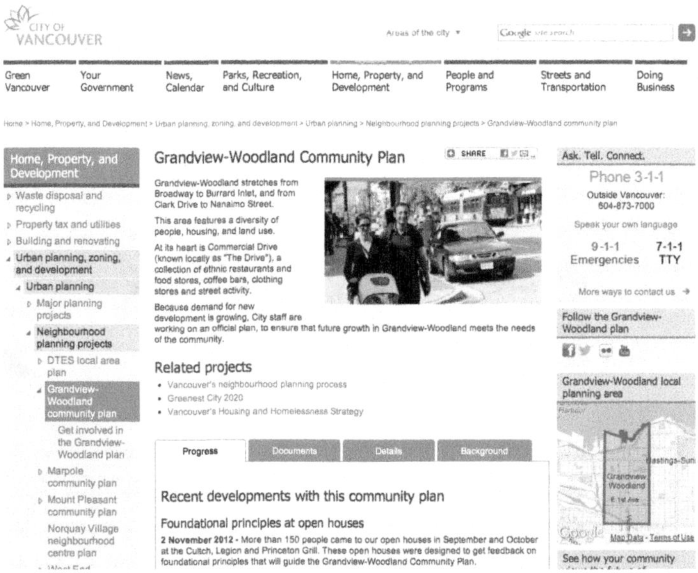

Figure 19.3. A web page about a city initiative on the City of Vancouver website

Figure 19.4. A community page on the City of Vancouver website

When the City of Vancouver curates content, they first build a page about a city project (see Figure 19.3). The page has a set of common building blocks: a heading, a photo, a description, and so on. The web page lives with all the other city projects, in a section titled, "Neighbourhood planning projects."

What is not visible on the project page (Figure 19.3) is a short project summary, which is a separate content module. That summary, plus a smaller version of the photo on the project page, is shown on the appropriate community page (Figure 19.4). Business rules programmed into the content management system determine which information to display. When the project is complete, the content management system can retire the project page and automatically retire all the corresponding instances where the summary is displayed across the website.

Fragments, Smaller than Topics

Up until now, the modules we have been discussing are technically *topics* – that is, modules that are stand-alone pieces of content. *Fragments* provide a way to share units of content that are smaller than topics. Examples include:

- A slogan
- A product name
- An image, for example a logo
- A feature overview
- A brief instruction or warning
- A legal notice

Fragments can be shared across an indefinite number of pages, but will often be displayed alongside content that was written specifically for those pages. Anyone who has tried to find and update all instances of a specific, small piece of content across a large content set can attest to how much work it can be. Reusable fragments can make this process significantly easier.

Traditional Methods have Dramatic Costs

One of our clients received an urgent request from its legal department to update the legal disclaimer on "every PDF datasheet and web page for every active product." Because the existing legal disclaimers were not shared and not managed with any thought to global updates, the only way to do the requested update was to copy and paste the same text over and over again for every deliverable.

The cost was estimated at almost $250,000 to do the following:

- Find all the instances.
- Make the updates.
- Push the updates through the corporate release system.
- Republish the deliverables to the users.

When told of the costs, the legal team decided that, in fact, the change was no longer quite so "urgent."

Using Structurally Consistent Content Models

In the IMRAD report example in Chapter 18, *Right Content, Right Context*, we were able to identify reuse candidates *before* the content in question was even written. We were able to do this because there was a well-defined, simple content model defined by IMRAD. We also saw how topics and fragments, properly written as reusable modules, could be leveraged as discrete units to accelerate creation of new or updated reports adapted for new audiences.

When we store and share content this way, we no longer need to engage in rote tasks such as manually copying and pasting or rewriting content, and we greatly reduce the risk of introducing errors. This last point is particularly important. Whenever authors rewrite copy, minor differences will creep in. On one project, a maintenance manual contained three conflicting procedures for the same task in three different sections of the book. Another industry professional ran an analysis tool on a large document set and found the same instruction written over three hundred ways. Even if these differences do not introduce errors – and they inevitably do – they make it impossible to update a procedure without resorting to costly, manual copy and paste.

We could identify reuse candidates before the content was written because we had a strong model in place.

Structured content models are the explicit expression of our editorial guidelines. These guidelines form a *schema* – a framework for how to interpret a document's structure and how to populate it. For any given genre and sub-genre, the guidelines describe how to build an acceptable instance: what modules should appear, what order they should be in, and so forth. Content should only be signed off for publication if it's valid against the guidelines.

In Chapter 15, *What Exactly Is Content?*, we defined content as "the stuff inside a container." Structure defines the contents, attributes, and ordering of the containers.

An easy metaphor that shows how structure benefits content strategy and content management is plastic storage containers.

An easy metaphor that shows how structure benefits content strategy and content management is plastic storage containers. Given the low cost and diversity of uses, a household can easily amass a large collection of storage containers – but how organized is that collection? Some households boast orderly stacks of matching containers, labeled and dated. When not in use, the containers are stored in neat stacks or nested by size, like Russian nesting dolls. Other households may have drawers or shelves spilling over with a chaotic jumble of colors and shapes, and matching lids to containers is a game of chance. You can see the contrast in Figure 19.5.

Figure 19.5. Container order vs. container chaos[1]

What makes some collections an exercise in wasting time and other collections an organizational aid? Consistency. Domestic organization specialists assert that the secret to a useful, manageable set of storage containers is to throw out the irregular ones. No matching lid? Throw it out. Not part of a stackable set? Throw it out. Get rid of it. Purge.[2]

---

1 Photo credits: http://bit.ly/museumstorage CC BY-SA-2.0 (left), Noz Urbina (right).

2 See *Organize your Tupperware Video,* [http://bit.ly/sortingcontainers] by organization blogger Sandy Jenney. Sandy's video provides an apt metaphor for dealing with corporate content.

This type of thinking applies to structured content.[3] Getting the right content into the right structures and enforcing those structures within the right governance framework makes an enormous difference in the effectiveness of a reuse strategy and the effectiveness of the team that manages it.

Inconsistency in structure, metadata, and terminology such hurt readability and manageability of content. Don't tolerate inconsistency.

When structures are content containers instead of physical containers, they still need to have consistent shapes and sizes and fit nicely into sets. When containers fit together, we can stack, sort, label, and arrange our content to fit our larger structure. We're not restricting the container size or purpose – we are still able to have a specific container type for every purpose – as long as the container fits within the larger set that is our overall information architecture.

In today's content creation and publishing systems, organizations have the ability to define structures according to organizational needs. However, looking at a larger picture, organizations can share structures between corporate divisions, with downstream partners, and within industries. For example, think of the automotive industry:

- Parts suppliers provide content to automobile manufacturers.
- Automobile manufacturers in turn aggregate that content into vehicle-specific manuals and supply those manuals to specialist third-party publishers.
- The publishers provide that content to auto repair shops in the form of specialized manuals for professional mechanics.

To do this they standardize, wherever possible, the content they exchange. From an industry almost synonymous with process refinement, we can learn an important lesson: if you build content with the future in mind, you create opportunities for new revenue, collaboration, and cost savings.

[3] We're not, of course, advocating that you deny users needed content just because it's inconsistent. However, because inconsistencies have a negative impact, delivering content without correcting the inconsistencies is dangerous. Consider the consequences carefully.

Realizing the Benefits of Structured Content

Structure isn't all rules and policing. There are benefits from the perspectives of the content authors, organizations, and end users. Using well-structured containers does not affect the quality or nature of the content inside, but it certainly improves your ability to create, sort, retrieve, and manipulate your content.

Structured topics and fragments improve your ability to deliver adaptive content into a responsive design, because different content can be delivered depending on the user's context and device configuration. There is still a balance to be worked out between content and visual style concerns. The mantra is that content is king, but content still should be tested across different deliverables to make sure that it displays and behaves as expected.

A modern content experience is not authored; it is designed, versioned, and tested much like a product.

If you're thinking that this is starting to make writing sound like building a software program, you're partly right. Content creators, strategists, and responsible decision makers do not need to become software or code experts by any means, but a modern content experience is not authored; it is designed, versioned and tested much like a product. Like a product, your content has defined users, use cases, and features. Thinking in a methodical and product-manager-like way about content helps deliver a strategically beneficial result.

Benefits to Content Teams

By defining the structure of the content containers before filling them with content, authors receive guidance for their writing. An author's content can automatically be validated against the official schema when a module is saved, and in some tools, even while the author is writing. We'll discuss specifically how structure enables this automatic validation in Chapter 20, *The Power of Semantic Content*, but for now, it's only important to understand that the schema is a codified formalization of traditional editorial guidelines. By formalizing the guidelines in the system, we can check against them and help writers keep to the rules.

If this all sounds a bit onerous, be reassured that structure can be implemented on a spectrum. The guidelines can be stricter or looser, as dictated by your unique business processes and situational requirements. To paraphrase Albert Einstein: "Things should be made as simple as possible, but not simpler."

Often, authors who initially resist separating content from format come to find the new way of working liberating, as it allows them to focus on the message and not waste time with the presentation, which varies from device to device anyway. Even though content must be validated on various devices to make sure it meets user expectations and business needs, this does not mean you must write different content for each device.

Content written against a defined structure also helps reviewers and managers. Content is created consistently from the start, which helps avoid repeated editorial cycle updates, and reviewers know exactly what the structure should be. Sign-offs can also be more efficient, since it may not be necessary to have every individual deliverable separately approved if they are all derived from a common source. Reviews and sign-offs, while necessary, are not any author's favorite part of the job. Minimizing both is a benefit to everyone.

Benefits to Organizations

Restricting the shapes and types of containers makes arranging and managing content simpler. It provides excellent control over consistency and avoids what would otherwise be a very large editorial and quality assurance workload. This is in addition to reducing or eliminating the need to manually rework, review, and format content for different deliverables.

At times, you may need to change content to make it fit a structural container.[4] The content might need a bit of a rewrite or trim – like cutting up food to fit a certain size of storage container. And from time-to-time, you may need a new type of container for a particular purpose. Part of governance is deciding what content structures you need and when you need to modify or extend those structures or bend the rules.

---

[4] That is a *structural* container, not a visual container in the deliverables.

Part of governance is deciding what content structures you need and when you need to modify or extend them.

A simple example of a content definition could be that all product overviews should consist of the following parts:

- A paragraph of 150 or fewer words that contains the full product name and code
- A follow-on bullet list of 3-5 key features

If a content creator submits a product overview with more than 150 words and without a bulleted list, a reviewer – or the software – could refuse to accept the topic until the overview is shortened and a list is added. Reworking for structure is no different. The business defines how it wants to communicate and then follows those definitions. When new needs arise, stakeholders can review them and decide how to address the need, which might or might not result in a change to the rules.

When a system is implemented well, the net result is an increase in productivity. Individual modules may actually take more effort to set up, but the asset amplification across various contexts is significant enough to offset the investment. In reuse-heavy projects using XML, especially where translation is involved, we have seen savings of 80% to 300% of the implementation cost in the first year. This means that some projects pay for themselves in just a few months. End-user satisfaction and internal operational benefits are the gravy.

Benefits for Users

Consistency helps with comprehension. Consuming content in a predictable structure becomes easier because you know where to look for the information you want. It allows readers to "skip, skim, and scan"[5] with more ease. Consider, for example, the comparative ease in finding information in highly structured, alphabetized, and indexed content such as catalogs, encyclopedias, phone books, and spreadsheets, compared to the other extreme: a novel where any page can have any structure or content and the sequence is defined by the author alone.

[5] UX Myths, *Myth #1: People Read on the Web* [http://uxmyths.com/post/647473628/-myth-people-read-on-the-web]

Predictable structures help you create content that adheres to the Principle of Least Astonishment.[6] The premise is that predictable content structures are easier to move through and consume than unpredictable structures. Predictability frees the user from distractions and uncertainty, which are obstacles to understanding your content. To illustrate this to content teams, we ask, "Consider two situations: one where you have a strong sense that you know where you are and what is going to happen next, and the other where you don't know where you are and feel like anything could happen. In which situation are you more comfortable, less stressed, and best able to focus on the task at hand or the message being conveyed?"

Consuming content in a predictable structure becomes easier because you know where to look for the information you want.

If you've ever tried to use a poorly structured website or application while attempting to accomplish something important – complete a transaction before a deadline, make a purchase, check in to a flight in a hurry – then you may have experienced user stress. Reduced user stress increases brand loyalty, which leads to more use, better use, more recommendations, and fewer support calls. Finally, if you share content across deliverables, the probability of customers encountering conflicting information in your content will be significantly reduced.

Component Content Management Systems

While we are not focusing on supporting tools and technology in this book, it is important to note that building content using modules requires tools designed for that purpose. *Component Content Management Systems* support structured content, give writers direct control over modules, and automate publishing through multiple channels. They are distinct from *Web CMS's,* which are focused on one delivery model (the Web) and the content types that support web delivery.

6 http://en.wikipedia.org/wiki/Principle_of_least_astonishment

CHAPTER 20

The Power of Semantic Content

> I once led a workshop with a client that was struggling to output old print content to multiple channels. It turned out they had migrated every last visual detail on their old printed pages to what they called *semantic* markup: list numbering was manual, as were page breaks, or "text decorations," as they called them. Everything was done by hand. What they did was not semantic markup, and the system not only provided no benefit, it was harder to use than the old one.
>
> —Noz Urbina

In Chapter 17, *Planning for Power Publishing*, and Chapter 18, *Right Content, Right Context*, we discussed the importance of separating content and presentation. In Chapter 19, *Making Content User-centric Using Modular Building Blocks*, we discussed how to make content more powerful using modular building blocks. We can now add a third dimension. We need to add clear labels to our modular containers so they are findable, sortable, and above all, meaningful to both users and automated computer systems. This labeling of content is called adding *semantics.*

What does semantic labeling really mean? This is an area of much discussion and confusion. You may have some familiarity with the Semantic Web, semantically structured content, XML, and related concepts. You may also have heard a range of conflicting opinions about those topics. In the context of this book, we provide a high-level view, starting with the abstract and working back to the concrete. This will provide enough context so that you can assess the degree to which these concepts can and should be applied in your content strategy.

Semantics is the discussion and study of "meaning"

Talking Semantics

In the vernacular, the expression "it's just semantics" means splitting hairs – talking at an irrelevant level of detail and not seeing the forest for the trees. Semantics is the discussion and study of "meaning" and, for our purposes, certainly not splitting hairs.

As content strategists, the semantics of our content is inextricably linked to our work and is a key attribute that helps us leverage content as a true business asset.

Computers don't know what anything we write actually means. Although search engines are a significant step forward in bridging the gap between people and machines, their ability to deal with semantics is very limited. This is why, when faced with a phrase like "Light Polish Shoes," they can't tell which of the following meanings is correct:

- Light-colored shoes
- Lightweight shoes from Poland

Similarly, without adding some explicit meaning to content at the time of creation, search engines can't differentiate the following possible meanings of the word "park":

- A space set aside for the enjoyment of the public
- The act of leaving your vehicle in a designated (possibly public) space

Unless we provide semantic information that computers can understand, they don't know what we mean.

Taken out of context, even a person can misinterpret cases like this. Search engines, even though they run some very clever algorithms over our content, use statistics and pattern matching to guess what we are after. Unless we provide semantic information that computers can understand, they don't actually know what we mean. In a business setting, missing semantics can translate into your content not appearing in searches, which can lead to missed opportunities and missed sales.

Search engines, Content Management Systems and modern publishing systems need context and meaning spelled out to realize their full potential. Enter semantic, structured content.

Semantics Change the Experience of Media

Let's look at a straight-forward, concrete example where semantics allows a computer to process content in powerful ways. We are using Facebook as the platform because it has become a familiar user experience world wide, but you should be able to follow the example even if you don't use Facebook.

This example looks at semantics applied to photographs.[1] When you have photos on your computer, you can look at the details or properties of the individual files. Most people don't bother looking, but if you do, you will see extra data about the file – this extra data is called *metadata*. Metadata includes things like the file name, file type, file size, date taken, and date modified.

More advanced cameras and operating systems automatically record additional metadata such as album, tags, camera maker, camera model, categories, resolution, GPS coordinates, and so on. However, a computer cannot automatically determine some of the most basic information that humans might want to know about their photos, including the following:

- Who are the people in the photo?
- Was the photo taken at a special event, like a birthday or wedding?

When you upload photos to Facebook, you have the opportunity to fill in this missing information (see Figure 20.1):

Figure 20.1. Facebook photo upload dialog with metadata fields[2]

[1] We address textual content in the section titled "Semantic Markup for Textual Data" (p. 192), but media such as photographs are a simpler place to start.

[2] Photo credit: Rahel Bailie

Metadata on the upload screen is divided into two content types, the album and photo. Some fields are shared, and some are type-specific:

- **Title:** Accepts text. Appears on albums only.
- **Description:** Accepts text. Appears on both photos and albums.
- **Location:** Accepts text, but tied to a global public index of places. Appears on both photos and albums.
- **Date:** A controlled field that accepts only a calendar date. Appears on both photos and albums.
- **Face tags:** Special tags that contain the name of a person in a photo and where the person is located within the photo.[3] Appears on albums only.

When you add a face tag – tag being synonymous with label – Facebook adds the information to an index that can be used to sort and display the photos. The indexing enabled by this new metadata then provides various navigational abilities that your local computer cannot. You can also set viewing permissions.

In this example (Figure 20.1), Rahel could set permissions to specify individuals or contact lists that would be denied access to the photograph of her grandchildren Ashley and Aaron.

On Facebook, you can:

- Browse all the photos in which you are tagged, no matter who took them.
- Remove your face tags from a photo; this removes the metadata from the index, so that this photo will no longer be found in a search for you.
- Browse all the photos where a particular person is tagged.
- Change certain metadata, such as photo or album descriptions, yet keep the content in the same collections and indexes.

---

[3] Face tags are selected either from your contacts or by entering a text string for those not in your contacts.

- Browse to public pages about the locations where the photos were taken; these pages use metadata to build up location-specific content such as who among your friends has worked in a location or "liked" a location (see Figure 20.2).
- Browse your albums and other collections on different devices, for example the following:
    - Mobile web browser
    - Native smartphone app
    - Native tablet app

We are limited only by the meaningfulness and completeness of our semantic labeling.

Figure 20.2. Using tags, Facebook connects people in photos and photos to places

If Facebook decided to, they could provide additional features. An example might be to integrate an automated print-on-demand service to make bound copies of photo albums. The content assets and necessary metadata are already there, and they could easily be sent to a photo printing service. In other words, the system could be easily extended to create different combinations of content. We are limited only by the meaningfulness and completeness of our semantic labeling. Semantic metadata allows this type of sorting – if you haven't tagged your photos, you can't benefit from the metadata.

This example makes the whole exercise of semantic labeling seem simple enough. Almost a bit too simple. Any database can facilitate this kind of technopower, right? Yes. Exactly. So why haven't we made the rest of our content that easy to manipulate and reuse? Is it the same reason we haven't all tagged our photos in Facebook – lack of interest or time – or is there a more complex set of tensions at work?

New user contexts, changing market demands, and the sheer volume of content and deliverables to be produced are pushing more and more organizations to the realization that their content must be more adaptable, agile and dynamic.

Textual content is far more complex than images or other media files, simply because of the complexity of natural language.

Textual content, however, is far more complex than images or other media files, simply because of the complexity of natural language. Content needs some additional work to get the technopower we're after.

Semantic Markup for Textual Data

We've seen that semantic content can enable computers to:

- Carry out more meaningful and complex commands.
- Produce new arrangements of content driven by metadata.
- Simultaneously output the same arrangement of content modules to multiple channels (smartphones, tablets, mobile apps, desktop websites, and PDFs).

The possibilities are endless.

Applied to all of our content, not just media files such as photos, this database-like ability to locate, list, converge, integrate, and manipulate our content can enable the kind of context-specific, adaptive, responsive power publishing that the modern consumer is after.

XML (eXtensible Markup Language) has become the de facto standard for doing just that. XML lets you add metadata and structure to your content so that computers can process all of your content in ways similar to what we just saw with Facebook and photos.

Semantic markup gives us a database-like ability to locate, list, converge, integrate, and manipulate our content, enabling power publishing.

Don't Google XML

You may have heard that XML is complex and difficult to use. This is usually because of an inadequate explanation, lingering bruises after a bad implementation,[4] or confusion about how XML contrasts with the newer HTML versions (XHTML, HTML5).[5]

Simply searching online for information on XML on its own is not advisable for beginners, since a search usually surfaces explanations developed by technical people for other technical people. Here we will try to explain XML in simpler, more relatable terms.

The Human Side of Semantic Markup

In our Facebook example, we looked at how meaningful, semantic labeling enables a computer to understand some of the things that people get immediately when looking at a photo. Our brains are trained to pick out faces and other meaningful attributes of a photo instantly and often unconsciously. The computer needs to be told, explicitly, what humans can tell from a glance. Similarly, when humans look at a text-based document or web page, they immediately understand many things about the document that a computer wouldn't.

---

[4] One of our favorite tirades against XML is "XML Can Go To H***" [http://www.webcitation.org/-6BrSghpBQ], where a long suffering designer is left to fend for herself after a poorly thought-out XML project gets rolling. It's a classic case that illustrates how process and technology change are not something that can be implemented casually by the inexperienced.

[5] HTML5 is sometimes positioned as the successor to XML, but that is inaccurate. HTML5 is an evolution of the previous HTML standards. Fortunately, there is an XML flavor called XHTML5, which can be manipulated using XML tools. HTML5, even in its XHTML5 form, is not a content-centric language; presentation is too ingrained. In short, XML is good for controlling and storing your content, and HTML5/XHTML5 are good for delivering or importing content. For the tech-savvy, there is more on the IBM developerWorks site [http://www.ibm.com/developerworks/xml/library/x-think45/] and W3C blog [http://www.w3.org/QA/2008/01/html5-is-html-and-xml.html].

From a life-time of looking at formatted documents, we develop an intuition for the meaning and significance of certain visual elements.

From a life-time of looking at formatted documents, we develop an intuition for the meaning and significance of certain visual structures. For example, looking at Figure 20.3, it is not difficult to identify the following types of blocks:

1. The text block at the top with the largest typeface is the document title.
2. Short text blocks in a smaller typeface separating paragraphs are headings.
3. Longer text blocks separated by a bit of white space are paragraphs.
4. Text blocks in a smaller typeface at the bottom of the page are footnotes.
5. Indented text blocks with bullets or numbers to the left are lists.
6. Isolated text blocks below images are captions.

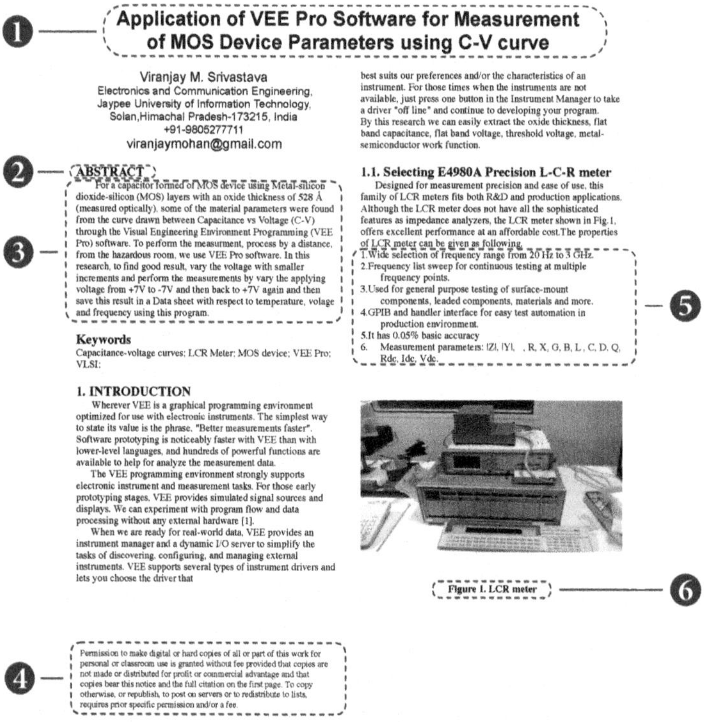

1 — **Application of VEE Pro Software for Measurement of MOS Device Parameters using C-V curve**

Viranjay M. Srivastava
Electronics and Communication Engineering,
Jaypee University of Information Technology,
Solan,Himachal Pradesh-173215, India
+91-9805277711
viranjaymohan@gmail.com

2 — **ABSTRACT**

3 — For a capacitor formed of MOS device using Metal-silicon dioxide-silicon (MOS) layers with an oxide thickness of 528 Å (measured optically), some of the material parameters were found from the curve drawn between Capacitance vs Voltage (C-V) through the Visual Engineering Environment Programming (VEE Pro) software. To perform the measurment, process by a distance, from the hazardous room, we use VEE Pro software. In this research, to find good result, vary the voltage with smaller increments and perform the measurements by vary the applying voltage from +7V to -7V and then back to +7V again and then save this result in a Data sheet with respect to temperature, volage and frequency using this program.

Keywords
Capacitance-voltage curves; LCR Meter; MOS device; VEE Pro; VLSI:

1. INTRODUCTION

Wherever VEE is a graphical programming environment optimized for use with electronic instruments. The simplest way to state its value is the phrase. "Better measurements faster". Software prototyping is noticeably faster with VEE than with lower-level languages, and hundreds of powerful functions are available to help for analyze the measurement data.

The VEE programming environment strongly supports electronic instrument and measurement tasks. For those early prototyping stages, VEE provides simulated signal sources and displays. We can experiment with program flow and data processing without any external hardware [1].

When we are ready for real-world data, VEE provides an instrument manager and a dynamic I/O server to simplify the tasks of discovering, configuring, and managing external instruments. VEE supports several types of instrument drivers and lets you choose the driver that best suits our preferences and/or the characteristics of an instrument. For those times when the instruments are not available, just press one button in the Instrument Manager to take a driver "off line" and continue to developing your program. By this research we can easily extract the oxide thickness, flat band capacitance, flat band voltage, threshold voltage, metal-semiconductor work function.

1.1. Selecting E4980A Precision L-C-R meter

Designed for measurement precision and ease of use, this family of LCR meters fits both R&D and production applications. Although the LCR meter does not have all the sophisticated features as impedance analyzers, the LCR meter shown in Fig.1, offers excellent performance at an affordable cost.The properties of LCR meter can be given as following.

5 —
1. Wide selection of frequency range from 20 Hz to 3 GHz.
2. Frequency list sweep for continuous testing at multiple frequency points.
3. Used for general purpose testing of surface-mount components, leaded components, materials and more.
4. GPIB and handler interface for easy test automation in production environment.
5. It has 0.05% basic accuracy
6. Measurement parameters: |Z|, |Y|, , R, X, G, B, L, C, D, Q, Rdc, Idc, Vdc.

6 — Figure 1. LCR meter

4 — Permission to make digital or hard copies of all or part of this work for personal or classroom use is granted without fee provided that copies are not made or distributed for profit or commercial advantage and that copies bear this notice and the full citation on the first page. To copy otherwise, or republish, to post on servers or to redistribute to lists, requires prior specific permission and/or a fee.

Figure 20.3. Example of structure implied by formatting[6]

[6] Image source: http://commons.wikimedia.org/wiki/File:Cmos_related_document.pdf. Public domain.

The human interpretations could go on and on, and experienced readers could make many of them even if the words are blurred out, too small to read, or even in a different language. If you have even a bit of contextual guidance, you can extract much more information. In Figure 20.4, even if you don't read Vietnamese (or even recognize that the text is in Vietnamese), you know you're looking at a product overview page because you can use visual cues to decipher meaning.

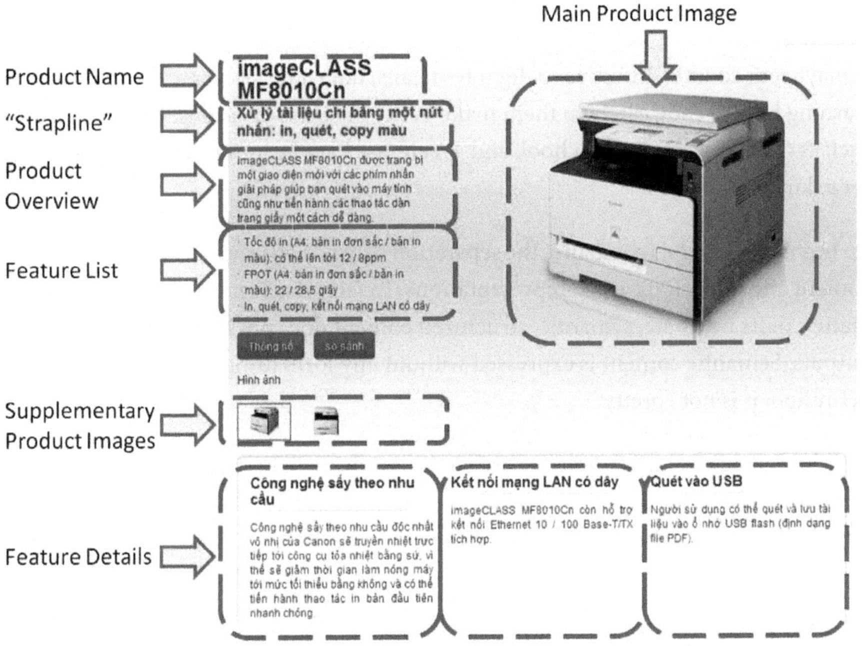

Figure 20.4. An arrangement of text and images that, together, are recognizable as a product overview page

Decoding the semantic and structural aspects of content like this is natural for humans. Computers, however, don't understand concepts like Product Overview or Feature List any more than than they understand who is pictured in the photo in Figure 20.1.[7]

[7] Face recognition software has advanced in recent years, but at the time of writing, it still relies on human intervention.

It may be tempting for some, but we strongly encourage you not to skip this section!

A First Real Look at Markup

This is the point where we draw back the curtain to see what semantic content actually looks like. We know some readers may be curious, while others will want to skip the details. We strongly encourage you not to skip this section. Markup languages, particularly XML and HTML5, are everywhere in publishing. The more you know about the power and potential of markup, the better prepared you will be to develop a strong content strategy.

It may seem counter-intuitive to dig into details, but some leaders are finding that learning how to code can help them make better business decisions. Organizations such as Codecademy, Code School, and Treehouse have been very successful offering these kinds of courses.[8]

To begin, it is helpful to visualize the separation between pure, unformatted, semantic content and its various visual representations. In fact, visualization is the crux of the matter; in its raw state, semantic, structured content does not look like any of its outputs. Semantic content is expressed without any formatting information, so by definition, it is not "pretty."

Let's look at a few real examples of XML markup that will help you get started. Don't worry too much about the exact details of every line. Instead, look at the overall structure and the highlighted items. XML is not as complex as some think it is.

Figure 20.5 shows the semantic, structured content, marked up in XML, for a product page similar to Figure 20.3:

1. **A title:** This consists of the title text surrounded by XML tags (`<title>` and `</title>`). The tags and everything between them is called an *element.*
2. **A short description, or abstract:** The `<shortdesc>` tags surrounds this text.
3. **A group of images:** Each image is identified in a separate element with the tag name `<image>`. The group is itself an element titled `<image_group>`. Yes, elements can nest, just like sections in a document.

8 "Leadership: CEOs Learn to Speak in Code"[24].

4. **A list of key features:** This is another example of element nesting, with `<feature>` elements nested inside a `<key_features>` element.
5. **A list of other features:** Again, nesting. Notice that we use the `<feature>` element again, this time inside a `<features>` element.

```
<product_overview id="4C42F4" productdivision="printers" productline="portable">
  <title>CS Strategist 4DM</title>
  <shortdesc>The CS Strategist 4DM is a super portable all-in-one printer
      that'll surprise you with its flexibility and ease of use. WIFI and
      Bluetooth, market-leading resolution… Everything you need!</shortdesc>
  <product_overview_body>
    <image_group>
        <image href="cs-strat4dm-image.JPG" role="main"/>
        <image href="cs-strat4dm-image2.JPG"/>
        <image href="cs-strat4dm-image3.JPG"/>
        <image href="cs-strat4dm-image4.JPG"/>
    </image_group>
    <key_features>
        <feature>Small and light, with 3" touch-screen display</feature>
        <feature>Powerful CMS extends your content into print</feature>
        <feature>Powered by Android OS for the latest apps</feature>
    </key_features>
    <features>
        <feature id="browser123">
            <name>Internet Browser</name>
            <description>A mobile browser allows you to surf and search,
                then print directly.</description>
        </feature>
        <feature id="touchscreen123">
            <name>Touchscreen</name>
            <description>Buttons take up space, the CS Strategist lets
                you work from one, easy-to-use touch screen.</description>
        </feature>
    </features>
  </product_overview_body>
</product_overview>
```

Figure 20.5. A feature description marked up in XML

Some of the semantics in Figure 20.5 can be derived from the tags themselves. For example the paired tags (`<feature>` … `</feature>`). Each pair surrounds the content in question, making it sufficiently clear to both a computer and a human what is inside.

XML explains to computers what humans immediately know about content just looking at it.

Other markup provides additional information. You may have noticed some markup inside the tags in Figure 20.5. For example, the `<image>` elements each contain markup like this: `href="cs-strat4dm-image.JPG"`. Those are *attributes*, and they provide additional information about the elements they are inside of. Between elements and attributes we are able to express – in a way computers can process – much more than could ever be expressed in just the text, even if that text is visually formatted.

Our one-sentence summary of XML markup is: XML explains to computers what humans immediately know about content just by looking at it.

XML vs. Other Markup

XML is an extensible language, as the acronym implies. XML is extensible because it's a meta-language. That is, it is a set of rules for building new markup languages. You can create an XML language for any subject area you like. For example, there are XML languages for music, business transactions, healthcare records, voting information, and dozens of other areas, including, of course, business-critical content.[9]

Other markup languages – HTML being by far the most famous – come with predefined tags that cannot be changed. HTML has tags like `<em>` or `<p>`, which are used by all organizations around the world using the HTML specification.

XML elements are defined in an industry-agreed or organization-specific set of rules, called a schema or DTD, which name each element and describe how the elements must be used and what can be inside them. An example rule definition might state that the `<feature>` element must appear inside a `<features>` element. Many elements can contain text, like `<description>` in Figure 20.5, but they may also contain other elements, depending on the schema.

The schema also defines attributes, which contain additional metadata for an element. In Figure 20.5, productdivision, id (identifier), and href (hypertext reference) are all attributes, and the values assigned to each can be seen inside the quotation marks.

XML is Easier Than it Looks

When we look at an XML file such as the one in Figure 20.5, we don't see the colors, fonts, sizes, layout, and other visual cues that normally help authors as they create content. This is why XML is rarely viewed and edited in its raw form by anyone except

[9] Some well-known XML languages for content are: DocBook, DITA, and S1000D. If you are starting a content strategy project, the odds are that one of these existing languages will be suitable.

technical experts. Most authors, subject matter experts, and customers use tools that hide the raw code.

In a well-designed system, authors should only need to understand the basic principles to contribute to a structured, semantic system. Authors should not be focused on XML, or any markup system. They should only need to understand the content model, which should be no more difficult than learning rigorous editorial guidelines.

Authors should only need to understand the content model, not the complexities of XML, to contribute to a structured, semantic system.

Semantic, structured XML content can be created in several ways that do not require direct editing of XML source:

- A CMS webform
- A PDF form
- A dedicated XML authoring tool (commercial and open-source options exist)
- An XML plug-in to MS Word (several options of varying quality exist today)
- An automatic export from a system like a database of product parameters, source code library, *Enterprise Resource Planning (ERP) System*, *Product Lifecycle Management (PLM) System*, or other content repository

Because XML is an open standard, many tools have been created to work with it, and you can mix and match tools according to the needs of your organization. Some organizations use XML so transparently that their authors, who are subject matter experts rather than professional writers, don't even realize they are creating XML content. You can even create structured XML content from user contributions, such as forum comments, if your content entry methods are well-designed and easy-to-use.

Changing the Format-first Mindset

In the section titled "Content Lifecycle Myths" (p. 243), we assert that technical staff often focus on the containers rather than the contents when building and rolling out content solutions. In XML, the containers – the content models – are specifically built so that authors can focus on the content and not worry about the presentation.

In projects where visual formatting is determined first, content becomes an afterthought.

In projects where visual formatting is determined first, content becomes an afterthought. The container defined by the visual presentation drives what should go inside of it, rather than the other way around. We call this design-driven content.

Instead, we want content-driven design. As you saw in Figure 20.5, the XML file contains no design whatsoever; it is pure content and structure, ready for design to be applied to match the output requirements.

With semantic content, the container isn't a generic, one-size-fits-all crate into which content gets packed. It is more like our example of stackable plastic storage containers, where we have the right size and shape for each purpose and need. The container was designed for the content, not the other way around.

Semantic content models are not designed for presentation; they're designed for advancing organizational goals. The visual container for any specific device or format comes last and has to mold itself to the content. The container on a web page or in an app is just formatting.

Semantic content models are not designed for presentation; they're designed for advancing organizational goals.

Semantic Markup in XML and HTML

Tagging can be more or less semantic. Looking at the example in Figure 20.5 again, but focusing on the mark-up of key features, we can compare how we have modeled key features in XML to how we would have to model them in HTML, which supports much less semantic information. Figure 20.6 is the key features part of our example:

```
<key_features>
  <feature>Small and light, with 3" touch-screen display</feature>
  <feature>Powerful CMS extends your content into print</feature>
  <feature>Powered by Android OS for the latest apps</feature>
</key_features>
```

Figure 20.6. Key features section in the product overview (XML)

In HTML, we would have had to use a generic unordered list (<ul>) and then fill it with list items (<li>). Figure 20.7 shows the key features part of our example marked up in HTML:

```
<ul>
  <li>Small and light, with 3" touch-screen display</li>
  <li>Powerful CMS extends your content into print</li>
  <li>Powered by Android OS for the latest apps</li>
</ul>
```

Figure 20.7. Key features section in the product overview (HTML)

From a semantic perspective, the difference between the XML and HTML versions is the difference between more or less semantically tagged content. What does that mean, you ask?

It means that <li> … </li> tells us less about the content between the tags than <feature> … </feature>. Similarly, the <ul> element tells us less than the <key_features> element. If you look at <ul>, you don't know what you are going to get or what you should put inside. If you look at <key_features>, you have a pretty good idea. That means there is more semantic meaning in the tag itself.

Consider the following three types of content: part number, invoice number, phone number. If you have the number 987-654-3210 out of context, neither a human nor a computer could identify whether it is a part number, invoice number, or phone number. With semantic labeling, it becomes clear:

- <part_num>987-654-3210</part_num>
- <invoice_num>987-654-3210</invoice_num>
- <phone_num>987-654-3210</phone_num>

The tags provide enough meaning for a computer to process the content correctly. With the tags hidden away in the final deliverable, they all might look the same to a person, but the intelligence is there behind the scenes, allowing the system to handle the content appropriately.

Responsive Design and Reuse with Semantics

In responsive design or reuse systems, content with embedded semantics allows you to pull out the right amount of the right content for the target device or deliverable. For example, with key features clearly labeled, it is possible to have the same responsive design web page display just the key features on a mobile phone browser and hide other features behind tabs that can be clicked. Similarly, for delivery to a print-oriented overview document looking at key features of several products in a family, key features could be used and other features could be omitted completely.

Responsive design and adaptive content reuse systems are so powerful because the logic needs to be built only once.

Responsive design and adaptive content reuse systems are so powerful because the logic needs to be built only once. After that, any number of content instances can be loaded and automatically mapped to the appropriate points in the output.

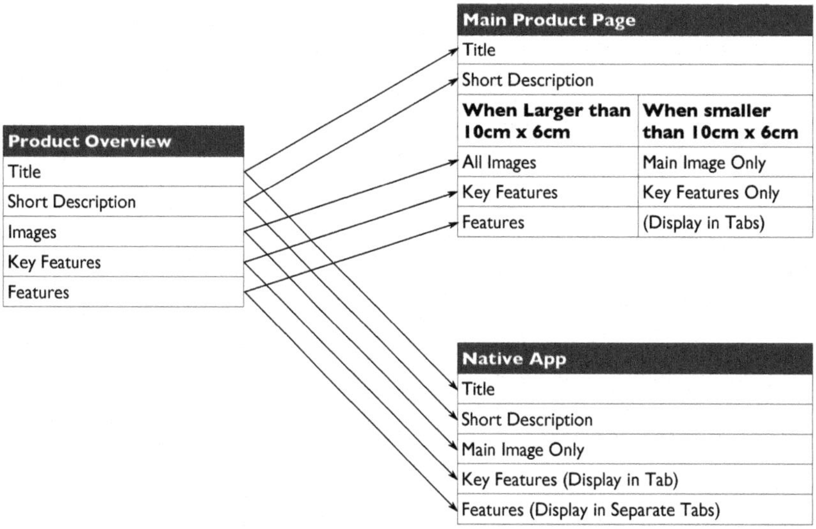

Figure 20.8. Content mappings between the content model and two different outputs

A diagram like Figure 20.8 can be used to show how structures in the content map to two different outputs help different stakeholders in a multidisciplinary team visualize content mappings. Other outputs like print deliverables or alternative web pages could be added to the diagram as needed. Filters and selection rules could also be added to outputs to select only content when certain attribute values are found – e.g. `productline="portable"` – or even more complex rules, depending on the metadata available in the content and the user's needs.[10]

Using the Right Amount of Semantics

You need to select an appropriate level of semantics. Putting carrots in a storage container and then labeling the container as "food" doesn't provide the information you really need. Better would be to label the container "carrots," and better still would be to add the date. Of course you can go too far. Adding the time of day and the visitors who were at your house when you served the carrots would be a lot of effort for no real return.

Normally, the model is created before very much of the content is written, and therefore helps authors write consistently. However, there should be enough options and flexibility designed into the model that it doesn't become a straight-jacket for authors. For example, you can control the number of items in a list or the number of features allowed in a product feature list, but should you?

In a structured authoring world, technical communicators can get by with three basic module types: concept, task, and reference, but there is often a need for additional semantic information within those types.

Deciding on the appropriate level of semantics is best left to a specialist. For example, you may have heard that HTML5 has certain semantic capabilities. Deciding whether those capabilities are sufficient for your needs, or whether you need more sophisticated capabilities, is a critical design decision that you need to investigate with a specialist. That is the only way to ensure you the technopower your organization needs.

---

[10] Diagrams like Figure 20.8 were used in the Vancouver municipal website project that was shown in Chapter 19, *Making Content User-centric Using Modular Building Blocks*.

HTML5 does have some semantic capabilities, but evaluate them thoroughly and carefully before assuming they are sufficient for your needs.

When tracing problems with semantic content in our clients' organizations, we've often found that the decision makers underestimated the importance of this modeling work, and the resulting models were either too lax or too strict to be workable. Too strict makes it impossible for the authoring team to have enough flexibility to do the content justice; too loose makes the technical teams struggle to process the content.

Both writers and technologists need to be able to work, and work together, to deliver the optimal experience to users. Both may need to be (re-)educated on the benefits and goals of semantic content so they buy into the process. Neither the author-first perspective of "Why can't we just write the way we've always done it?" nor the technology-first perspective of "Why can't everyone just populate a database with data?" should be allowed to dominate the conversation.

As the decision maker, it will be up to you to make the call as to whether you have the appropriate skills on your team to do an unbiased assessment or if you will need to bring in an outside perspective to analyze and develop your content models and to mediate – some would say interpret or translate – between the worlds of technology and content.

Why Semantics Matters

To summarize, let's take a look at some of the things a computer system can do with semantic content:

- **Future-proof:** XML is an international, text-based standard not owned by any one vendor. There is no license to pay or commercial tool required to create it. This protects content against format lock-in and tool changes, as many tools can process XML. Many organizations even use XML to retire and archive entire systems, because they know that their content won't be at the mercy of a proprietary standard that might change or disappear at the whim of some other company.
- **Validate:** Computers can check for structural issues. For example, the rules of a content module dictate that there should only be one title and one short description. If an author includes two titles or two short descriptions, the software will flag this as invalid. Validation is what makes it possible for an application to create XML that will be compatible with downstream processes.

- **Find:** Semantic content provides information that makes it easier for search engines to locate information. You can tag modules, parts of modules, or fragments with semantics that help search engines. For example, if individual details about a product differ from region to region – this often happens in travel, automotive, governmental, and legal content, to name a few – then location-specific metadata can help a search engine serve content that is appropriate to the user's location.
- **Filter, transform, and format:** Computers can automate formatting, reducing costs significantly. And they can generate multiple deliverables for print, web, and mobile from the same source. Responsive design systems can feed back device details and deliver the right content for that device. For many organizations, formatting costs can drop to the point where the only cost is maintaining the overall system. This is a big win compared with the hours involved in transforming content from unstructured MS Word files or manually re-adjusting thousands of formatted documents into their desired output deliverables. For very exacting and customized layout scenarios, like visually rich catalogs or magazine content, some human tweaks and polish may be needed, but for many applications, the process can be fully automated.
- **Manage translation:** Because items are labeled and identifiable, sending exactly the right content to a translator and getting back a production-ready deliverable becomes much easier. Some organizations have saved upwards of 50% in translation costs because of how much formatting and quality assurance work was removed from their processes. Translation accuracy is also increased, because semantic information helps translators just as much as it helps readers.
- **Reuse:** Because of the clear, tree-like hierarchy of XML content models, everything in an XML file has a type of address that lets you look up items by their location in the tree in addition to finding them through attached metadata. For example, if you have a list of features, you can locate any feature based on its location in the file (first, second, … last).
- **Enrich:** Metadata is the key to filtering and sorting large masses of content efficiently. In addition, it can be used to automatically create relationships among similarly tagged items. This can help create taxonomies, folksonomies, and structural metadata that work together. Semantic content also provides a way to standardize labeling systems so they can be shared across genres and deliverables.

Attribute metadata can be used to micro-target content. For example, by putting a "region" flag on an element, content can be hidden or shown depending on the audience. Even without knowing XML markup, you can probably tell that the product overview in Figure 20.5 should be indexed with other printers, in the subcategory for portable printers (see Figure 20.9).

```
<product_overview id="4C42F4"
                  productdivision="printers"
                  productline="portable">
```

Figure 20.9. Semantic information in a product overview element

- **Create new deliverables:** Modules are not particularly adaptive if you can't combine them in a mix-and-match format to create new context-appropriate deliverables. XML can be used to standardize both the module structures and the overall deliverable structures for sites, books, apps, or whatever you need. Sometimes it means using all the same content, sometimes it means adapting what is delivered by demographic, context or some other variable.
- **Define deliverables independent of any software system:** You can select an industry standard or define your own XML standard for describing a content "story" for a user. If you look at the product overview page example, you will see that you might have several possible stories. You might create a catalog story that pulls together product information and short descriptions from multiple product overviews. In parallel, you could create a portable printers story that pulls, from the same body of product reviews, information for just the portable printers.

  Both stories could then be automatically published in print, mobile web, and desktop web forms. Like a table of contents or site navigation map, the XML file describing the story contains little or no content but maps out relationships between modules, metadata keywords, and the order and hierarchy of content. Again, the details of this are best left to an information architect experienced with cross-platform semantic content design. What is important to know is that the labor of formatting a whole end-user story for a device or platform can be automated once the story and modules are defined in XML.

The semantics of your content is the intelligence that makes the content manageable and consumable. In many projects, a large proportion of the content's intelligence, structure and relationships is described only in the software that manages it – that is, a content management system. The implication and risk in having all the intelligence in the content management system is that changing software would mean extensive rebuilding of the content just to make it work like it did before. Similarly, when that intelligence is not embedded in the content, adapting, transforming, and filtering the content to deliver new experiences is a costly and labor-intensive exercise.

The semantics of your content is the intelligence that makes the content manageable and consumable.

Deciding to invest in semantics means that your human resources are focused on what they're most needed for – writing and optimizing content to support the organization and user goals. Redundant tweaking of text and visuals, and pouring resources into manual processes related to administration and translation burns through budget with no value-added return.

Developing a Content Strategy

If you are fortunate enough to have a skilled content strategist on staff or on contract, that person should know a lot of the information in this chapter and should be able to run the project with minimal guidance. If you don't have someone with this level of skill, then this section will guide you through the process of implementing a content strategy, a culmination of everything you've learned so far in the book. This final stage includes a look at:

- How to assess your organizational maturity and readiness for change when it comes to content strategy
- Customer and content lifecycles – what they are, what they aren't, and how they interact
- Relevant performance measures, information architecture, audience and task analysis, and content design principles
- The kinds of skills you will need to find or hire to take a content strategy from theory to reality

CHAPTER 21

Leveraging Content Strategically

> Remember back in the 1990s, when companies first started commissioning websites to be built? Remember how no one really understood where this web thing was going or where it would land? Sometimes I'd hear the head of marketing or product development or the CFO ask, "When will this budget line item go away – when will the website be done?" A few years later, it was a rude awakening to realize that it would never be "done." Today, no one asks that question; in fact, the website is often recognized as the most important vehicle for a number of operational channels.
>
> —Rahel Anne Bailie

In this chapter, we look at content strategically. We consider business management methodologies as applied to content, organizational readiness, and the mind shift needed to begin thinking of your content as a strategic asset.

Today, an organization's website is often recognized as the most important vehicle for a number of operational channels.

While business management methodologies such as Lean, Six Sigma, Balanced Scorecard (to name a few of the most popular models at the moment) differ in their details, they have some common denominators:

- Start with your current corporate goals.
- Analyze your business requirements.
- Analyze the assets in question.
- Select the most efficient and effective solution.
- Formulate a strategy, including metrics.
- Determine how to implement the strategy, which may include selecting technology.
- Carry out the implementation, which may be an iterative process.
- Measure success and prepare for the next phase – a new version, upgrade, maintenance, and so on.

The same principles apply to content strategy. In other words, figure out why you need to change, how you need to change, what you need to change, and then change it and show where the changes worked and what still needs to be done.

There's an ad where a guy builds the frame for a shed and gets stuck inside. He hadn't planned for doors or windows.

However, as the saying goes, the devil is in the details, and that's where a lot of the problems lie when it comes to content. Starting too far down the chain causes all sorts of problems. We have seen some groups start at the implementation phase and simply work from their existing strategic assumptions. This is reminiscent of the television advertisement where a fellow builds the frame for a shed only to discover that he's stuck inside the frame – he didn't plan for doors or windows. This error stems from the traditional treatment of content as a deliverable in a larger supply chain.

You can see examples of this when staff discuss how their companies won't invest in component content management for their product content. Yet if you were to wander into the financial departments of those same companies, you wouldn't see accounting staff manually making account entries into ledger books. And those financial systems are neither cheap nor simplistic. So what did it take for those companies to move forward? Company decision makers understood the business benefits of speeding invoices, tracking and collecting money, and managing financial assets in the best possible way.

Financial assets are common to all businesses, and executives understand that. Similarly, a content strategy needs to make the case for tracking business-critical product content – specifications, how-to instructions, training material, user support content, and so on – within the larger customer lifecycle to demonstrate that good content is worth the investment. The decision maker must understand the business benefits in order to to make such an investment.

Assessing Your Organizational Readiness

A common reaction to the idea of tackling content strategy is the fear of having to "boil the ocean" – that is, having to adopt a full-fledged content strategy immediately and apply best practices to all content throughout the organization. If that is your reaction, stop and breathe. That would be an overly ambitious goal, even for an organization that has a pressing need. The ideal way to tackle a content strategy is to have a short-term goal and a long-term goal. Once you identify the long-term goal, then break down the steps into manageable short-term goals. This makes the path to success seem less daunting and allows you to iron out the wrinkles in your content strategy before widening its scope.

A good exercise to identify the readiness of your organization is to assess your organization against a content strategy maturity model like the one in Figure 21.1. Determine the stage your organization is at, the stage that would best serve its needs, and the work needed to be done within the organization to reach the desired stage.

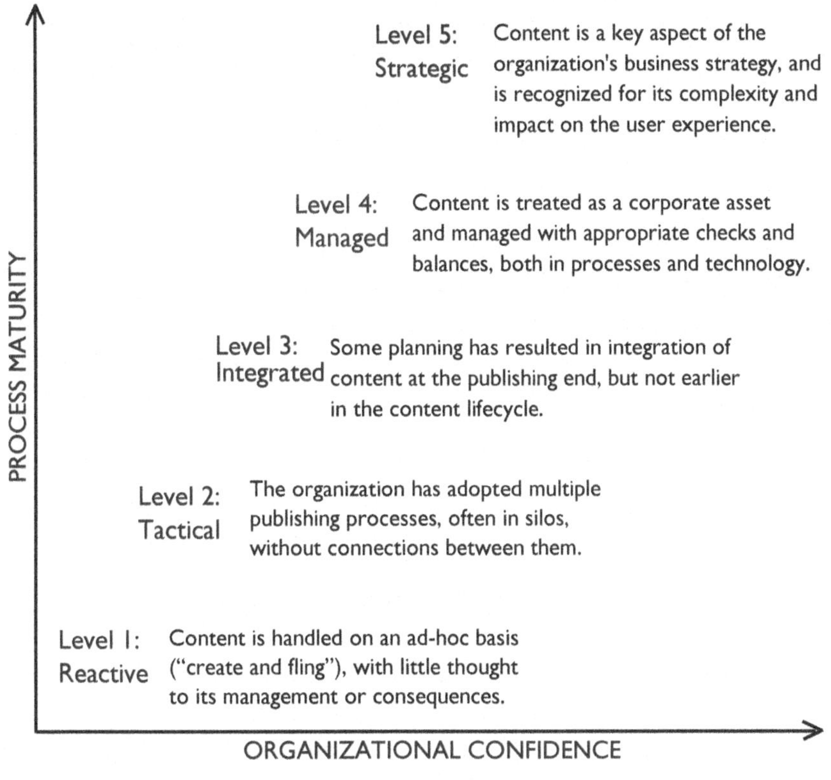

Figure 21.1. Content Strategy Maturity Model

The maturity model describes the degree of formality and optimization of processes within an industry or profession. In the area of content strategy, the maturity model is a tool for assessing progress in improving content-related processes towards the goal of managing content as a corporate asset.[1]

Unless your organization is a newspaper or producing content is your primary product, there likely hasn't been real impetus to pay much attention to content.

It is not unusual for organizations to be at the first or second stage of the maturity model. After all, unless your organization is a newspaper or has a business model where producing content is your primary product, there has likely been little impetus to pay much attention to content. And it's not necessary to try to jump to the highest level. Even one step up can make an exponential difference in content quality and delivery. The improvements in processes will have an effect on your organizational confidence and vice-versa. It will inform the level and sophistication of your content strategy.

Thinking of Content Strategically

Readers may look at this heading and wonder how content can be strategic. Marketers might argue that keywords designed for search engine optimization are strategic, but that doesn't make the content itself strategic. Content can be accurate or inaccurate, help or hindrance, easy-to-read or a hard slog, clear or vague, skimpy or detailed, convincing or lackluster, but "strategic" and "content" make an uneasy pair.

Thinking of content strategically means planning how to deal with content from cradle to grave, throughout the content lifecycle. As with most business lifecycles, there are inputs (analysis), outputs (production), and feedback mechanisms (reactions).

What makes the content lifecycle different from other lifecycles is that content generally has more than a single life; there are multiple iterations and reincarnations along the way. And there is another twist in the plot. As discussed in Chapter 5, *Content as Part of a Complex System*, content has to adapt to whatever shifts have happened in the business landscape, These shifts may be straightforward and require a simple ad-

[1] The model was developed at Carnegie Mellon [http://www.sei.cmu.edu/cmmi/] in the 1980s to measure improvements in software development and has been adapted for many other areas of business.

aptation, or they may be complex and require adaptations that will have a ripple effect on other content or on future content iterations.

Thinking of content strategically, then, is an important step toward developing a content strategy. It means looking upward and outward, placing the strategy within the context of the corporate business model. Thinking of content strategically is, in effect, the analysis phase of the content lifecycle, discussed in more depth in the Chapter 24, *Centering the Strategy Around a Content Lifecycle*. The analysis quadrant of the content lifecycle becomes the cornerstone of a content strategy.

What makes the content lifecycle different from other lifecycles is that content generally has more than a single life.

Is Your Content Strategy Really Strategic?

Strategic content has a well-defined purpose. Each piece of published content should be traceable to some business requirement. Here are some questions you can ask:

- **Which requirement does this content satisfy?** You should make sure that the business requirements are articulated and prioritized.
- **Who would use this content?** You can use behavior-based personas to identify different user types: novice, impatient user, expert, and so on. Then you can tailor and position your content for those user types.
- **What would someone use this content for?** Analyzing what users want to accomplish provides insights into the content they need and helps match their needs to the needs of the organization.
- **Why would someone use this content?** Understanding users' motivations can help you make content easier to find and use.
- **Are users connected to other useful content?** Content needed to complete a transaction or round out an experience may exist in disparate places; surfacing that content in useful ways is an important aspect of strategic placement.

Some organizations have no strategy beyond maintaining the status quo. Other times, content authors may want to develop a strategy, but don't feel they have the power to effect change. In both of these cases, organizational decision makers – marketing managers, product managers, and engineering managers – may ignore requests to review content for accuracy or relevancy, but then spring to life when anything more than superficial changes to content are proposed.

Many of the questions that purport to be strategic are actually tactical – but can be recast as strategic when analyzed.

Many of the questions that purport to be strategic are actually tactical. Here are a few examples of tactical questions that should be recast as strategic questions:

- **Should linear content be moved to topic-based content?** This depends on how the content will be used and, more specifically, reused. This in turn depends on the business case, which is the strategic part. How you rework content is part of the implementation of your strategy.
- **Should we use an XML standard such as DITA?** This goes back to your business case; how you structure your content depends on what you need to accomplish. There are many reasons to move to structured content, but realistically, if there is no business case or if you don't have the technological infrastructure to support structured content, then you won't be able to leverage your effort. Again, it goes back to making the business case for why structured content will result in ROI.
- **How do we create content for multi-channel publishing?** While multi-channel publishing is an important part of leveraging content for multiple audiences in multiple media, it is still part of your implementation, not your strategy. You must know what your content needs to do, from a business perspective, before you address editorial and technological questions.

There is no denying that these questions are important; the answers to them can make or break a content strategy. Yet if you have not done a fundamental analysis of your content requirements, you have no way of knowing the right or best way to implement your content strategy.

Putting the Strategy into Content Strategy

If you've read this far in the book, it's a safe assumption that you are starting to see the value of a content strategy. The experiences, if not always the theory, have resonated enough that you kept reading.

You may already have a team – user experience or usability professionals, marketing communicators, writers, web designers, product or marketing staff, technology or IT professionals – that has presented you with a content strategy proposal. If so, we hope you have a better understanding of the implications of having a content strategy and why your team is asking for time and resources to tackle the content challenges they see. Or you may be the one trying to resolve what you know is a problem, but you haven't yet quite figured out an entry point for tackling it. Or you may be the decision maker who wants to know whether you're done yet and can retire that line item on the budget. Or you may understand that content is a pain point in your organization, and you are trying to wrap your head around how to solve the challenges and issues presented by it.

In other words: where do you go from here?

Content strategies, like the organizations that implement them, are unique. The needs of organizations are highly situational. The benefits that a particular content strategy brings to one organization may not work for another organization. This statement may seem obvious when comparing organizations with different business models – for example, a manufacturer versus a government agency. But even between two similar companies – competitors, perhaps – the content strategies will differ because of variations in their public operations, their internal processes, and a host of other differences. As in medicine, no two patients are alike. When it comes to content strategy, there is no single prescription that will make everyone's content pain go away.

Yet there is some common ground and some basic principles, backed up with diagnostic methodologies, that can lead to prescriptive measures that can help you leverage your investment in a content strategy. The return may be immediately evident or might not make itself apparent until later. Developing a content strategy that helps you lead a team or project through the process is, from the perspective of a decision maker, a way to maximize your ROI on your content investment. Doing some up-front assessment can help speed that return on investment, and the rest of this section will show you how to do just that.

CHAPTER 22
Feeding the Customer Lifecycle

> Grr! I hate shopping online. Hardly anyone writes product descriptions that answer my basic questions. #ux #contentstrategy
>
> —Twitter post viewed 18 Jan 2011

The quest for the right mix of content on a corporate site is like the quest for the holy grail, particularly for marketers. Marketing departments develop content that is clean, crisp, clear, and designed to lead visitors down a compelling and attractive path to the shopping cart. It's a little like dating: use your best line and hope you get a date. In reality, however, consumer behavior doesn't work that way.

Pick-up lines don't always turn the heads of prospective dates, and marketing material doesn't always turn browsers into buyers. Marketers may think they know what content consumers want, but marketing copy often doesn't address the needs of those who see their purchase as the beginning of a relationship with your organization.

The marketing side of your website may be the first place people look for information, but it is certainly not the last.

The marketing side of your website may be the first place people look for information, but it is certainly not the last. Sole reliance on traditional marketing material to promote and sell a product is short-sighted. Customers don't use marketing content alone to make their purchasing decisions, and increasingly, they don't come to a website through a home page or meekly follow the crafted path to the shopping cart. Instead, as shown in a usability study conducted by the Nielsen Norman Group, consumers determine their own path, and rely on alternate content sources, such as search, reviews, vendors, and retailers, to reach what they feel are informed decisions.[1]

Marketing departments may think that "dating" content converts browsers to buyers, but, in reality, it's often "relationship" content that closes the sale. This happens because relationship content answers questions consumers want to know, like: When

---

[1] Read the transcripts of the Nielsen Norman case study [http://www.useit.com/alertbox/-cross_site_behavior.html] and usability session [http://www.useit.com/alertbox/-sites_visted_transcript.html].

I need product support, can I find the content I need? Can I find what I need online, quickly, and freely, or is it hidden and unavailable? Will I regret buying this product when it comes to figuring out how it works or how to fix it?

Consumers won't change their information gathering behavior patterns, so it's up to us to anticipate their natural behavior patterns. Understanding how consumers get information about your products is part of brand management and is important to building a relationship between consumer and organization.

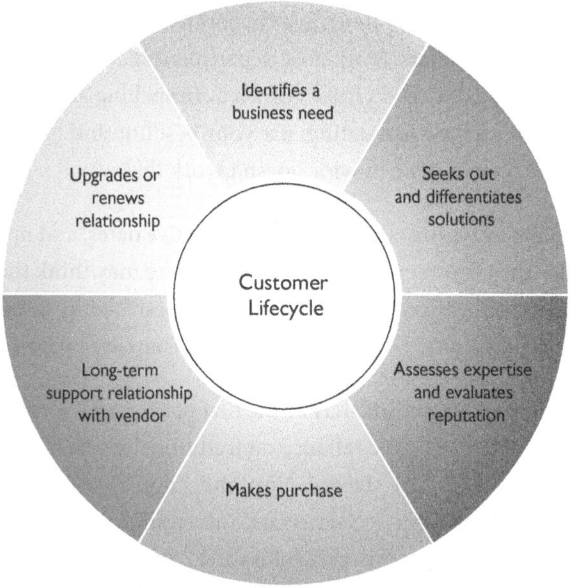

Figure 22.1. Customer lifecycle

To continue with the dating metaphor, focusing on the sell is like focusing on getting the date. Presenting best-foot-forward content is the courtship approach to winning someone over. Managing content is like the hard work of marriage: long-term success requires an ongoing effort. Figure 22.1 shows that the customer lifecycle is a continuous, iterative process over the course of what is, one hopes, a long relationship.[2]

[2] Note that the *customer* lifecycle is distinct from the *content* lifecycle, which is discussed in Chapter 24, *Centering the Strategy Around a Content Lifecycle*.

A customer makes a first purchase only once. The real work is keeping existing customers, maintaining relationships, and building enough brand loyalty to ensure repeat business, garner positive analyst and consumer reviews, and promote goodwill.

In the customer lifecycle, the bulk of the customer's time is spent on the post-sales side, and that side determines the longevity of the relationship. Much of that relationship depends on good communication: listening to our customers and having good information ready when they need it.

Notice that in the customer lifecycle, the bulk of the customer's time is spent on the post-sales side

A recent example comes from a medical device manufacturer. Despite their sophisticated marketing content, product sales were slumping. Their website featured 3D animations of whirring brain scanners and a virtual treatment center where users could browse marketing blurbs and bullet points about product features in an interactive Flash-based world.

So why were product sales slumping? A primary reason was that potential buyers could not make the connection between the beautiful marketing content, the product they would receive, and the after-sales relationship. This manufacturer lacked a strategy for updating marketing content as the product line got updated. As it acquired new product lines, which it did regularly, there was no way to update the content to reflect the new products. It became too expensive to populate the animations with the new product data.

This is in a market where repeat business and upgrades form a significant share of revenue. Customers, and even internal staff, were unable to navigate the web resources and find the content required to maintain equipment. No amount of seductive marketing material was going to pry money from hospital budgets if buyers felt the down-time for this company's machines might be higher than the down-time for a competitor's product.

Content that leads to a sale is just the first step; the after-sale material and third-party influence is what many consumers investigate before they make their purchase.

The after-sale material and third-party influence is what many consumers investigate before they make their purchase.

Develop Your Own Customer Lifecycle

Learn what kind of content your customers really need. Get to know your customers and what content they want. The case study in Chapter 10, *All Content is Marketing Content*, recounted a usability study for a company that markets power inverters. The site had white papers, testimonials, product descriptions, and case studies. But the test subjects looked for purchase-decision content by searching for terms like "1000 watt" and "surge capability." They didn't need to learn about inverters, they simply wanted to find the right inverter for their needs. This knowledge triggered the company to include detailed product information and technical specifications. Instead of uploading PDF files into an obscure folder, the site was redesigned so each product had tabs for content such as product information and specifications. That way, technically savvy consumers could easily find the product best suited to their needs

Companies focused on the long-term relationship, not just the courtship, know that for their prospective customers, the detailed product specification is the decision-making content. User experience consultant Daniel Lafreniere points out that it's consumers who decide what content is important.[3] Therefore, it is important to really know what information your potential customers are looking for and to make sure they can easily get answers to their most pressing questions.

There is a joke about how women find men more attractive when they do the dishes. In other words, it's the comfort found in thoughtful, everyday gestures that makes someone good relationship material. Matching the content to the entire customer lifecycle gives potential (and repeat) customers the information they need to make an informed decision about their vendor of choice. Likewise, smart organizations pay attention to useful, everyday content – technical, training, and support center content that consumers need to assess a product. Trying too hard to impress can backfire. Ensure that you are not only creating "shiny" content, but also providing "nuts and bolts" content that your audience really needs.

---

[3] Daniel Lafreniere discusses Extreme User Research on the Boxes and Arrows site [http://-www.boxesandarrows.com/view/extreme-user].

CHAPTER 23

Implementing a Content Strategy

> The analysis is the strategy part; the rest is implementation.
>
> —Rahel Bailie

Knowing how to design information is a critical part of a content strategist's skill set. However, it is only one part. The content strategy must also be integrated into the organization's larger processes. Since there is an established process for user-centered design (UCD),[1] it seems logical to extend the design process to include content.

Chances are that the need for a content strategy will be articulated during a larger undertaking, such as a web refresh project or a content architecture overhaul. Content strategies follow their own processes that include conducting a content inventory, an audit, and an analysis, plus work on the metadata, content structures, and content architectures. Yet this often happens outside of the rest of the project, with the end result being wireframes that don't accommodate the content, content that doesn't work with form fields, or content that is served up in less-than-optimum ways. There is an alternative.

Join a User-Centered Design Process

Because content strategy is rooted in user experience, the implementation of a content strategy is directly related to some sort of design and development process. A user-centered design process generally looks something like Figure 23.1. The graphic is somewhat simplified but makes the point.

[1] The latest standard for UCD is ISO 9421-210, *Human-centred design for interactive systems*[9]

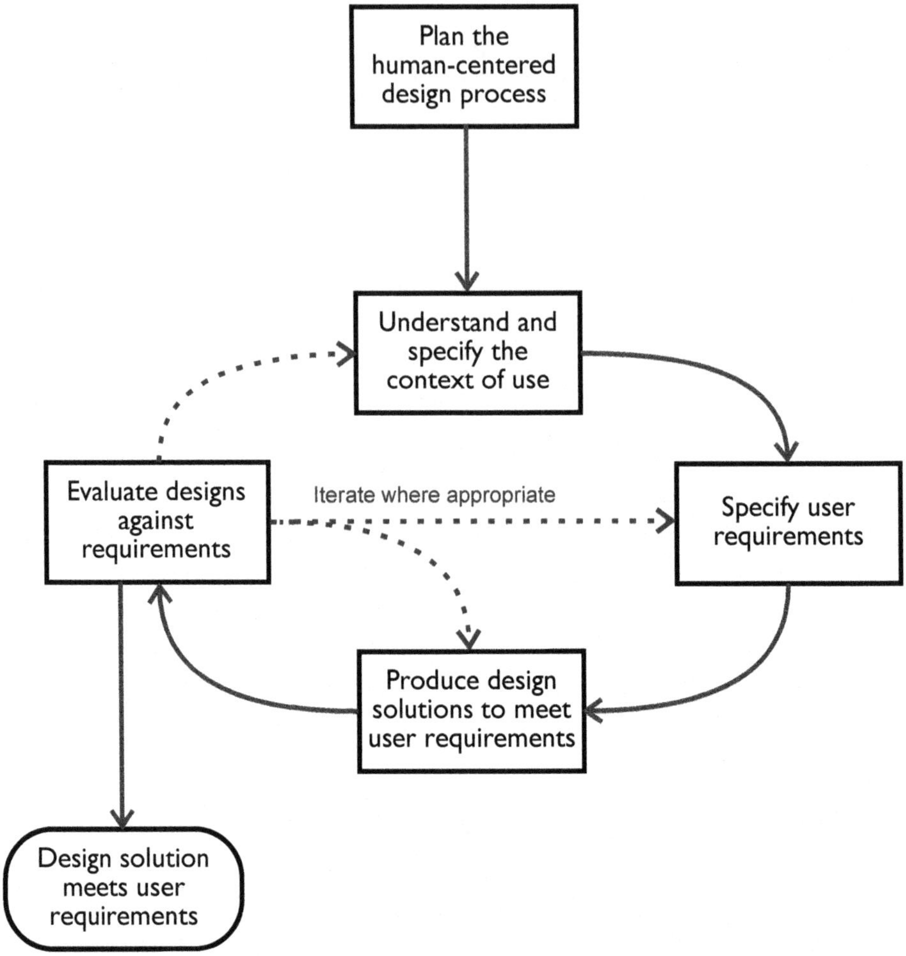

Figure 23.1. Human-Centered Design Process as per ISO 9421-210 standard

There is no ISO standard for developing content, and it's unlikely there will be one soon. Content is sufficiently complex that the closest the industry has come to creating standards are style guides. The missing piece here is the usability of the content itself. All of the design and interaction elements that surround the content have been considered, but not the content itself. Yet the people who come to your site (or knowledge base or support site) do so to consume content.

While the execution of a UCD process on a project may vary between organizations, the common tasks remain constant and can be adapted or extended with relative ease to encompass content. Here are examples of this for some common UCD tasks:

- **User research:** Extend research to discover anticipated content.
- **Personas:** Include content needs for each persona.
- **Scenarios:** Extend to include logical content, content format, and placement.
- **Wireframes:** Ensure that the website architecture supports content needs.
- **Design:** Check that the design allows enough space to fit content.
- **Usability:** Test the content for readability, accessibility, and appropriateness.

If the content is not tested, the process is not complete. We can easily link good content to project goals. Consuming content – whether it is videos on a site like YouTube, music on a site such as iTunes, or product content on the many sites we sift through with each search – is connected to the primary goals of consumers. This makes content an equally important value proposition for our organizations.

If the content is not tested, the process is not complete.

The wall between user experience and content practitioners is coming down. User experience professionals have awoken to the fact that content must be an integral part of the design, and that content should take its place at the center of the user experience. Once you decide to undertake a content strategy, determining whether there is an existing user experience project underway and joining forces with the design team is key to starting the strategy in the right phase.

Look for a Framework that Fits

An organization that intends to manage its product content strategically will need to implement its content strategy within an appropriate framework. If there is no existing project with a UCD process in place, it will be important to determine certain baselines for content within the context of how that content will support the brand. For example, the user experience must be designed around the content that consumers need at any given time, and today, that means a strategy for mobile.

The walls between user experience and the content sides are coming down.

- **Availability:** Considerable thought gets put into the various audiences, how they want to use information, and what they use on which devices. For example, developers of mobile applications may choose to create an iPhone app, but if the customer base includes a significant percentage of users of other devices, or functionality that differs between devices, there may be a need for multiple applications for the web and various mobile devices – each with a slightly different content need. A strategy to feed all the apps from a single content repository will likely be needed.
- **Functionality:** The most common tasks for consumers may be quite specific, and the content must support that functionality. For example, consumers may use one of the new barcodes, the square QR code, to pay with a swipe of the phone. This is an innovative convenience for customers, as well as an efficiency tool for the organization; it keeps the check-out line moving and delays to a minimum. There must be content that explains how to use the functionality, and there must be content that encourages adoption.
- **Brand strengthening:** Enabling access through mobile apps doesn't preclude consumers from viewing the full complement of content on their mobile phones. In fact, many organizations optimize their sites for mobile devices such as tablets and smart phones. But a smart organization understands the difference between what content users want to access from a mobile screen and what content they are likely to access from their larger-screen devices.

Consider the Performance Measurements

One of the basic principles of performance models is this: input affects output. It seems simple, then, to say that analysis affects production and reaction to content, yet analysis is the most likely phase of a lifecycle to be skipped.

Analysis is the most likely phase of a lifecycle to be skipped.

It's not surprising, as the staff with the mandate to consider business ideas strategically is small compared to the number of staff involved in implementation. And the staff whose job descriptions include corporate strategy probably don't think corporate content assets are important enough to be managed by staff at their level, if they even think of content as a corporate asset to begin with.

In the many years of observing and participating on email lists where content developers congregate, in communities where content developers connect, and in forums where communications managers come to share and develop new ideas, we've noticed that the bulk of the discussion is about the collection and management aspects of content. Many of the discussions are about what technology to use to develop, manage, and deliver content. The common thread is that the content itself rarely comes into question; you see comments such as, "We've always sent press releases to key media." and, "We just make manuals and throw them over the wall."

The most startling example of this attitude we have seen came from a writer who expressed indignation on a mailing list at being asked to think about his content strategically. His post – the details are being kept vague to protect the author – ridiculed his boss's request that the writer describe how he planned to contribute value through his work. He deemed his manager a fool for asking because it was obvious that year in and year out he documented products by writing manuals.

By dismissing the request, he lost an opportunity to step up and build a rationale for delivering the content within his purview. Even if his analysis concluded that the existing content was the best possible for his content consumers and that it was being delivered with optimal efficiency, his analysis would have demonstrated the value his manager had wanted to see.[2]

For a content strategy to be effective, you need to measure and demonstrate the strategic value of the content. But because many line staff, like the writer in this anecdote, feel more comfortable operating at a tactical level, the job of implementing a framework that measures effectiveness and performance usually falls to team leads, product or project managers, and other decision makers.

The sole reason we create content is to be ready for its consumption by the right audience at the right time. That is the connection to user experience, and the tie to measuring content effectiveness.

---

[2] In fairness, an analysis might have taken place offline, and at the time the questions were asked, there may have been a content strategy in place. But judging the questions and response comments, the writer's comfort zone was to operate squarely within the implementation arena.

Content in the Context of User Experience

Content strategists are, in effect, designers or architects of content – professionals concerned with content in the broader scope of how it performs to support business goals. The need to integrate content strategy into the user experience process has become pressing, and forward-thinking designers and organizations are beginning to look at ways to incorporate content strategy into the design process.

UX is concerned with keywords, taxonomy terms, and other metadata. But that content doesn't build brand reputation.

The term "user experience" conjures up a vision of interaction designers, information architects, web developers, and graphic designers crafting ways that end-users interact with a website. Until recently, the missing piece was the content. The user experience team looked at placement of content, and typing of content, but not the actual content. They might be concerned with the keywords, the taxonomy terms, and other metadata. But that's not content that builds brand reputation. It's just data used by systems to make the back end run.

In other words, user experience professionals have traditionally been concerned with how content gets tagged so that it can automatically be pulled into the right place at the right time for the right audience, but they haven't been concerned about the content itself, the stuff between the tags.

The silo that separates the "word people" from the people involved in the technical side of site development remained, while the divisions between the other groups – information architects, transaction designers, web developers, database designers, graphic designers, and so on – began to blur. The content itself was treated like BLOBs (Binary Large Objects). BLOBs are usually files – images, PDFs, or other documents – that got used as provided. As long as the content appeared in its appointed spot and fit into the allocated space, it was considered A Good Thing.

Content Architecture and Information Architecture

The term "information architecture" was adopted by the user experience community and became a well-defined term that is used to signify "the art of expressing a model or concept of information used in activities that require explicit details of complex systems."[3] Information architecture is an integral part of the overall user experience.

[3] http://iasaglobal.org/iasa/Information_Architecture.asp.

There is an ongoing debate within the profession about what constitutes "little IA," which focuses on the organization and structure of information spaces, and "big IA," which encompasses a broad range of responsibilities, including business strategy, information design, user research, interaction design, and requirements gathering.

In many ways, content strategists are like the big IAs of the content world, combining responsibilities from areas such as business analysis, user research, information architecture, interaction design, library science, and presentation design. By the time a content strategist gets to the actual content modeling – a type of content architecture – significant research has been done on the users, the content, and the infrastructure that influences the content potential.

The Role of Content

An alternate perspective of the user experience is to reframe end users as consumers who are on a hunt for content. They are, in effect, content consumers. All of the elements that we traditionally see as part of the user experience are the treasure hunt, and the content is the treasure.

Consider this common UX situation, abbreviated for this book:

The UX team establishes personas, scenarios, and use cases for users of a site. These typically look something like this: A middle-aged man, Sam, goes to the home page and enters a search term. The system returns two results in the main column, and Sam clicks the title to display the chosen content. End of use case.

Now, consider this alternative:

Sam goes online to make sense of a diagnosis given to him by his doctor. He enters a search term. The system returns two results in the main column, and Sam clicks the title to display the chosen content. The content doesn't answer his question, and he proceeds to another site. End of use case.

When Sam got to the content and discovered that it was not helpful, he could have been thinking one of two things, "Great navigation, wonderful colors, love the affordance on the buttons," or "Well, that was a waste of two minutes of my life."

My guess is that user tests would yield the latter response. So where is the disconnect?

Despite the adage, "Content is king," the designers who hold the responsibility and the budget for the UX project are actually the kings. Their perspective generally excludes content, at least content quality. As long as some content was delivered, they consider the user experience complete and they tick the "task complete" box.

However, if you consider our alternative scenario above, the need for content strategists to work on content architecture becomes clear. The types of content, complexity of content, and delivery methods have all become more challenging to manage. The ability to do a quick programmatic fix of content has proven unsuccessful. The need for content architecture by strategists who have an intimate understanding of the nature of content – not only its complexities, but also its potential – is pressing.

Before getting into the nuts and bolts of the content strategy deliverables, then, a content strategist will need to extrapolate the content needs from some of the work done by the user experience team.

Audience and Task Analysis

You need to identify who comes to your site, why they come to your site, and, what they want to accomplish. What is the call to action: are they primarily looking for information or is there an online transaction involved?

As playfully illustrated through the xkcd comic in Figure 23.2, there may be a significant disconnect between what your organization thinks users want and what users really want. You need to help your audiences get in, get what they want, and get out. To do this, you need to find out who your primary audiences are and what they actually want to do on the website. Then you can prioritize your audiences and prioritize their tasks.

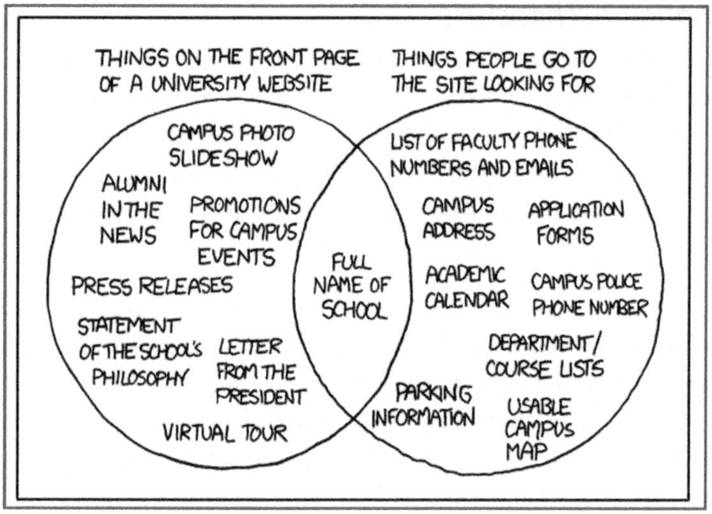

Figure 23.2. The comic site xkcd.com pokes fun at university websites[5]

The next consideration is to determine how consumers view your site. Are they using a large screen or a mobile device? Keypad or touch screen? This makes a difference in how the information is presented.

The cool factor of a Flash page falls flat when it shows up as a blank screen on an iPad. This is where it's important to create personas, scenarios, and use cases. This technique is used by a variety of user experience practitioners and is discussed in depth in *The User is Always Right: A Practical Guide to Creating and Using Personas for the Web*[17].

The cool factor of a Flash page falls flat when it shows up as a blank screen on an iPad.

Creating these artifacts will give you an idea of real versus theoretical site use. Using the restaurant example from Chapter 3, *Understanding the Disconnect between Content and User Experience*, or the university site example in Figure 23.2, we see the disconnect between what organizations and their site developers think is important and what people really want. This problem is ubiquitous; virtually every project begins with a discussion with the project sponsors about what *they* think they want to do and what would be most effective, when they should be discussing what their *users* want to do.

[5] Credit: http://xkcd.com/773 CC BY-NC 2.5.

Information Architecture

Once you understand your requirements and you have planned the content needed to support those requirements, then – and only then – can you start to develop your content strategy. Much like an architect creates blueprints for a house based on the environmental landscape and the requirements of the inhabitants, user experience professionals begin drawing out how the sites will be structured, how the interactions will work, and how the content will be delivered.

At a high level, information architecture (IA) resembles a site map and determines which pages fit within which menu items on a site. For the information architecture to be useful, it should do more than just determine which pages go where. It should also specify what type of content should go onto each page. You need to know what type of content visitors expect to see when they reach a page. Do they want an overview? Overview plus details? A comparison chart? A link to a shopping cart? The details aren't as important as getting the type of content identified.

Content Design

Once you have worked through the preliminaries of the user experience, you can begin to design the content. You need to match the type of task with the type of consumer and the type of use. This might be called the technical side of content, and it is an important, but largely invisible, aspect of your content. In addition to the technical side, there is an editorial side, which we will discuss in the section titled "The Editorial Side of Content."

The Technical Side of Content

The technical side of content includes the following:

- **Content types and content models:** A content model guides authors as they create content and tells a CMS how to make similar pieces of content behave the same way. For example, in Chapter 15, *What Exactly Is Content?*, we saw that the content model for a news release guides authors to always include the appropriate pieces of content for a news release, and it guides the CMS to treat all news release content according to the same rules.

- **Content structure and metadata:** Meaningful labels (metadata) allow a CMS to automate content delivery to different outputs. These structural elements separate text from format and allow metadata to be added. For example, consider a product that has some features that work on a touch-screen phone and other features that work on a non-touch-screen phone. If your content structure includes metadata that identifies which content applies to which phone, your publishing pipeline can be automated to create a deliverable tailored for each phone.
- **Taxonomy and semantic tagging:** Meaningful terminology enables search engines to deliver more meaningful search results. Search engines use hundreds of criteria to generate search results. The ones we have control over include vocabulary, short descriptions written for search engine results, and tags that help categorize content on a site.

Delivering content has become complex, and being an expert in a subject area doesn't mean you have expertise in the technicalities of content delivery. Just as an organization wouldn't expect its subject matter experts to be expert accountants or lawyers, it should not expect its subject matter experts to be expert content strategists.

We don't expect subject matter experts to be accountants or lawyers; we shouldn't expect them to be content strategists, either.

For example, in a content management world, content can seem to be on a page, when actually it's dynamically generated from somewhere deep within a content repository or database. Visit the site of any large online retailer and you'll notice that there are many products on a page, with basic parallel elements: a photo, a description, and a price. A quick look at the web page code will reveal a series of calls that populate the page with content. For an online retailer, the calls might pull photos from a photo database, descriptions from a content repository, and prices from an ERP system. We can conclude, rightly, that creating web pages is of diminishing importance. It is more important to focus on issues such as the following:

- Understanding how content should be delivered to meet business and user needs
- Creating business rules that feed content into web pages on demand
- Working with web programmers to ensure that templates support the content that will be fed into them
- Working with the content creators to ensure they create content that will fit into the template areas reserved for that content

The difference between a smoothly run system and a nightmare for authors depends on the skills of the person putting together the delivery strategy.

It is important to entrust the architecture and delivery of content to content strategists who understand how content management systems work and how content flows. This is part of what a content strategy helps figures out: where the content should live, which pieces will be delivered, where will they be delivered, and how the developers should program the system to make it easy to maintain the content. The difference between a smoothly run system and a nightmare for authors depends on the skills of the person putting together the delivery strategy.

The Editorial Side of Content

The editorial side of content spans a wide range of concerns, from staying on-brand to staying within the style guide. Designing content within a CMS means re-imagining the way content is structured so it can be leveraged to help meet your business goals. Some of the basic editorial principles include the following:

- **Language:** Is the content relevant, accurate, informative, timely, engaging? Is it on-brand and does it have a clear call to action? Does it follow guidelines for tone and voice, readability, plain language, accessibility, and house style?
- **Page structure:** Does the page structure follow best practices for the content format? Is the content "just enough" and presented as part of a clear task path? Does the content have enough navigational aids to encourage reading and to guide users to their destinations?
- **Images:** Are images used to support and explain and do they follow best practices for accessibility? Do the images have captions and descriptive alt tags? Do they work for people who are color-blind?
- **Metadata:** Is the page optimized for search? Does each page have sufficient metadata to facilitate filtering and findability? Do pages have the right metadata for a CMS to use to route content through the system?
- **Links:** Do links follow best practices for navigation? Are they optimized for search, and do they have descriptive link text?

A good content strategist will look at a wide range of editorial concerns that affect content. From a decision maker's point-of-view, it is important to recognize that there are significant factors to creating well-formed content, and dealing with those factors will require a significant investment of time.

CHAPTER 24

Centering the Strategy Around a Content Lifecycle

> I don't need to know the ins and outs of content strategy. What I do need is assurance about two things: that we can deliver the expected results – in other words, give the public what they need – and that there is some methodology behind the process that I can get behind, understand, and monitor to see that the project gets completed on time, on budget, and with quality results.
>
> —Jonathan Ainsworth, Project Manager

In the introduction to this book, we stated that this is not a how-to book for practitioners. A number of those books have been written, and we predict they will continue to proliferate as the field of practice matures. So why talk about the content lifecycle? Isn't that getting a little too specific? It depends at which level the content lifecycle is considered: at the practitioner level of detail or at the level that allows decision makers to manage content more successfully.

Simply acknowledging that content has a lifecycle is a step in the right direction. Content production and publishing were traditionally considered a linear activity. The supply-chain model assumes that content is a single-use commodity that has a clear beginning and end. This may have been true in pre-web days, where the content process had a single, final delivery: the printed page.

Product content follows a very different rhythm from a linear supply-chain model. It's cyclical and iterative.

Today, product content follows a very different rhythm. It's cyclical and iterative. Content follows a lifecycle, whether that lifecycle is acknowledged or not. In fact, as a decision maker, you probably already manage content through an informal lifecycle.

Decision makers do not need to understand every detail of what happens to content throughout its lifecycle, but it is a tremendous help to understand the lifecycle in situational contexts and to understand how the various stages support your organization's objectives. Moving from a supply-chain model of content development to an iterative lifecycle model is a profound shift. That shift affects how content is planned, created, managed, published, and governed as part of a content strategy.

The Content Lifecycle

The content lifecycle is the core of a content strategy. From cradle to grave, the journey of content through each stage of the lifecycle determines its capabilities and potential and, ultimately, the success of your strategy.

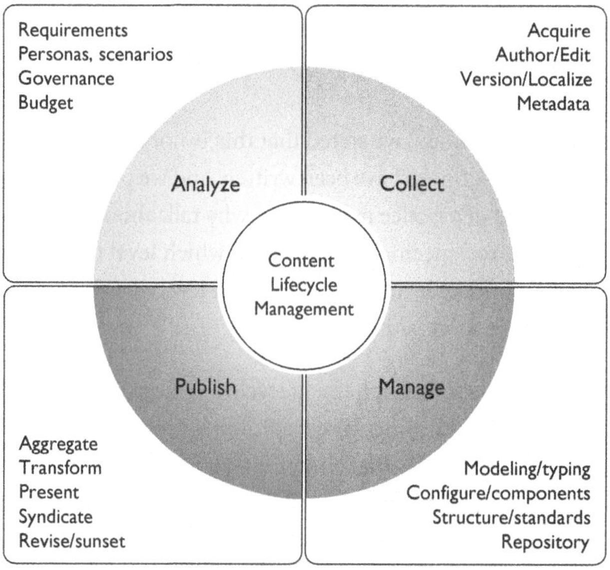

Figure 24.1. The Content Lifecycle

The content lifecycle has four quadrants: analysis, collection, management, and publication (including post-publication maintenance) followed by a loop back to analysis for the next cycle. You need to make decisions in each quadrant. Let's look at the questions that need to be addressed in each quadrant.

Analyze: Examining Business Drivers

Every content strategy begins with the analysis quadrant, starting from the business requirements. The types of issues that require consideration at this stage include: requirements, user experience, governance, and budget.

Requirements: The business drivers may have been considered, but putting them into context helps clarify them. The following questions help determine how content will get authored, produced, and delivered, so this analysis should be done with each project where content is requested.

- What drives the need for content?
- What type of content does marketing think is needed, based on market research?
- What content do competitors provide, and what content is needed to raise the bar to stay competitive?
- What markets do you serve, and how do they expect their content to be delivered?
- Is localization needed? If so, at what stage and into what markets and languages?
- Is any content being shared with other divisions or sister companies?
- Is content being provided to suppliers or partners downstream?

User experience: The following questions should be posed to the sponsoring group – probably marketing or product development – and will need to be validated by the user experience group.

- Who are the typical audiences and what makes them tick?
- What types of content do they expect, when do they need it, and what format should it take (text, audio, video, etc.)?
- How will the content be used?
- How is the interface being designed, and will audiences expect to access content as part of that interface?
- Do the use cases handle what happens if content is not available, and in that case, what is Plan B?

Governance: The following questions address governance, which includes ownership of content, decision-making authority, and review policies:

- Who owns which content?
- Who makes decisions around the publishing of content, and who has veto power?
- Are there any inter-departmental politics that could jeopardize the publication processes or content in any way?
- Is there a periodic review policy, and is management willing to enforce it?
- Have all the stakeholder groups bought into the project, or will the project be jeopardized if a critical group gets cold feet and decides not to cooperate?

Project budget is always discussed, but content budget is rarely discussed.

Budget: The project budget is always discussed, but the content budget is rarely discussed. It's amazing how many projects are scoped without a line for the production or migration of content. These questions should be addressed to make sure content is fully considered as part of your budget.

- Is there a budget for creation and ongoing maintenance of the content?
- If a new tool needs to be adopted to automate content processes, is there budget to implement it and integrate it with other tools already in play?
- If certain activities, such as content migration, need to be outsourced, which department has the budget for it?
- Where do annual maintenance costs and upgrade expenses get allocated?
- If more content developers or content strategists are needed, will a budget be made available?
- If retooling processes result in a large savings in translation in one department's budget but a modest expenditure in another department's budget, is there a provision to re-allocate funds so that project needs can be met?[1]

[1] This could apply to any line item where the cost is charged to one department and the benefit to another.

Collect: Creating or Gathering Content

This quadrant is called collection because all content is not created from scratch; content may be acquired from many sources. There are many questions to be asked to establish both qualitative and quantitative aspects of the body of content.

Quantitative: The quantitative questions help determine size and scope.

- Just how much and what types of content are being discussed?
- Is all of the content going to be created in-house?
- Is all content created by a single group, or will the content come from multiple authors or departments?
- Can the existing content be used as is, or does it need to be edited?
- Is the existing content in a format that is usable in the new system, or will new content types and content models need to be developed?
- Will content be imported from other sources? If so, does it conform to a standard that makes it easy to migrate, or will it need lots of work to make it usable?
- Will imported content need to be brought into line with the content standards being used going forward?

Qualitative: The qualitative questions have more to do with content expectations.

- Is the content relevant, accurate, timely, engaging, and standards-based?
- Will the content need to be rebranded?
- Do content gaps exist? If so, how will those gaps get filled?
- Where does the content come from?
- Will third-party content need to be edited to conform to existing content tone and voice?
- How many content types will be included, and do content models exist for them?
- How many genres will the content need to accommodate?
- How much work will be involved to single-source the content to all the outputs?
- Are there technologies that can automate this?
- Is there enough technical capability and organizational capacity to handle all the content, or is outside expertise needed?

- Are all the authoring groups on board, or are there rogue authors or developers creating content?
- Are production processes in place to handle the content with the efficiency that the project demands?
- Are processes in place for localization of the content?
- How soon are the other languages needed after the source content is ready?
- Are the language deliverables staggered, or are they all due at once?
- How are changes in the target languages handled after changes have been made in the source language?

Metadata: Metadata is one of those unseen, yet critical, aspects of content creation. The key to content findability is high recall, retrieving as many relevant results as possible, or high precision, retrieving a handful of the highest-relevance results. The effectiveness of information retrieval is only as good as the metadata and the systems that support it. The following questions are related to metadata and especially findability on large-scale sites.

- What types of metadata are needed?
- Whose responsibility is it to work with the integrator to ensure that the right metadata fields are created?
- What is the best way to structure the metadata to suit the publishing variants?
- Can the content inherit metadata from broader categories?
- What about content that fits multiple categories?
- How comprehensive does the metadata need to be?
- Does the organization have a robust taxonomy?
- Is a *taxonomy* (controlled vocabulary plus hierarchy) enough, or is a thesaurus (taxonomy plus related concepts) or an *ontology* (thesaurus plus scope notes plus keyword guidelines) required to meet business and user requirements?
- Do adequate controls exist to attach metadata to content? If so, are they enforced, or can authors bypass those controls?
- What systems will be reading the metadata?
- How will the metadata be validated to ensure that it is solid?

Manage: Improving Production Efficiency

The management quadrant has to do with production efficiency and assumes that there is some underlying content management system. The management questions mostly revolve around adoption of standards and technologies.

- How will content be componentized and modularized?
- What level of content granularity is needed?
- How will business rules get written and implemented?
- What type of author support will be available, and what is the impact on content production?
- How far up or down the publishing pipeline should specific techniques be implemented?
- How will the system and processes allow for content to respond to rapid changes in business requirements?

Publish: More than Presentation

The publishing quadrant deals with all the aspects of content that happen after the authoring is done and the content is ready to be sent to its destination. Some of the questions may overlap with those in the previous quadrant, but are posed in this context to stimulate discussion of the future of your content.

- How is content aggregated for publication?
- Is the content presented in a consistent way to help users succeed at their tasks?
- Is the content able to be discovered and syndicated?
- How does content get retired, archived, or deleted?
- What are regulations or policies around content retention?
- Is there a way to help authors meet the review policy?
- When the content is reviewed, is there a process to revise and republish?
- When content enters a new iteration, what are the implications for related content or downstream processes such as localization?

Once the content has been published, this is not the end of the process. Content needs to be controlled post-publication so it can be located, reviewed, and either archived or revised and republished. Otherwise, the content will become unsynchronized and be open to the introduction of errors or omissions. It could also leave the organization open to customer dissatisfaction, brand damage, or even legal liability.

The Decision Maker and the Content Lifecycle

The content lifecycle is proof that creating and publishing content can follow recognizable, predictable, repeatable process. The content lifecycle is one tool you can use to help decide whether to control content within a content management system or not, whether to translate content or not, and whether content gets deleted at the end of its life or revised and reused. Your strategy comes from your work in the analysis quadrant. The other three quadrants are more tactical in nature, focusing on the implementation of the strategy. However, planning for the activities in the collect, manage, and publish quadrants up front will make the implementation go far more smoothly. The success of a content lifecycle is directly related to the effort put into planning the content strategy.

The stages within the lifecycle may be subject to variations. Variations are common between content genres. For example, the lifecycle of a white paper may be very different from that of a training module. There are also situation-specific variations. For example, one organization may require a translation stage whereas another organization produces single-language content. Despite these variations, the overall process remains consistent and stable.

Laying a Sound Foundation

The various components and intersections of content are complicated, too complicated for you to think that you can begin implementation without a plan and then hope to connect the dots later on. When constructing a house, a builder works from a plan that specifies not only the structural dimensions, but also the heating, ventilation, and plumbing. In a similar manner, a content strategist creates the blueprint by which designers, writers, and developers can build a successful model for delivering content.

As you get deeper into the process of developing, managing, and publishing content, you will need to deal with technology such as a content management system. However, before you get to that point, there are a few things to keep in mind about the content lifecycle:

- **It is software-agnostic:** The stages of the lifecycle address a comprehensive set of issues, that must be addressed no matter what software is adopted.
- **It is extensible:** The cycle is not limited to content within a silo, whether a departmental silo or genre silo; the lifecycle is used to plan for use of content where needed, as needed.
- **It is iterative:** Content lives on through multiple iterations, whether the iteration is a translation, a revision, or other type of variant.

When constructing a house, a builder works from plans that specify not only the structural dimensions, but also the heating, ventilation, and plumbing aspects to be built.

The content lifecycle exists whether content is managed manually, with some assistance from technology, or with full automation. The content lifecycle is about content, front and center. The definition assumes that content is recognized to be a corporate information asset and requires the same level of custodial care as other types of corporate assets. The content lifecycle is about more than getting content to work within a content management system; in the bigger picture, the content lifecycle is about implementing a content strategy to follow a repeatable system that governs the management of content throughout its existence.

Content Lifecycle Myths

Until recently, descriptions of the content lifecycle were written up by technologists, usually content management consultants, who described the content lifecycle in the context of a content management system. For their purposes, this description was apropos. Content, for them, was a single object – in technical terms, a BLOB (Binary Large OBject) – that the content management system would route from place to place based on some built-in business logic. The content types were irrelevant, as long as they behaved as BLOBs within the CMS transportation system. The content could be a graphic, a document, or fields of text that traveled together.

This placed the focus on the containers rather than the contents of those containers. The assumption was that forcing the containers to comply imbued the contents of those containers with quality. The endeavor was considered successful when the system worked as intended, and the contents delivered according to the rules written for the CMS. This is an upside-down view of content, where the tail wags the dog. It is time to dispel some of the most common myths around content and the content lifecycle.

A content lifecycle must be tied to a CMS: No, not at all. Content has a lifecycle, with or without a CMS; a lifecycle is an organic system. Before content could be managed by technology, the lifecycle was manual. Often, the lifecycle is still largely manual and depends on human intervention to move content from phase to phase. Organizations with large amounts of content have recognized that maintaining the content lifecycle manually is not cost-effective and that a CMS is the logical vehicle to corral and guide the content throughout its lifecycle.

The success of a content lifecycle depends on the quality of the CMS: Well, to an extent, but not really. It's important that the CMS is able to support the content lifecycle, so having a CMS that is robust enough to meet the content needs of the organization is important. But having a quality CMS does not guarantee the success of the content lifecycle. A CMS can only be programmed to support the process decisions you make. The success of the lifecycle depends on the content strategy that you formulate at the beginning of the lifecycle.

If the strategy is flawed, then the content models, work flow, business rules, and so on, programmed into the CMS will reflect those flaws.

If the strategy is flawed, then the content models, work flow, business rules and so on, programmed into the CMS will reflect those flaws. So while the quality of the CMS is important, even the most sophisticated CMS cannot save a flawed strategy.

We only need look to the horror stories of the uber-CMS implementations of the early 00s to see how this played out in the past. Those projects were all about the containers and not the contents. The system sales were often made on the basis of features and ill-suited to the content that needed to be processed. To use a metaphor, customers would ask for a vehicle to transport their content – a sedan, or a minivan, maybe – and be sold a ship, complete with the need for a harbor to dock it in, a crew to build it, and staff to maintain it. Analysis of the content and the content lifecycle would have illuminated the disconnects between the system and the requirements.

A content lifecycle can always be supported in a single CMS. Once the content lifecycle ties to a CMS are severed and we understand there is no dependency on having one, then nothing dictates that there must be only one CMS.

In this book we have generally used the generic term, CMS. However, there are actually several types of systems which might manage content at different stages of the lifecycle.[2] Especially in large organizations, these other systems may be managing large content sets whose deliverables end up being presented to the user on the website, in print, and on other delivery channels alongside other content.

In years past, vendors and CIOs alike were pushing for a single vendor, single system paradigm where all content needs would be handled in a single system. Because the content lifecycle is organic, system-agnostic and quite often extensible, the single-system approach waned. Today many departments such as technical communications, support, and training generate content in their own tools. Those different streams of content must mesh seamlessly with each other and with additional streams of content to prevent the user from seeing internal silos.

Sometimes, the right family of CMSs sharing metadata and content from different parts of the organization is what's really needed. The lifecycle is the overarching concept that encompasses all organizational content systems that share content or deliver content to the same audiences.

Sometimes, the right family of CMSs sharing metadata and content from different parts of the organization is what's really needed.

Content can be produced independently of the user-centered design process: You may rightly point out that content gets created independently of the user-centered design process all the time. We would counter that this is why many websites are in the mess they're in today. The user experience professional designs for the process leading up to the content, but not the content itself.

[2] For example, a *Web CMS* is a specialized CMS for managing web delivery. Because they are so common, the generic term CMS has become almost synonymous with Web CMS. The existence of *product lifecycle management systems* (PLMs) serves to further perpetuate the myth that there is a one-to-one relationship between the content lifecycle and a piece of software.

Common disconnects include the following:

- **Too little space to display content:** This could result in displaying only a list of titles when having a content preview might be critical to a smooth user experience. Or limiting allowing space to an arbitrary number of words or lines of text leaving only a non-helpful half-sentence displayed.
- **Obscuring or deprioritizing the highest-value content:** If content has not been taken through the UCD, it's up to the designer to guess what content type goes where. Some UX professionals do this better than others. However, nature abhors a vacuum, and when there are no guidelines on where content types should be shown, that vacuum will be filled by other criteria – for example, attractive screen composition – that may not serve the needs of users.
- **Ignoring or overlooking certain content types:** Without a content inventory and analysis, the designer may not know about the actual content types and their purposes. The content types could be grouped incorrectly or presented in inappropriate ways.

The organization doesn't need governance to manage the content lifecycle: Governance is a critical success factor. In too many cases, a project has gone sideways or been abandoned because the chain of authority has not been explicitly set out or because the processes have not been established and approved organization-wide. The governance model defines a web that controls your processes. In this light, the need for operational processes is not optional. In other domains, there is clearer, more intuitively obvious, delineation of governance – for example, only developers can write code – but when it comes to content, everyone is a writer. The guidelines to be established include the following:

- **Ownership:** When there are differing opinions about who gets to make decisions around the publishing of content, who prevails? A clear set of protocols around content publication needs to be established. Too often, content is created and maintained within silos, and without a governance model, there can be a stalemate. A group can decide that they like recreating content in their little silo, and their circumstances are special enough that they get to operate according to a different set of rules. If that is the case, then those circumstances and exceptions must be established as part of the governance model.

- **Processes:** What are the review and sign-off processes that establish how content gets created and produced? Unless there is an organization-wide understanding of how content gets created, it leaves room for waste. Are there any inter-departmental politics that could jeopardize the publication processes or content in any way?[3] Is there a periodic review policy, and is management willing to enforce it? Have all the stakeholder groups bought into the project, or will the project be jeopardized if a critical group gets cold feet and decides to pull out?
- **Budget:** This may not be as straight-forward as it seems. There is likely a budget for creating content, but what about training or maintenance? Or you may decide to adopt a new process that will result in significant improvement in localized content, but the localization budget may reside within another department. There may be a provision for cross-departmental sharing of the expenditures and savings, but without an agreement, departments can get very territorial about their budgets. In other cases, the funds for implementing a tool may come from a project budget, but the annual maintenance costs are assigned to another department. These issues are all too common and all too commonly ignored until a problem arises.
- **Operations:** Each organization has a distinct set of tensions that require operational guidelines. If you are new to governance, see Welchman Pierpoint's excellent white paper, "Web Operations Management Primer"[23].

The next set of myths has more to do with content than the actual lifecycle. However, some of these myths indicate a lack of content strategy. A lack of strategy could mean a lack of editorial strategy, a lack of social media or collaborative documentation strategy, deficiencies in content modeling, lack of a technology strategy, or some combination. The technology aspects of the content lifecycle may be addressed quite thoroughly, but that only deals with the containers into which the content fits. There are separate aspects of a content strategy that address the aspects to which the content itself needs to adhere.

---

[3] On a client project, for one content type, we managed to reduce the meeting times by 84% and approval process by 99% just by enforcing a governance model that eliminated some serious political ping-pong between two engineering groups.

We have yet to be shown a content-free experience, let alone a satisfying content-free experience.

Our site is about experiencing brand, not providing content, so there is no need for content strategy: This is every marketing executive's dream: all brand experience and no content. In our many collective years of experience, we have yet to be shown a content-free experience, let alone a satisfying one. YouTube wouldn't be nearly as compelling if all the video content was missing, and a sports site would be nothing without highlights and score updates.

The bottom line is that the experience is the treasure hunt, and the content is the treasure. Site visitors come to find some sort of content, whether it is persuasive, instructional, or entertainment. That is the treasure they're hunting down. The process of finding the content influences the user experience. But, to be clear, ask anyone who has gone on a hunt – from the six-year-old at a birthday party to a site visitor looking for content – if the search comes up empty, the dissatisfaction is palpable. You won't hear about the great navigation or the affordance on the buttons or the whiz-bang Flash on the home page. All you will hear about is the information that couldn't be found.

Social media is a bit of a misnomer. It should be called social content.

We have a social media strategy so we don't need a content strategy: Social media is a bit of a misnomer. It should be called social content, because the text, photos, video, and other contributions by the various participants are all content, and that content needs to be managed. And not to belabor the point, it needs to be managed through a content strategy. For example, if your social content consists of user-generated product discussions, your social content likely supplements, extends, or at least supports the official documentation provided by the organization.

Unless there is a content strategy for presenting both types of content in context, there is the potential for chaos. The organization needs to make decisions around content creation, curation (how to wrangle all that contributed content so it is useful for content consumers), presentation, preservation, reviews, and retention plans. The social content cannot be divorced from the rest of the corpus; the content strategy should look at the lifecycle of all content types and the interactions among them.

We know how people read our content, and that's mostly what content strategy is about: This myth encompasses a number of assumptions – often unsubstantiated, but that's a whole other book on usability and user experience – about how content consumers access, read, and otherwise use content. It's worth looking at some of these assumptions before discussing how they fit into a discussion of content strategy and the content lifecycle.

- **The only content people see is "above the fold":** Actually, the research tells a different story. Without diverting into the topic of scanning versus reading and how people navigate browse paths, let's say that you've adjusted your content to optimize its use by your primary user groups. This is a single aspect of a content strategy that effects one quadrant of the content lifecycle: Collection.
- **Good content fits within the site design constraints:** If you constrain content to the number of words that looks right with the graphic design, rather than creating a graphic design that accommodates the number of words the content requires to make its point, you've succumbed to a classic case of the tail wagging the dog. The site architecture should start with the content that needs to be presented, and the design should support that.
- **We can leave it to users to create the content:** A naïve assumption is that if you build it, they will post. If you think that users just can't wait to contribute awesome articles to your wiki-powered tabula rasa, you may be in for a nasty shock. There are success stories about organizations whose users clamored for a collaborative space to share information, but these are success stories because the implementation came after the content strategy was formulated. The Web is littered with not-so-successful stories, where a wiki was slapped up without a sound strategy behind the implementation.

Constraining content to the number of words that looks right for the graphic design is a classic case of the tail wagging the dog.

We can implement a content lifecycle without doing the basics: content inventory, audit, and analysis: Definitely not. If you're going to start by launching your site for France, don't start with a file scrape from Brazil (because it's smaller, so therefore supposedly easier to categorize) and expect to come up with a proper inventory, an accurate number of content types, or a migration strategy. This statement may seem so obvious that it doesn't need to be stated, but this scenario comes from a client (sanitized to protect the guilty parties, of course).

The more content is version-controlled by conventions (version number, file name, URL, and so on), the harder it is to maintain: The inability to manage properly versioned content is no more than a lack of imagination. Or a lack of willingness by corporate or departmental policy to accommodate it. Or both. Corporations that are vulnerable to negative consequences arising from delivery of incorrect content have figured out how to manage content versions in an appropriate way. They've realized that the ROI on investing in processes and/or technologies that support managing content is far more advantageous than saving $100,000 only to lose $1 million to a lawsuit. These are not fictitious numbers; these dollar amounts come from clients who have had fines levied by regulators, lost lawsuits by injured customers who inadvertently misused a product, or lost the confidence of potential clients because of adverse publicity arising from negative reports. All these examples are content-related disasters, some of them compounded by a lack of an audit trail or poor versioning. A good content strategy should address these issues; it will pay for itself in no time.

More content is better content: This myth should be called the "compensate for lack of quality with copious quantities of content" myth. When you can't determine which content is appropriate in which places, that points to a lack of strategy. You can't compensate with unfocused content, inaccurate content, wordy content, or other sleight-of-hand techniques.

Can you imagine looking for a specific piece of information and finding all sorts of irrelevant content? Oh, you probably have.

Can you imagine looking for a specific piece of information, and finding all sorts of irrelevant content? Oh, you probably have. And you have made fun of the site, and perhaps told your friends in a ditting[4] contest for who's had the worst user experience. Or perhaps someone has told the world in a fit of pique through a Twitter post. And if this is your site, then it could be the butt of some of the same jibes, too.

Take the opportunity to watch fourth-year engineering students, employed part-time as computer technicians for organization such as Best Buy's Geek Squad, look for content on the Web. They are likely searching for a solution to a technical problem, and how they search for content is a microcosm of a larger audience. They put some keywords into a search engine and choose the top search result. If the content fills the screen, they immediately click the browser's back button and go to the next search result. When challenged to read the entire screen in case the answer is near the end

[4] For those who haven't had the privilege of serving in the Navy, "ditting" is a Navy term for a form of story telling where each anecdote "one ups" the previous one.

of the article, they brush off the suggestion with a terse, "Oh, it takes too long to read," or "I'll find something shorter."

From their reactions – and what we know as the browsing pattern of skip, skim, and scan – we can conclude that readers often find it faster to look through search results for the page with the shortest, most concise and focused answer, than it is to read one or two longer pages. You may not agree with this, but usability research has observed this frequently enough that it is considered the norm, not a behavioral anomaly.

New Strategies, New Lifecycles

As the discipline of content strategy develops, the usefulness and sophistication of the content lifecycle develops along with it. Long gone are the days where a web publishing hobbyist could cobble together some HTML and copy-and-paste from the corporate brochure to a website and call it a day. Even hiring a team to do a website refresh project is becoming a thing of the past. Instead, we are looking at a situation where content comes in from multiple sources – created in-house, generated through social channels, and imported from other sources – and gets published to multiple channels – web, mobile, ebooks, sent to other systems for publication and, yes, print.

But to take content in and push it out the other side, the content must pass through a checkpoint of sorts, where content is made publication-ready from a technical standpoint as well as an editorial standpoint. That checkpoint is where content often gets stuck because it turns out not to be publication-ready. Just as a border checkpoint can get backed up during peak periods, content can get backed up waiting to be vetted for publication readiness.

It's not incumbent on the decision makers of a corporation to know how to implement a content strategy, any more than it is for them to understand the details of double-entry bookkeeping.

It's not incumbent on the decision makers of a corporation to know how to implement a content strategy, any more than it is for decision makers to understand the details of double-entry bookkeeping (though budgeting is very much within the scope of decision makers). It is critical, then, to have a high-level understanding of what goes into developing and implementing a content strategy. It helps validate that the team knows what it is doing, that there is some science behind the methodology, and that, as a leader, you can be confident that the investment in a content strategy makes a contribution to the bottom line.

CHAPTER 25

Finding the Content Strategy Skills You Need

> Content strategists are the management consultants of the content world. There are many specialties within the broad field of content strategy, but the commonality is that practitioners specialize in improving performance of content.
>
> —Rahel Bailie

Good content doesn't just happen; it's the result of questioning and planning – in other words, developing a strategic view. In Part IV, "Content Under the Hood," we illustrated how creating and managing content has become increasingly complex, and as a result, the strategies needed to manipulate content have become increasingly sophisticated. Chapter 24, *Centering the Strategy Around a Content Lifecycle*, makes it clear that you need both in-depth knowledge about your organization's business plans and content strategy expertise to produce a body of content that could be considered a corporate asset.

Your company has in-depth knowledge about its business plans, but does it have the content strategy expertise?

While you certainly have writers of various stripes – copywriters, marketing writers, technical writers, social media monitors, and user community managers – most of these writers do not have a strategic view of content. They know how to create informative copy and how to apply good principles of communication. But as discussed in Chapter 15, *What Exactly Is Content?*, they may not understand that copy has become a subset of content.

In the days when the responsibility for strategic-level content decisions rested elsewhere, having writers "just write" was a viable approach. Those were simpler times – like back in the days when a website could be built by "just coding some HTML." Now, it's more likely that strategic decisions around content need to be made by an intermediary – someone who has both a strategic view of the business goals that content is expected to support and an intimate understanding of the implementation side of content. What is important is that a writer is not a content strategist. The skill sets may overlap, but the focus of the role is quite different.

The Content Strategist's Role

There are two basic types of decision makers:

- **Immersed in the content world:** This is the decision maker who comes from the content, communications, or support side of the house. This person may already be a content strategist or have the skills to become one. The challenge for this decision maker is to help the organization rethink the roles of writers and separate the strategic from the logistic and the copy creators from the content managers.
- **From outside the content world:** This is the decision maker who comes from the marketing, engineering, or business side of the house. This decision maker has the same challenges as the one who has been immersed in the content world but has the additional challenge of finding a content strategist or developing those skills in-house.

Content strategy has become too complex to be left in the hands of the inexperienced.

Content strategy has become too complex to be left in the hands of the inexperienced. We don't expect writers to be experts at information architecture just because they know how to create folder structures on shared drives. Similarly, we shouldn't expect clients to be experts at content strategy just because they know how to use a word processor. Writers cannot be expected to know enough about content standards and content modeling, reuse models, metadata best practices, microformats, writing for syndication, and componentization for content management systems to make informed decisions about how to pull all of the pieces together to support business directives.

This is where content strategists come in. At the forefront of the movement to treat and manage content as a corporate asset – to understand the nature of content and the ways that content can be leveraged, editorially or technically – are people who have recognized that they relate to content strategically and have hung a content strategy shingle on their skill sets.

The role that content strategists perform within an organization is much like the role of a management consultant. A good content strategist is a management consultant with a specialty in improving the performance of content. In other words, content strategists are practitioners who understand content, often at a level that professionals in adjacent fields never stop to consider.

Content strategists understand how content connects to other content, how the development and delivery of content affects, and is affected by, practices connected to other professions, and how content connects to content consumers.

Content strategists are specialists who understand content at a level that professionals in adjacent fields have never stopped to consider.

However, as in management consulting, there is no common skill set. Content strategists come from diverse backgrounds: technical communication, marketing communication, social media, or enterprise content. They come to the table with their specialties, but they have stretched their skill sets beyond their existing fields of practice. Content strategists specialize, but they also share some common underlying qualities (see Figure 25.1 (p. 256)).

Skills and Aptitudes for a Content Strategist

For some careers, there is an established path. There are educational programs, professional development paths, professional association training programs, and mentors to guide those wanting to make a career transition. In the world of content strategy, as of yet, there are no college programs, professional certificates, or training courses through professional associations. Given the lack of readily-available information, what does one look for when engaging a content strategist?

A single content strategist likely will not be a master of all the details of every aspect of content strategy. Instead, a content strategist uses core consulting methodology to determine how content should be delivered, why, and to what benefit. The core consulting methodology – simplified here for sake of space – determines current state, analyzes the requirements (of the business, content, and users), determines future state, identifies gaps, and creates a roadmap from the current to the future state. Understanding the nature of content – from genre analysis to taxonomy to delivery models to line editing – is a given.

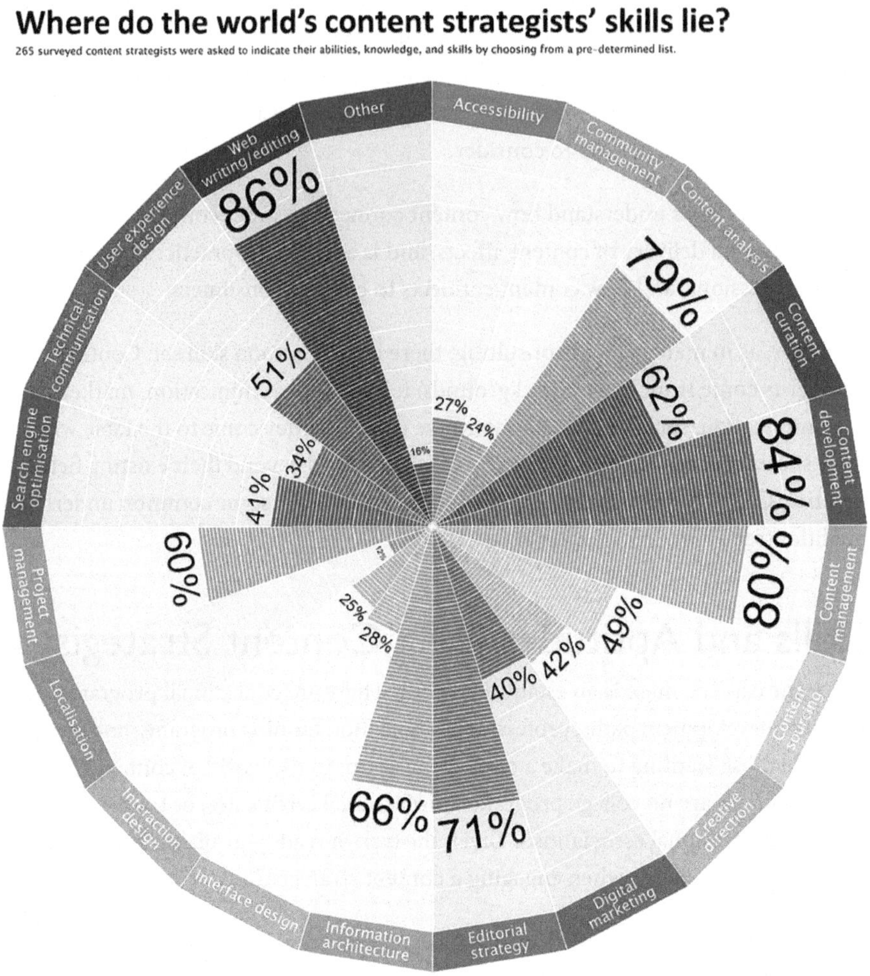

Figure 25.1. The content strategist's skill sets[1]

[1] Contributed by Richard Ingram [http://www.richardingram.co.uk/] CC-by-SA 2.0.

Processing content is not like processing data; it's a lot more subtle and complex. A content strategist needs to have some sort of content background – English, writing, journalism, library sciences, translation, or related fields – to understand the qualities and properties of content. To undertake any sort of content analysis or taxonomy effort or content rewrite requires some measure of skill at content development.

Processing content is not like processing data; it's a lot more subtle and complex.

The content strategist should be able to work as part of the larger team – engineering, integration, user experience, communications, and so on – More important, a strategist should understand how important it is to be part of the big picture, and understand how to integrate the content strategy within the larger organizational plans. This requires an understanding of traditional and emerging business models and communication paradigms that support marketing and customer relationship efforts.

Content strategists may also be called upon to create information architecture artifacts: conceptual IA models or wireframes. This may be a small part of the overall activities, but being able to carry out user-centered and experience design processes is an important part of a content strategist's toolkit, and knowing how to apply those processes to content is definitely worth bonus points.

It is definitely helpful when content strategists are technology-aware – in other words, knowledgeable enough about current and emerging technologies that they can recommend strategic ways of implementing content.[2] Otherwise, the strategist is like the carpenter who only owns a hammer; every problem looks like a nail.

This is different from technical acumen – there are way too many complex software apps out there to be both a content strategist and a technologist. But the strategist should have enough conceptual knowledge to understand how content should or could flow through a system and which types of systems will deliver the goods for a particular business need. This means system awareness, along with knowledge about implementation best practices, content migration techniques, and content standards. In addition, the strategist needs to understand the interrelationships between people, processes, and technology.

---

[2] One director of content strategy at an interactive agency asserts that a content strategist, by definition, must have a working knowledge of XML; without it, you have a writer, not a strategist.

Different Skills, Different Solutions

A content strategist should have a range of skills that span the particular practice area. Going back to the metaphor of the management consultant, an accounting specialist will have a different set of skills than a process engineering specialist. Similarly, a content strategist in a PR agency will require different skills than one working with a manufacturer. While the two content strategists will share a set of common baseline skills, their specialist skill sets could be significantly different.

The temptation to hire based on software skills is counterproductive. Instead, hire for aptitude and an understanding of principles.

For example, a content strategist working in an industry, like software, that focuses on user assistance – technical documentation, help, training, support, and related content – should know enough about the differences between major content development processes and technologies to understand content migration, optimization, workflow, delivery, and management within that realm. Does that mean a deep knowledge of all the major tools on the market? Not in the least. However, the strategist does need to have enough experience with these tools to know the differences between how they process content, and through that, how to make sound assessments of new tools. The strategist also needs to know how to exploit the content and how to determine which system works in which situation.

The temptation of organizations to want a laundry list of software skills underlines a lack of understanding about the field and about the benefits that a content strategist can bring to a project. Just as "the music is not in the violin," the ability to use a range of software tools is not what makes a good strategist. Many industries "hire for aptitude; train for skills." This seems like sound advice for the practice area of content strategy, particularly because so much of the work is tied to aptitude. [3]

As your organization looks at getting more out of its content, it's important to ensure that the content strategist brings the right mix of aptitudes and skills to the table to deliver the appropriate solution for your body of content within the context of your business goals.

[3] For more information, read the four-part series [http://intentionaldesign.ca/2010/06/09/-world-of-content-strategists/] about skills needed to practice content strategy on IntentionalDesign.ca.

CHAPTER 26
Basic Principles Toward a Quick Start

> If you don't care where you're going, then any road will take you to a destination.
>
> —Emma Hamer

Our industry has reached a stage where we recognize that we are corporate publishers and that the time has come to adopt a more strategic approach to create, manage, and publish content. It's not enough to take any old road and hope to get to the destination we want. We have also realized that if we don't get our content strategy in order, others in the competitive landscape will. As explained in the introduction, this is not a how-to book; it's for anyone who needs to understand content strategy and talk about it intelligently with staff and other stakeholders.

We are well into the decade where content is recognized as a valuable business asset and where management of content deserves the same level of care and attention as the management of any other business asset.

Content is recognized as a valuable business assets, and management of content deserves the same level of care as any other business asset.

It's no longer a question of when content strategy is needed, it's a question of how to adopt a content strategy framework that provides reliable, repeatable, effective, and efficient processes – and results. To paraphrase Winston Churchill, "This is not the end. It's not even the beginning of the end." We hope it is the end of the beginning and that you are now armed with enough information to go out and put a content strategy into place.

If we were to distill the lessons from this book into some basic principals, the focus would be on creating content that is sustainable, reusable, and leverage-able. This realization doesn't mean ignoring the editorial side of content; we are going into this with the assumption that your content is already written for your particular audiences and can be adapted for the medium used to deliver the message. What we're getting at is getting your body of content into top shape so you can put some technopower behind it and leverage it as a valuable business asset.

With some strategic planning, the challenge of creating a long-lasting content strategy is not insurmountable. As a starting point, you can get your content strategy off the ground with these basics:

- **Analyze your content:** Understand your current content landscape. Create an inventory, carry out an audit, and then analyze the content from qualitative, quantitative, and technical points of view. Look at all the content, not just the content for one medium or one project. Informing that analysis is research – typically done ahead of time by business analysts – about the needs the organization hopes to address through a content strategy and a user analysis to determine the who, what, when, where, why, and how of the audiences who will consume the content. Audience, in this context, is both internal and external.
- **Separate content from format:** Resist the temptation to give meaning to content through inline formatting. Content should be as plain as possible. No desktop publishing, no inline formatting. Plain content can be leveraged far more easily than content with embedded formatting. Format-free content is easier to migrate between systems and interchangeable between systems that use common standards.
- **Know your content standards:** It's one thing to have great editorial standards, and those should not be sacrificed. But for content to be leveraged as part of a content strategy, it needs to conform to any applicable international standards. This means getting familiar with content standards – from Dublin Core to schema.org[2] to DITA – and knowing when to use them and why. This also means understanding the competitive landscape and where the differences are between what you offer and what your competition offers.
- **Marry the technical with the editorial:** The focus of this book isn't on the editorial quality of content,[3] but it's worth mentioning. It's not worth investing in the technical side of content if the sole purpose is to move ineffective, inaccurate content more efficiently.
- **Make good use of semantics:** A good part of what will allow you to leverage content, beyond the combination of good content and good technology, is

---

2 schema.org provides a collection of vocabularies you can use to add metadata to HTML documents.

3 Editorial quality is well covered in books such as *Clout*[10] and *Content Strategy at Work*[3]

metadata. Without good metadata, your content will be hobbled: your technology won't understand what to do with your content and search engines won't understand your content. There are three basic types of metadata: administrative, structural, and descriptive. All three are needed to make your content meet your business objectives. Working with semantics isn't a single skill set, either; the different types of metadata may well fall within different disciplines.

- **Build an extensible, scalable foundation:** Build a strong foundation for your content solutions, and make the foundation as extensible and scalable as possible. A firm foundation should allow for growth, such as adding templates to build new types of modules. Create content solutions that can draw from a technology-agnostic single source and that can be easily published to many different platforms. Build traceability into this process.
- **Implement the right technology:** The whole purpose of a content strategy is to support business goals and user needs, so adopting the right type of system – one that allows content to be presented, moved around, reused, aggregated, converged, integrated, syndicated, and so on – is critical. The "we have [name your existing software here] so let's use that" approach lets the tail wag the dog. Get a thorough set of user requirements, business requirements, and content requirements, and use them to figure out the technology requirements. Then, and only then, choose the system you intend to adopt.
- **Measure, assess, and maintain:** Evaluating the performance and effectiveness of your content is crucial. Enforce a process that measures content and its effectiveness for all of its audiences, both internal and external, and continue to refine the success metrics and key performance indicators.
- **Adopt a governance model:** As you develop a content strategy, you will need to decide how content will be managed throughout the content lifecycle. Making these decisions as soon as the issues arise is a good insurance policy that avoids the tendency to make snap decisions later on or capitulate to the loudest voice in the room.
- **Employ the right skill sets for your project:** Developing a content strategy requires a specialized skill set. It goes well beyond having professional writing skills. Content strategists may have a core set of skills that give them a deep understanding of content, but not all content strategists are cut from the same cloth.

> To implement an entire strategy, you will likely need skill sets that include information architecture (to organize content), analytics and search engine optimization (to make content rank properly in search engines), library sciences (to develop indices and taxonomies), curation (to keep your content relevant, fresh, and fully connected), and technology (to create content types, models, and other structures). This is in addition to content creation skills such as writing and creating graphics, illustrations, and other media.

We live in a world where the only constant is change, a world where technology continues to emerge, content and information are being produced at exponential and uncontrollable rates, and customer expectations keep getting higher and higher. Given this environment, you'll want a content strategy that has some longevity. Future-proofing your content strategy, however, may mean preparing for a future a mere couple of years away. That's an even more compelling reason to start working on your content strategy – now.

Glossary

Adaptive Content

Most commonly attributed to Ann Rockley. In her book, *Managing Enterprise Content: A Unified Content Strategy*[19], she defines adaptive content as follows: "Adaptive content is format-free, device-independent, scalable, and filterable content that is transformable for display in different environments and on different devices in an automated or dynamic fashion." Adaptive content is maintained as a single source that can be delivered to a range of output formats and channels for a variety of different audiences without having to be rewritten or reformatted.

Agent

In complexity theory, an agent is a person or thing that can have a purposeful response that changes the system it is acting within. Agents have certain attributes, such as a location (where the agent operates), capabilities (what the agent can do), and memory (impressions from that past that affect the decisions made in future). In software systems, an agent would be called an actor. In content strategy, an agent could be anything that has an impact on the content itself, the way content is managed, or the larger system in which content exists.

Amplification

An action or circumstance that causes an increase in the magnitude of a result. Amplification can have positive or negative results. In finance, amplification refers to factors that cause prices to be more volatile or to change with greater magnitude. In content strategy, amplification refers to a disproportionate benefit or disadvantage that results from a change in how content is managed.

Attribute

A way of adding extra information to elements in markup languages. Attributes consist of a name and value pair. In the example below, the `<img>` element has two attributes, named `src` and `alt`, with the values `bookcover.jpg` and "The Joy of Cooking":

```
<img src="bookcover.jpg" alt="The Joy of Cooking"/>
```

See also *Element*.

Attribution Theory

Attribution Theory is a term used by psychologists for a variety of models that try to describe the processes people use to explain the causes and effects of events. In content strategy, Attribution Theory has been used to explain the role content plays in purchase decisions.

Business-Critical Content

This is an arbitrary boundary for a body of content directly related to a company's primary business. Business-critical content is whatever your organization uses in the context of forming and maintaining persistent relationships with consumers of your product or service. This body of content could include user guides, operating guides, training material, customer support material, and customer updates, plus marketing material such as product descriptions, feature-and-benefit descriptions, catalogs, and so on.

Channel

The route that communications take from a source to a destination. Channels are defined according to how the organization needs to communicate, and include routes like a partner extranet or a social media app. Many different deliverables in different formats can be delivered over a given channel. If deliverables travel via the same route, even if they vary widely in content and format, they are going through the same channel.

Complex Adaptive System

A Complex Adaptive System is a system where the interactions among agents change the system itself. Complexity theory explains that this means a dynamic network of interactions.

Component (also, Content Component)

See *Module*

Component CMS

A type of Content Management System (CMS) that automates the publishing of content to websites, print, and other media, through a series of publishing scripts. The distinguishing functionality is that the shaping of the published content is controlled by the writer. Content is entered into an XML editor and then manipulated at a granular, component level. The content is then processed by publishing scripts. Changes to the publishing model are controlled by the author.

See also *Modular Content.*

Component Content

See *Modular Content.*

Content Lifecycle

A content lifecycle describes the phases that content goes through from planning and creation to various manipulations to publication to post-publication processing to retirement or iteration through another cycle.

Content Management System (CMS)

A software application that automates the storage and publishing of content. Software vendors have created a wide range of functionality to try and differentiate their products and gain a competitive advantage. However, there are two basic types of content management systems: Web CMS and Component CMS.

See also *Component CMS* and *Web CMS.*

Content Module

See *Module.*

Content Object

See *Module.*

Content Repository

A storage mechanism for digital content that provides access to content, including search, retrieval, and modification capabilities. A content repository provides asset storage but few, if any, management features. A content management system typically uses a repository such as a database or folder system to provide access to content. End users interact with the CMS and don't directly see the repository.

Content Strategy

A content strategy is a repeatable process that governs the management of content throughout the entire content lifecycle.

Content Strategy Audit

An initial review of an organization's content strategy or readiness to adopt one, looking at business goals, processes and high-level needs.

Dynamic Delivery

Publishing is considered to be dynamic when the actual deliverable – the arrangement and collection of content components delivered to the user – does not exist as a unit until requested by the user, at which time the deliverable is assembled by software. A software system that builds a weather report or calendar by reading data feeds or databases is one example of dynamic delivery. Another would be a system that builds a product manual for a custom-built product by searching a content repository for content about the features in that product.

See also *Adaptive Content.*

Element

Elements are the basic construct of text-based markup languages like HTML, XML, or RSS. They are labels which surround content to give it extra meaning. Elements are marked with angle brackets around the name of the element, for example, an element named paragraph would be `<paragraph>`. Elements can be more or less semantic (See Also *Semantics*), which means that the meaning of the contained content is reflected by the element name itself. For example using an element named `<Step>` in an ordered list of steps is more semantic than using an element such as `<ListItem>`.

See Also *Attribute.*

Embedded Assistance

Messages that give hints to, or guide, someone to have a more successful outcome while using an application. An example is the pre-populated text within a form field that indicates the format to use when entering your phone number. Embedded assistance provides "right time, right context" content and more immediate help than the older model of help files, where clicking an icon opened a separate set of files where users could search for the desired topic.

Enterprise Resource Planning System

Enterprise Resource Planning (ERP) systems integrate management information processing across an entire organization – finance/accounting, manufacturing, sales and service, customer relationship management, and more – into a single software platform. ERP systems can make it easier to create centralized management dashboards and select the right content for the right customers.

Format

Noun: A format provides a standard and predictable way to encode information for storage in a computer. A file format specifies how bits of data are used to encode information on a storage medium like a DVD or computer hard drive. Common file formats in the world of content include XML, HTML, MS Word, and PDF. Some of these formats include visual presentation information like color, font, and layout in the same file with content.

Verb: To format means to apply visual presentation information to content according to a visual specification. This can be an automatic process using templates and stylesheets or a manual process where people apply style information to individual pieces of content.

Fragment

A small piece of content that, unlike a *Topic*, is not intended as a stand-alone *Module*. Examples includes, warnings, notes, or taglines. Fragments are intended for reuse but not as a stand-alone unit; they must be used in other larger units to be useful.

See also *Module* and *Topic*

Genre

The structure of content that conveys social meaning. Fiction is a genre of literature that has sub-genres such as mystery, adventure, romance, and so forth.

Governance

A set of decisions, policies, and guidelines that define operational boundaries and expectations and allow staff to operate with confidence. Governance is a core function of decision making in leadership, where the corporate-level decisions affect authority, responsibilities, and processes. Governance may also include laws or regulations that affect how businesses operate. In the content world, a governance model extends to how content is acquired, how it is managed, who is responsible for it, the systems that manage it, who has authority over which areas of the corporate body of content, and what risk management measures are in place.

HTML

Acronym for HyperText Markup Language. This is the markup used on the Internet for most websites. HTML markup tags define how content will be displayed on the Web. The latest version of HTML, HTML5, adds tags that give writers greater control over the structure of content

Metadata

Data about a web page or piece of content. Metadata can include information about content such as the date it was created, what type of content it is, and what topics it covers. For example, a page about tablets might have metadata that identifies it as related to mobile devices.

Modular Content

A method of structuring content using standard pieces (modules) that can be assembled into larger units of content or deliverables.

Module

A general term for an independent unit of information that can be used with other modules to assemble end deliverables. Modules can refer either to *topics* – say an entire product overview or task – or *fragments* of content as small as a warning, a disclaimer, or even a single word such as a product name. Modules make it easier to build different outputs as required.

In this book, the terms *Module* and *Component* are synonymous. You may also see the term *Content Object* in other publications.

See also *Topic* and *Fragment*

Multimodal

Users can access content using many different modes of interaction. In addition to the common visual computer mode – where interaction is through a screen, mouse, and keyboard – you might have voice recognition software, screen readers, gesture modes with facial-expression interactivity, and more. Content that is designed to support multimodal interaction can offer significant ease-of-use benefits for hands-free operation, mobile devices with limited keyboards, and other situations where the common visual mode won't suffice.

Multiplicity

A large number. In the content world, multiplicity refers to the large number of deliverables you get when you multiply content assets by the number of versions by the number of output media by the number of languages.

Ontology

A formal classification system that uses shared taxonomies and vocabulary to explain relationships between concepts. An ontology can help deal with terms that may have multiple definitions. For example, the word "dough," which has one meaning within the context of baking and another (slang) meaning in the context of money.

Persona

A fictitious person created to be representative of a type of user, customer, or other participant. Typically, personas are created as part of a user experience design to help plan an application or website. A real user might be represented by different personas at different times depending on needs and context.

Portlet

A portlet is a small, self-contained window within a web page where a service runs or information is presented. An example of a portlet would be a web page that has a stock ticker or a window that shows current weather conditions.

Power Publishing

Modern, technology-enhanced publishing for complex communication requirements including single source publishing to help address situations with a high degree of multiplicity.

See also *Multiplicity*.

Product Lifecycle Management System

Product Lifecycle Management (PLM) systems support the management and control of data and processes related to a product or service throughout the entire lifecycle. PLM brings together individual applications that support various parts of the product creation process. However, it does more than just combine different IT applications. It also reflects the fundamental philosophy of a centralized, open, end-to-end system that helps identify opportunities for managing the complexity of the product creation process and improving cooperation across business units and company boundaries.

Progressive Disclosure

A design principle for both content and applications that centers around the idea that it is often best to initially present a user with only a subset of the available content or user interface. Then, let the user decide whether to look at – i.e. have disclosed – more content or capabilities. This allows users to consume only the content they want, without worrying about being overwhelmed by additional content and complexity.

See also *Adaptive Content*.

Responsive Design

A collection of digital design principles and coding techniques that allow content to display differently in response to the device being used. Although usually discussed in relation to small versus large screens, the principles apply to setting up a wide variety of different kinds of interfaces (Ethan Marcotte's *Responsive Web Design*[13] is an excellent resource for more information about responsive design).

SaaS (Software as a Service)

Software that is delivered as an online application rather than being run on a desktop or other local computer. SaaS is an aspect of cloud computing, which is a generalized term for services offered through online platforms. Gmail is an example of SaaS, while Outlook is an example of a desktop application.

Schema

A standardized representation, or set of rules, that helps organize content. An XML schema, such as DITA or DocBook, defines a set of elements and attributes along with rules for how those elements and attributes can be combined to create valid units of content. A schema can be used by a software validator to determine whether a particular unit of content follows the rules of the schema.

Semantic Labels

See *Element*.

Semantics

Literally, "meaning." Semantics in content strategy means the encoding of content with meaning, to facilitate the findability of content. The richer the semantics associated with a body of content, the easier it is to manipulate the content to serve users better. Semantic encoding is generally done through the use of metadata.

Syndication

A mechanism that allows your content to be made available to designated sites, content repositories, email addresses, or designated destinations within a content management system.

Tag

See *Element*.

Taxonomy

A taxonomy is terminology within a hierarchical classification system. In a technology context. it is often defined as structure plus controlled vocabulary.

Technopower

The use of the power of various publishing technologies to amplify, reuse, or re-publish content beyond its original appearance.

Topic

A stand-alone *module* of content. Although intended to be assembled and reused with other modules to create a deliverable like a website or technical manual, a topic is a unit of information large enough to be independently useful to a user. Examples could include an introduction, a concept description, a product overview, or a reference topic.

See also *Module* and *Fragment*.

Transactional Content

Content built into software applications that users see during their interactions. Examples include the prompts during account setup, the feedback message after a successful setup, and the error messages when something goes wrong.

Triumvirate

The three common publications that share content for the same product: an operating manual or user guide, a training guide, and customer support material.

Web CMS

A Web CMS (Content Management System) is a content management system designed to make it easy to create and manage a website. The typical Web CMS provides collaboration, authoring, and administration tools along with a content repository that lets users manage documents and web pages. Unlike a Component CMS, a Web CMS typically stores content using web standards like HTML and does not support creating documents from components.

Web Operations Management

A term coined by Lisa Welchman to describe the combination of strategy, governance, execution, and measurement required to successfully manage a company's online operations.

Wireframe

A wireframe is a blueprint of the layout of a web page before any graphic treatment is applied. The layout includes general placement of page elements such as headers and footers. Wireframes include areas for including content and specifying which content fits in which area of the page. Wireframes may also indicate different information states such as the look of a page before, during, and after a transaction. Wireframes are used by content strategists to determine whether all the desired content has a placeholder on a web page.

XML

Acronym for eXtensible Markup Language. XML defines a set of rules for creating domain-specific markup languages using a common syntax. XML languages, such as DITA or DocBook, define a set of elements and attributes that allow you to encode your content.

Bibliography

[1] Axelrod, Robert and Michael D. Cohen. 2001. *Harnessing Complexity: Organizational Implications of a Scientific Frontier*. Basic Books.

[2] Besen, Stanley M. and Joseph Farrell. 1994. "Choosing How to Compete: Strategies and Tactics in Standardization," *Journal of Economic Perspectives* 8, no. 2, (Spring, 1994):117–131. http://www.webcitation.org/68raKQzik

[3] Bloomstein, Margot. 2012. *Content Strategy at Work: Real World Stories to Strengthen Every Interactive Project*. Morgan Kaufmann.

[4] Chapman, C.C. and Ann Handley. 2012. *Content Rules*. John Wiley.

[5] Cooper, Alan. 2004. *The Inmates Are Running the Asylum: Why High-Tech Products Drive Us Crazy*. Sams – Pearson Education.

[6] Donoghue, Karen. 2002. *Built for Use: Driving Profitability through the User Experience*. McGraw-Hill.

[7] Eisenberg, Bryan and Jeffrey Eisenberg. 2006. *Waiting for Your Cat to Bark?* Thomas Nelson.

[8] Halvorson, Kristina. 2010. *Content Strategy for the Web*. New Riders.

[9] International Organization for Standardization. 2010. *Human-centred design for interactive systems*. International Organization for Standardization (ISO). http://www.iso.org/-iso/iso_catalogue/catalogue_tc/catalogue_detail.htm?csnumber=52075. ISO website to purchase the standard.

[10] Jones, Colleen. 2010. *Clout: The Art and Science of Influential Web Content*. New Riders.

[11] Kurts, C.F. and D.J. Snowden. "The new dynamics of strategy: Sense-making in a complex and complicated world." *IBM Systems Journal* 42, no. 3, (September, 2003):462–483.

[12] Kissane, Erin. 2011. *The Elements of Content Strategy*. A Book Apart.

[13] Marcotte, Ethan. 2011. *Responsive Web Design*. A Book Apart.

[14] McLuhan, Marshall. 1967. *The Medium is the Massage: An Inventory of Effects*. Random House.

[15] Morville, Peter. 2005. *Ambient Findability: What We Find Changes Who We Become.* O'Reilly Media.

[16] Morville, Peter and Louis Rosenfeld. 2006. *Information Architecture for the World Wide Web: Designing Large-Scale Websites.* 3rd edition. O'Reilly Media.

[17] Mulder, Steve and Ziv Yaar. 2007. *The User is Always Right: A Practical Guide to Creating and Using Personas for the Web.* New Riders.

[18] Resmini, Andrea and Luca Rosati. 2011. *Pervasive Information Architecture: Designing Cross-Channel User Experiences.* Morgan Kaufmann.

[19] Rockley, Ann and Charles Cooper. 2012. *Managing Enterprise Content: A Unified Content Strategy.* 2nd edition. New Riders Press.

[20] Sheffield, Richard. 2009. *The Web Content Strategist's Bible.* CLUEfox Publishing.

[21] Singh, Mohini and Dianne Waddell. 2004. *E-Business Innovation and Change Management.* Idea Group.

[22] Thompson, Isabelle. "The Given/New Contract and Cohesion: Some Suggestions for Classroom Practice." *Journal of Technical Writing and Communication* 15, no. 3, (1985):205–214. http://baywood.metapress.com/index/C2H7Q757JYDD7K2Q.pdf. Note: requires subscription or purchase for online version.

[23] Welchman, Lisa. 2010 "Web Operations Management Primer." http://-www.welchmanpierpoint.com/article/web-operations-management-primer. Full text available online.

[24] Woyke, Elizabeth. "Leadership: CEOs Learn to Speak in Code." *Inc. Magazine*, (May 29, 2012):205–214. http://www.inc.com/magazine/201206/elizabeth-woyke/-speaking-in-code.html. Full text available online.

[25] Zhang, Hongjiang. 2000. "Adaptive Content Delivery: A New Application Area for Media Computing Research." http://research.microsoft.com/pubs/68791/-adaptive_content_delivery.pdf. Full text available online in PDF form.

Index

A

B

F

G

H

I

N

O

P

R

S

T

U

V

W

X

Y

Z

About XML Press

XML Press (http://xmlpress.net) was founded in 2008 to publish content that helps technical communicators be more effective. Our publications support managers, social media practitioners, technical communicators, content strategists, and the engineers who support their efforts.

Our publications are available through most retailers, and discounted pricing is available for volume purchases for business, educational, or promotional use. For more information, send email to orders@xmlpress.net or call us at (970) 231-3624.

Lightning Source UK Ltd.
Milton Keynes UK
UKOW07f1533070317
295980UK00001B/4/P

9 781937 434168